The Guardian Book of ROCK & ROLL

theguardian

The Guardian Book of ROCK & ROLL

edited by **Michael Hann**

Aurum

First published in 2008 by Aurum Press Ltd
7 Greenland Street, London NW1 0ND
www.aurumpress.co.uk
in association with Guardian Books
Guardian Books is an imprint of Guardian Newspapers Ltd

The pieces in this book were first published in the *Guardian*

A catalogue record for this book is available from the British Library.

ISBN 978 1 84513 397 9

10 9 8 7 6 5 4 3 2 1
2012 2011 2010 2009 2008

Text sourcing: Sally Watson-Jones
Text design: www.carrstudio.co.uk
Typeset by SX Composing DTP, Rayleigh, Essex
Printed and bound in Great Britain by
Cromwell Press, Trowbridge, Wiltshire

CONTENTS

INTRODUCTION

by Michael Hann

The *Guardian*'s news editors in 1963 and 1964 knew how to liven up the pages of the paper. Got an unpromising subject? Find a Beatles angle! So a report on a convention of drapers would concentrate on the effects on the British tailoring industry of the popularity of Beatles suits among young people. That rather suggests there is nothing new in one of the common complaints the paper receives: love the politics and comment, but why do you feel the need to drag Amy Winehouse (or Lily Allen, or whoever might be the media pop darling of the day) into so many stories in the paper? I advise those readers to visit the *Guardian*'s digital archive, where they will discover that little has changed; that music has long been a special interest of the newspaper.

In fact, the *Guardian* has been covering rock music in its many forms, and in many ways, for as long as rock 'n' roll has existed. This book is one version of the story we have told over those years (a version that leaves out the report on the drapers' convention). It contains no album reviews and no gig reviews, whereas another book could be made up entirely of reviews of releases and events both momentous and long-forgotten. This book contains few of our more egregious errors of judgment, whereas another editor's version of the story could have dredged up plenty of them.

Hence you will not find our year-end round-up of pop in 1970, in which the writer flitted across albums by the Velvet Underground, Neil Young and Joni Mitchell, before announcing that the now-forgotten rock 'n' roll revival band Sha Na Na had made the best album of the year. Nor have I made space for our review of 1976, which advised readers to ignore 'those boring Sex Pistols', for it had been 'the year of Jackson Browne'. However, I couldn't resist including the historian D.W. Brogan's dismissal of rock 'n' roll, not least for its insistence that aficionados of the music held more respect for Bill Haley than for Elvis Presley.

In truth, this book concentrates on two periods: the first 10 years of rock music, and the past 10 years. That's not a comment on the music, so much as a reflection of how the *Guardian* covered it.

In that first decade, rock 'n' roll was still a novelty; there is a breathless delight in much of that early coverage at having something new to write about, even if the journalists sometimes didn't appear to have much comprehension of what it was they were covering, and believed the hysteria surrounding the first stars was of more interest than the stars themselves.

The first *Guardian* writer to realise that rock 'n' roll was a significant and permanent part of our culture was Stanley Reynolds, whose debut in the pages of the paper coincided with the rise of the Beatles. Stanley, an American who came to live in Britain in 1960, joined the *Guardian* in 1963. He'd been at the *Liverpool Post and Echo*, and had been trying to persuade his bosses to let him write about the emergent rock scene in the city, but they told him the Mersey Tunnel was more interesting to the readers. He found a more receptive editor at the *Guardian* in Alastair Hetherington, who allowed him to write about Merseybeat, and about the fighting between mods and rockers.

'There were no other writers doing anything similar,' Stanley told me. 'They saw popular culture as an amusement. But I thought it was more interesting than that, and more important for the *Guardian*. I sometimes thought I was making a mistake, giving more cultural depth to it, because few of the groups seemed to last for very long.'

Stanley's career writing about rock 'n' roll was short-lived. He was an arts feature writer, not a specialist rock writer, so only a fraction of his work was about rock 'n' roll, but even so, the other newspapers had realised he was on to something and, within a couple of years, were employing their own, full-time rock writers. Stanley, no longer ahead of the game, chose to write about other subjects and tell other stories.

Nevertheless, I think Stanley Reynolds is the father of modern rock journalism, certainly rock journalism in Britain. He didn't review albums or gigs, but he reported: he looked behind the music and the screams, to try to work out not what was happening, but why it was happening. Like the Velvet Underground, the body of work is sparse, but hugely significant. And I'm delighted to say he's still writing today – his work appears on the *Guardian* obituaries page, and he had a second novel (only 45 years after the first), *Death Dyed Blonde*, published in 2008.

After the breakthrough made by Stanley, rock music became a staple of newspaper coverage. Something was lost as that happened. Because it entered the workaday news cycle, the sense of excitement was lost: it had become just another subject to be covered.

Though the *Guardian* carried plenty of music coverage through the 1970s and 80s, it somehow looks like a bit of an afterthought when one revisits those pages. The biggest stars were interviewed, and records were reviewed, and although rock 'n' roll had its own dedicated space within the paper, there was never enough space for the writing to stretch out, or for unusual subjects to be explored thoroughly – this despite having writers such as Robin Denselow and Mary Harron (who went on to become rather better known as a major film director).

The big change, the one that gave rock writing a new lease of life in the broadsheets (with the *Guardian* leading the way, though I would say that), was the advent of the multi-section paper. The *Guardian*'s Weekend magazine provided a forum for lengthy interviews with pop stars, the kind we had never published before. Friday Review (now Film&Music) became the place for newer bands, or reports on the music business, and the Guide took an altogether different, quirkier view of the industry. Hence the number of articles in this book from the past 10 years.

Now, again, that is all changing. The internet has become the new force in the media's coverage of music, and if a new edition of this book is published in 10 years' time, it will doubtless be groaning under the weight of pieces that have never actually been published in print before.

The influential music industry commentator Bob Lefsetz, in his Lefsetz Letter email, often mocks print music writers. You have no influence anymore, he taunts us. People buy records despite you, not because of you. Maybe so, Bob. But you're missing the point. The music writing of the *Guardian*, certainly, isn't intended to help record companies sell records. It's to tell stories. Yes, we do the interviews with big bands before they release their latest album. Yes, we review all the major releases. But we also do things just because we want to, which was what Elvis and Little Richard and Jerry Lee and Buddy wanted us to do, all those years ago. If rock 'n' roll has a message, and I choose to believe it does, that's what it is.

Dave Simpson didn't spend two years trying to track down all the former members of the Fall because he wanted Mark E. Smith to have a few more quid in his pocket. Nor did Laura Barton attempt to drive every road mentioned in every version of Jonathan Richman's 'Roadrunner' in a desperate effort to double sales of his latest album. Those were missions carried out in the truest spirit of rock 'n' roll, and resulted in memorable pieces that said something about music that a thousand album reviews could never manage. And that's why pieces like those get remembered, while the review of the second Libertines album gets forgotten.

This book, I hope, contains the breadth of rock 'n' roll music. It has its silliness, its tawdriness, its funniness. It has obsession, disgust and bafflement. It has money, politics and manipulation. And it has some of the very spirit of the music. In one of the final pieces in this book, Craig Finn of the Hold Steady writes about the Replacements, from his hometown of Minneapolis, and how they changed his teenage years. His own band, he says, want to do the same thing: 'Let people know that everything is going to be OK. And when it isn't, rock 'n' roll can help.' I hope it can.

MORAL PANICS

10 September 1956

ROCK DEVOTEES TURN HOSE ON CINEMA MANAGER

by our own reporter

Frenzied rock 'n' roll fans snatched up fire hoses and sprayed Mr Tom Boardman, manager of the Gaiety Cinema, Manchester, during the first showing of *Rock around the Clock* yesterday afternoon. He had been trying to stop a mob of youths from 'jiving' on the stage in front of the screen, where they had climbed to get away from the police and attendants in the aisle.

At this point the film was stopped for 18 minutes, in the hope that uproar among the audience of 900 would subside, but each time one of the rock 'n' roll bands interrupted the story of the film boys leapt from the front stalls into the front aisle and stamped their suede shoes in the 'jive'.

Frequent fights broke out between the dancers and the seven policemen called in to bolster up a corps of 20 special ushers. Under the good-tempered command of Inspector J. McLoughlin constables pushed the boys back into their seats, shook them a little to drive out the spirit of the 'rock', and returned to the side where they could look at the film – and wonder. Only once, during the second showing, the waving of a boy's arm could be clearly distinguished as fighting, rather than jiving – the two look very alike.

Young people at the back of the cinema, where they were not training fire hoses, gave vent to their emotion by stretching their arms out to the screen like savages drunk with coconut wine at a tribal sacrifice. Sometimes they flung their lighted cigarettes about; always they chanted the songs and banged out the insistent beat on the carpet. Even two usherettes were seen tapping their hands against the side of the chocolate trays.

Mr Robert Weatherill, general manager of the Buxton Circuit, which controls the Gaiety and the Burnley cinema where *Rock around the Clock* was shown last week, said the reaction was 'just about as I expected', but he could not understand the audience.

'When there is no music they hiss so that you cannot hear the dialogue, and when the music starts they shout so much that you can't hear it. What do they want?'

Reporters who have seen the film several times (and the fact that they have had to should dispel some of the profession's glamour) say that trouble always breaks out at roughly the same points in the story and particularly when the rock 'n' roll bands perform at an exclusive girls' school dance. The stuffy parents, of course, disapprove but the children love it.

The rhythm of the music suggests quite as much as any reaction of the audience, what rock 'n' roll is all about. Indeed the meaning of the slang words would horrify most parents more than the behaviour of the children, which was open enough. Few people have stated the musical meaning of rock 'n' roll better than one of its masters in this film. Mr Bill Haley explained: 'It's easy, Alligator, you take the music and play it upside down.' Rhythm, made by guitars and a bass, underlies it, with melody from the tenor saxophone. The urgent snarl of this instrument scurries about like a big dog getting excited by a children's game, snapping at their feet and knocking them over.

Rock around the Clock holds its audience long after they have left the cinema. After the second showing hundreds of youths blocked Peter Street between the Midland Hotel and the Free Trade Hall with frantic jiving. Strangest of all was a woman's shout that scattered the pigeons in Albert Square – 'We're gonna rock, rock, rock till broad daylight.' John Bright's statue did not quiver. Obviously he was a 'square.'

After the first burst of community singing at the beginning of the last showing of the main film there was another relatively quiet spell, broken by a shower of sparks as a firecracker sailed over the stalls. Policemen who had been standing near the exits moved forwards as it exploded, and two youths were pulled out to the cheers of the audience.

Each time the theme song reappeared there were disturbances, dancing in the aisles, and scuffles near the exits as the police removed the ringleaders. These reached a climax during the last five or ten minutes of the film, when most of the audience was on its feet. There was a brief pause when the audience got outside, and then a crowd of several hundreds moved into St Peter's Square.

While policemen tried to clear youths and girls from the bonnets of cars and buses, the leaders of the crowd formed a circle round the Cenotaph. Thirty or forty youths rocked and shouted and waved their arms under the dedicatory legend engraved on the column until they were removed by a police sergeant and several constables. Most of the crowd then moved down Oxford Street into Piccadilly, where it was dispersed by the police.

Councillor B.S. Langton, chairman of the Watch Committee, said last night: 'Obviously if this sort of thing is going to go on, we or the police, or we and the police, will have to do something about it. Exactly what action we shall take will depend on the report.'

8 November 1956

'ELVIS THE PELVIS' AND THE BIG BEAT

D.W. Brogan

The American people have a great many serious things to think of now, but one of the less serious, but not totally unimportant, things they debate is the Elvis Presley phenomenon. Is he a credit to his state, as the Governor of Mississippi has asserted, or is he only too representative of that most backward and savage of American commonwealths? Should he be paid nearly as much as Miss Mary Martin on television? Is he going to get married? Is he about to be drafted?

Such are some of the questions that the American public, in a muddled and often angry frame of mind, puts to itself. It rejoiced when it learned that teenagers in Manchester wrecked a cinema under the inspiriting influence of *Rock around the Clock*, and that our adolescents are ready to give to 'Elvis the Pelvis' the same adoring reception that the two-way stretch girdle age-group gave to Liberace. We are all in the same boat, so it is gladly believed. Not only American kids are crazy.

The Presley boom recalls Frank Sinatra of ten years ago. 'The Charleston' and 'The Black Bottom' were as much a source of scandal as 'Blue Suede Shoes', and the American child is ready to tell Mom or Grandma where she gets off. These infatuations are no novelty, and having to listen in to only too many discussions on Elvis, I recalled that day in New York when Sinatra fans stormed Times Square, tearing each others' clothes off when deprived of the chance of stripping and perhaps dismembering their hero.

After all, the Bacchae had been there before. And my taxi driver, philosophical in spite of the hold-up, had found the right answer for a sulky colleague: 'What has he got that we haven't got?' 'I don't know, but I sure wish I had it.'

As we all know, Mr Sinatra has gone on to become a very serious actor, and Mr Presley is following in his first footstep. Has he not announced that 'I didn't take a singing test when I had my screen test. It was an acting test.' Well, seeing will be believing, but in the meantime Elvis is a symptom all right. A symptom of what?

In one way it is easy enough to answer. The screaming adolescents who wreck cinemas and terrify ministers and parents are disciples of the goddess 'to whose bright image nightly by the moon/Sidonian virgins paid their vows and songs.'

'What,' asked a lawyer friend of mine of his Irish-Catholic office girl, 'does your mother think of your rushing off to see Elvis Presley?' 'She doesn't mind; she doesn't know anything.' 'But what about the wiggle?' 'Oh, that's just his way of expressing himself.' Today, as we know, to cripple self-expression is a sin.

In spite of the prayer meetings and the refusal to hire halls, self-expression rages. Yet Elvis is a *good* boy; he doesn't smoke or drink – so what? In the William Faulkner country which he comes from that is all the law and the prophets. It is probably only an accident that has made him a master of rock 'n' roll and not a gospel-singer or a minor warbler of 'country music'.

Already someone unknown is on Elvis's trail. For leadership in this world is 'a garland briefer than a girl's'. Only death can confer real immortality, as the cult of James Dean shows. 'Somewhere some young musician is working on something which will make rock 'n' roll sound like the genteel tinkling of a spinet,' says a rock 'n' roll organ. This is the Big Beat that is on the way. We have been warned.

But Presley is not all of rock 'n' roll. Although the claims to have originated the style are now as numerous as those of the cities that were Homer's home town, scholars, like the erudite members of the Institute of Jazz Studies, are nearly unanimous that the inventor is Mr William Haley, or 'Bill' Haley as he is known to his fans, learned and unlearned alike. To Mr Marshall Stearns and his colleagues the Presleys do not matter. They are concerned with masters like Messrs Haley, Broff, Clayton and Baker. They are keen students of the drumming techniques of Cuba and Haiti, to which centres of the new music pious pilgrims now go as once they went to Dresden and Bayreuth.

It is easy to write this off as a fad, but the faddists are not naïve; they are not 'Douanier Presley' types. I have known highly cultivated professional musicians turn from a learned discussion of a Mozart concert conducted by Sir Thomas Beecham to the future of 'progressive jazz', the 'California' style, and the probable future of Mr Dave Brubeck – to most of them a 'lost leader'. Psychologists discuss rock 'n' roll as a therapeutic discharge and, unless you are careful, you may get in for an evening of the most advanced jazz records as an alternative to a night of *My Fair Lady*. This may not be the true succession to 'Bach, Beethoven, and good old honest Brahms', as they sang in 1936 in 'On Your Toes', but it is raging.

And yet, and yet . . . Never has popular singable music been at a lower ebb than in this year of grace. Many hours of research spread over months in jukebox joints in a dozen states have convinced me that this is a lean year. Only one song has held its own, a melancholy piece of Abbey Theatre keening called 'The Wayward Wind'. Religion has slid. 'My Heart Is a Chapel' or even a conducted tour of heaven cannot compete with 'The Man Upstairs' of 1954. Possibly in desperation, radio, jukeboxes, sing-songs, have fallen back on old classics like 'Daisy, Daisy'. The hits of 25 to 30 years ago like 'Five Foot Two' are now ripe for revivial. But, in spite of the success of *The Boy Friend*, there has been no revival of the hits of *The Girl Friend*, although 'Blue Room' is surely schmalzy enough? I attended more than one 'community sing' and thought how superior, in singability, those classics were to 'Heartbreak Hotel'. So at Avalon, on Catalina Island, we sang of Casey and his 'strawberry blonde', of Lucille and 'the Oldsmobile'. We sang 'Tea for Two' and, of course, 'Avalon'. And in Boston, stronghold of the true, the beautiful and the archaic, they have revived 'Does Your Mother Know You're Out, Cecilia?' Who will sing 'Blue Suede Shoes' ten years from now?

14 February 1964

GOOD BEATLE MATERIAL IN RUSSIA, TOO

Victor Zorza

The true causes of Beatlemania, which have eluded the painstaking researchers of sociologists, musicologists, and anthropologists, can at last be revealed by the Kremlinologist.

What, a Moscow paper asked yesterday, was the attitude of the British authorities towards the Beatles? 'The British authorities do not interfere,' it answered its own question. 'Moreover, they encourage the Beatles. Why? Because this diverts the attention of the young people of Britain from politics, from bitter reflections about their deserted ideals and shattered hopes.'

The newspaper is *Moskovsky Komsomolets*, the Moscow youth paper. Of course, it tells only half the story. As so often happens with Soviet papers, the other half has to be read between the lines. Clearly, Moscow is concerned at the change in the balance of world power that will result from the recapture of Britain's lost American colonies by the Beatles. Hence its attempt to discredit them before they have time to accomplish their imperialistic transatlantic mission.

Moskovsky Komsomolets ought not to assume so readily that communism could not beat the imperialists at their own game of exporting counter-revolution. There is good Beatle material in the Soviet Union, too, though sometimes the information about it is hidden in journals so obscure that even *Moskovsky Komsomolets* might not subscribe to them. Its editors ought to obtain a copy of the *Kulturno-Prosvetitelnaya Rabota*, which stands for 'cultural enlightenment work'.

In Issue No 5 for last year, the magazine complains that Mr Khrushchev's memorable words – 'we stand for music that is melodious and rich in content, we are against all kinds of cacophony' – and the party's struggle against this kind of music are having very little effect on Soviet youth. Mr Malev, the author of the article, who investigated the officially sponsored clubs of Tula province, heard in one of them Western dance music which was notable for its 'spasmodic rhythms and banal intonation'.

In the House of Culture of Chemical Workers, Mr Malev reported, the story was the same: 'As a rule, there is no melody, the music is dissonant. Noise has been substituted for music . . .' The bands played even Soviet tunes in this Western style, but on the whole, little Soviet music was played, because the young people demanded foreign melodies.

In clubs that had no band, young people danced to homemade recordings. 'The main source of new music,' Mr Malev wrote, 'is the tape recorder, on which the melodies caught on the [foreign] radio are recorded.'

This, it should be reported in all fairness, is an improvement on the previous position, when homemade recordings were made out of X-ray film and sold on the black market. In the past year or two, Mr Khrushchev's drive for more consumer goods has made recorders and tapes available to those who have money for such things – and, incidentally, has helped to defeat his own musical commandments.

Youth organisations, pressed by the party to keep the young people ideologically pure, have tried to open clubs which would cater officially to the changing tastes. One such was the 'Café Red Sail', the opening of which in Odessa was described in the Soviet press with painful irony: 'The celebrated moment arrived. The first visitors were sitting at their tables. Then the first strains of the music were heard. Nothing like this has happened since the Flood. Drums crashed, Trumpets blared wildly. The singer pined for the Paris boulevards . . .'

The article described the lovers of such music as 'isolated individuals alien from head to toe', who also 'tell apolitical [read: political] jokes, pass around silly rumours, and scorn our laws and systems.' It looks as though the 'Soviet authorities' might have more of a musical-political problem with their young people than the British.

5 June 1964

MODS AND KNOCKERS

Stanley Reynolds

Liverpool, once known for having the hardest teddy-boys in the country, has so far sent no phalanx of Mods to Blackpool or New Brighton. At Scarborough not a deckchair has been flung in anger. The North, apparently, is immune to Clactons and Margates.

True, a gang of Rockers on 21 May forced their way into a house in Cheadle Hulme where Mods were having a party; in Sheffield the next weekend 50 youths marched down a street chanting, 'We hate Mods'; and last week timely police action in Matlock was said to have stopped another 'Clacton or Margate' – one 18-year-old was arrested for carrying an offensive weapon, a bottle. But one robin does not make a spring, and one Mod with a bottle in Matlock does not make a Margate.

The police do not seem to know why the North has been so far untouched by Mod and Rocker battles. 'I'll tell you why it happened after it does,' a spokesman for the Blackpool police said. A police spokesman at Scarborough said, 'I'm just at a loss to say why it hasn't happened here, and I'm a little afraid that if we give it any publicity they'll pick us for the next trip.'

The Manchester police are more definite. 'As far as we're concerned,' a spokesman said, 'they do exist, and we've had no trouble with them, but as long as we know where they are going to congregate we can move them along.' Certainly, anyone walking through Albert Square, Manchester, over the Whitsuntide weekend could not help but notice the extra police on duty – some with dogs. 'We heard they were coming into Albert Square,' an inspector said, 'and we moved them along. We didn't want to arrest anyone but we wanted to stop trouble before it started.'

In Liverpool, the police, naturally enough, like to think it has been due to their efforts, and particularly the efforts of Liverpool's juvenile liaison officer scheme, while others, Mrs Elizabeth Braddock, the Liverpool MP, for one, like to think it is because of the popularity of beat music in the city. Beat music has already been widely praised for contributing to the death of the city's once vicious street gangs. And, indeed, with an estimated 350 beat groups on Merseyside you would assume the young have time for little else but playing or listening to music.

This opinion is held by most teenagers in Liverpool, who have a habit of crediting beat music for all good things. It is not, however, shared by the adults who work with the 'beat scene'. Mr Ray McFall, the owner of the Cavern Club in Liverpool, which is famous now as the starting point of beat music in Britain, claimed that if there is any short answer it is because there are hardly any Mods in Liverpool.

'We certainly get girls in the club wearing long skirts,' he said, 'but if you go by the "classical" definition of a Mod, we don't have them. The Mods and Rockers style of dress hasn't come up here. If it does come North, then maybe we'll have trouble. Put any teenagers, who are very impressionable, in a uniform and they will get a pack mentality. If the leader of the pack says they should fight Rockers, then they will fight Rockers.'

In attempting a definition of a Mod one seems to fall into jargonistic quicksand. It turns into a ridiculous race to keep up with ephemeral teenagese. One feels tempted to dismiss Clacton and Margate as some sort of spring mating ritual among fancy plumed Modcocks and Modhens.

Indeed, some authority claims that one cannot be a Mod unless one owns a scooter and does not repair it oneself. A pseudo scientific approach, however, seems to indicate that the Mods all go in for a peculiar type of sartorial elegance, and, perhaps more important, are middle-class, while Rockers are slovenly dressed and basically working-class. The class aspects of Mods and Rockers are probably a good means of explaining away their absence in the North. And, after talking to Northern teenagers, a strong North v. South rivalry over Mods is also apparent. The Mod cult is seen as a sort of London counter-attack to the commercial success of the North in the 'pop' field.

'This Mod gear,' a 19-year-old Manchester Labour Exchange clerk said, 'is all a con job, a confidence trick, by the clothing manufacturers in London.' There is a definite commercial air about the London Mod scene and it seems to jar head-on with the Northern beat which had something happily amateur about it – even Epstein was an amateur when he stumbled by chance upon the Beatles.

The fact that there are more Mods in Manchester than in Liverpool could merely be because Manchester has more middle-class money than its sister city. But even the Manchester Mods seem at best a pale imitation of their London leaders. This idea of London leading in the Mod biz seems to irritate Manchester youths. One 18-year-old, who said everyone in the North was a Rocker at heart, said: 'I saw this guy in the Twisted Wheel the other night and he had on all this Mod kit, and I walked up to him and said, "What are you doing, imitating London?" That shattered him.' 'Of course,' another said, 'some of them are too daft, you can stand there taking the mickey out of these Manchester Mods and they don't twig. We had a good thing here until this Mod thing came up from London. We were listening to good blues and now these idiots dome in with "MOD" written across their shirts and all they want to do is listen to the Beatles. They're too stupid to see it's all a con.'

Given this hard and cynical and very Northern attitude towards the Mods business, one can be optimistic about Mods and Rockers battles staying South. But, perhaps, the best deterrent is the Northern Mods themselves. There is something endearingly pathetic about the North when it tries blindly to ape London. One tiny 16-year-old girl with a Tom Jones bow in her hair and a Mod T-shirt under her duffle coat, when asked if there was anything that set Manchester Mods apart from the London ones, said: 'Yes,' in a little high-pitched voice, 'We're scruffy.' One felt like running out and buying her an anorak.

3 December 1976

GRUNDY BANNED

Philip Jordan

Bill Grundy was yesterday suspended by Thames Television for two weeks after being accused of 'sloppy journalism' over his controversial interview on Wednesday with the Sex Pistols pop group. Mr Grundy was due to introduce another edition of the *Today* programme this evening. He spent two and a half hours with senior Thames executives for a postmortem on Wednesday night's programme and was told of the decision during the afternoon.

A Thames spokesman said: 'Precisely what measures have been taken is a confidential matter between us and our staff.' But the director of programmes, Mr Jeremy Isaacs, has expressed his views firmly to all on the *Today* programme, describing last night's incident as 'a gross error of judgment' caused by 'inexcusably sloppy journalism'. The Independent Broadcasting Authority (IBA) has accepted assurances from Thames that the incident, in which foul language was used by the group, was regrettable but unavoidable.

One early consequence for the group is the cancellation yesterday of a tour arranged by Rank Leisure Services. They said they did not wish to be associated with the punk rock group's type of stage presentation.

Viewers heard Mr Grundy apparently goading the members of the group. But Mr Grundy said yesterday that what he was doing was 'to prove that these louts were a foul-mouthed set of yobs. And that is what I did prove.'

He agreed that he had told one member, 'You're more drunk than I am.' But this was a witticism. He did his programmes 'stone cold sober'. His image as 'the greatest drunk in the world' built up by himself in his articles for *Punch* magazine was an image, like those built by Dean Martin or Robert Mitchum. 'You cannot do a job like I do without being sober.'

Immediately after the programme the 12 lines to the studio switchboard were jammed with complaints. One viewer said that he had been so outraged that he had kicked in the screen of his new £380 television set. Mr Ray Mawby, Conservative MP for Totnes, said that he would be lodging a formal complaint with Lady Plowden, the chairman of the IBA.

The BBC issued a statement saying that it played records on radio according to their musical merit 'regardless of arbitrary classifications'. 'Radio 1 considers that some records now being issued which are described as punk rock are arguably not in this category.' A Sex Pistols record was not being played on daytime radio programmes, although it had been heard on the specialised John Peel late night show. The group have been banned from the council guildhall at Preston. Mr Vin Sumner, the council's entertainments officer, said: 'We don't ever want them here.'

Ms Vivienne Westwood, who has lived with Malcolm McLaren, the leader of the group, for 10 years, said her two children watched the *Today* programme. McLaren is the father of one of the children. She used swear words in front of the children and they also swore. 'It is quite normal,' said Ms Westwood, who described herself as an anarchist.

She said of the 'be nasty' philosophy of the punk rock groups: 'There is nothing wrong with being nasty and rude. It provokes reactions from other people, it leads to release. It ends confinement by inhibition and hypocrisy. People are hung up about sex. All this protest is very hypocritical. I want to change things and let kids realise themselves and their own potential. If you want change, the best thing to do is to attack sex because there is so much hypocrisy about sex in Britain.'

Ms Westwood said that if Thames had been worried about people swearing, the show should have been videotaped. It was not true that at one concert a girl lost an eye in a melee or that someone else had an ear bitten off. Allegations that a third person had been hit by flying glass were 'completely wrong'.

Johnny Rotten, a member of the group, said in a BBC radio interview that he had launched himself to stardom by walking up and down the King's Road in Chelsea, spitting at people. 'I did it because they were stupid.'

10 January 1977

SOMETHING ROTTEN

Robin Denselow

Late last Friday night in the Paradiso club in Amsterdam, and from across the canals the cognoscenti of pop sub-cultures are gathering for what promises to be a bizarre experience. The Paradiso is one of the last hippy haunts left in Europe, an old chapel complete with stained-glass windows, that in the late Sixties became the shrine of flower-power and underground music. Somehow, the place has hardly changed. There are still old-fashioned hippies outside, openly selling drugs, and inside the smell of pot wafts from the bar to the pin-tables around the gallery. The atmosphere is friendly enough, but just a little uneasy.

What's so special about tonight is that the much-publicised, little-listened-to 'English punk rock package' is about to make its impression on Europe. Leading the tour, who else but the band with the remarkable distinction of being currently the most talked about group in Britain, despite the fact that few people have heard them play, and many suspect them incapable of doing so. Fresh from Bill Grundy, the KLM desk and his sacking from EMI Records, Amsterdam welcomes Johnny Rotten. 'Ullo,' he mutters, in an exaggerated East End accent, 'we're the Sex Pistols.' The crowd, who have read the band's press cuttings stuck up on the club's front door, murmur with interest. 'Shut up,' says Mr Rotten. A new wave of British culture has crossed the channel.

The show that followed was neither as inept, atrocious, violent, obscene nor brilliant as the Pistols' critics or enthusiasts might like to claim. Musically, it was not up to much, but good enough to knock down the rumours that the band didn't play on their one, strong single (now rapidly being withdrawn) 'Anarchy in the UK'. It was what might be expected from a bunch of aggressive teenagers with a few months' consistent performing behind them, and a record company advance to help them get reasonable equipment.

Not that the standard of the musicianship is the first quality

Pistols audiences go looking for. As the fashion for fast, raw, do-it-yourself music (now called 'punk' or 'new wave') spread from the remnants of the pub-rock circuit to an even more energetic following of teenagers and schoolchildren, the Pistols happened to be the first of the rapidly growing bunch to surface. They are by no means the best of the new wave acts who take as their heroes earlier American punks like Lou Reed or Iggy Pop, but the Sex Pistols have something the others can't match – Mr Johnny Rotten.

This night, the pallid youth in the tie-dye shirt with a sewn-on picture of Marx, who is now cleverly moving his bottom lip in an ape-like way to gibber at the audience, is giving his performance in the knowledge that EMI, the world's largest recording organisation, have decided they cannot handle him. His act, the television show, and the airport scenes were apparently too much.

Mr Rotten makes no comment on the situation, says nothing to suggest that today he is front-page news, but goes ahead with his usual stage show. The band crash into 'Anarchy', with Rotten singing well out of tune, staring wildly at the audience, and moving around like a leering hunchback. Words like 'piss' and occasional obscenities can sometimes be heard through the noise, while Mr Rotten, contorting himself into odd shapes and singing at one point with his head hanging upside down, leaves rivals like Steve Harley standing in the rock-cripple stakes.

He crashes with some conviction and considerable excitement through the old Who number 'Substitute', before embarking on a work entitled 'No Hope, No Glory'. This is based on a thunderous version of the National Anthem, with such screamed lyrics as 'God save the Queen, a fascist regime,' or – rather more to the point – 'tourists are money'.

Towards the end of this, any ideological barriers are broken down. The audience, which has obviously been studying how to behave, starts throwing beer at the band. The band start hurling beer back, followed, a lot more dangerously, by a microphone stand. The musical accompaniment to all this is a grinding, crashing ditty with the repeated line, 'The problem is you.'

The Sex Pistols were slightly unpleasant, but looked more like effective stage villains than revolutionaries. I have to admit (and I say this despite myself, having been utterly bored by all their press coverage) that in patches they were entertaining and exciting. They were certainly never dull for long. The notorious Rotten turned out to have a considerable stage presence, in his bizarre, insulting way, and he already knows how to handle an audience.

He may upset a lot of people, but then traditionally the beginnings of every new wave in rock always do. And far from being something totally different, he fits into the pattern of English rock's wild character actors, from Screaming Lord Sutch to Arthur Brown and Alex Harvey. As for real outrage he does nothing yet that compares with Keith Moon, let alone Iggy Pop.

Across town, while this was going on, two embarrassed top executives from EMI were worrying about how to get rid of this rather too successfully publicised band. Managing director Leslie Hill had flown in with his legal adviser to try to get the Pistols' manager Malcolm McLaren to agree to the already announced 'mutual separation'.

The meeting went badly, for in the early hours of Saturday morning a clearly upset McLaren was to be found standing on the edge of a canal, in the freezing cold. He and the band were staying in a cheap boarding house, the EMI executives were at the Hilton, and he was furious.

McLaren just stood there and talked non-stop, and despite his wild reputation (for being 'into anarchy' and running a kinky boutique) he sounded like any upset manager. He claimed that his boys 'were goaded' into their notorious TV utterances, and 'what they did was quite genuine – being working-class kids and boys being boys. They said what they felt was OK. They don't regret it.' He said the airport incident was 'fabricated up to a point. They may have spat at each other and been a little drunk, but they weren't flying the plane.'

Mr Rotten walked by as we were talking, looking surprisingly frail and quiet. Asked what he thought of EMI, he said he didn't. McLaren knew what he thought. According to him, EMI had known exactly what they were getting when they signed the band. 'Hill said he was thrilled. He was fully aware of their image, and had all the tapes of their songs. Now we have come over to

Holland promoting their record. And find they have "mutually terminated" the contract, and put out a statement without our knowledge. How can they "mutually" end it when we haven't signed to end it. Legally, we are still on EMI Records.'

According to McLaren, EMI's move has split its employees. He says the band has strong support among the company's A&R and publishing departments (they recently signed an additional contract for £10,000 for publishing), and says he had had messages of sympathy from inside the company. At the same time, he claimed – giving a possible new reason for EMI's action – 'EMI contends that there are international pressures on them, from all the Top 20 sort of acts, saying they don't support this sort of music. Some artists have said they won't renew their contracts if EMI continues with it.'

Whatever the real reason EMI find it 'not viable' to support the Pistols, they have been quick to act. The 'Anarchy' single is not being released in Europe as planned, and McLaren says it is being withdrawn in England and Holland, 'so last night we ended up selling fucking records at the bloody door. It's a joke.'

As for quickly re-signing with another company, he was surprisingly gloomy. 'I've told them to find us an equivalent contract, but we've had word that most of the major companies won't touch us with a bargepole. There's nobody after us. If we walk into another record company, what are they going to say – you can't play anywhere and we can't hear your records on the radio.'

That, I simply refuse to believe, especially when in the depths of his despair McLaren announced that 'NBC are flying in tomorrow to make a half-hour documentary on us that will be screened in America coast to coast.' If EMI are not very clever, they could come off looking more foolish than Rotten, for whatever else, the Sex Pistols are rather more than a publicity stunt.

21 September 1979

A GIRL WITH A PINK CREW CUT . . .

Val Hennessy

Flamboyant posters, punk slogans and other intimations of adolescence erupt suddenly, like acne, across my daughter's bedroom walls; the late Sid Vicious with scabs on his arms and a virulently pimpled chin supersedes the ubiquitous Snoopy. As I crawl about the floor rounding up soiled undergarments and dirty socks, bizarre unsmiling groups like the Boomtown Rats, the Stranglers and the Clash gaze down at me and, frankly, they get on my nerves.

Yet I should be the very person to understand. At my daughter's age, I possessed a collection of rock 'n' roll records that was the envy of a neighbourhood where winning the Co-op Saturday night jive contests was life's ultimate goal. Photos of Elvis, Ricky and Cliff were Sellotaped to the lid of my school desk and my idolatry offered to Conway Twitty, the Everley Brothers, the Beatles and Mick Jagger.

According to my daughter, Mick Jagger's a wimp, Cliff Richard's a wimp, and I'm the biggest wimp of all, handing round the digestive biscuits to her friends as they shriek 'I'm a laz-z-y sod' in unison, pogoing across the Criterion Cord in their sparkle-sox and bondage trousers.

Those effervescent happenings which in my day were called 'concerts' are now called 'gigs' and from these my daughter occasionally returns flob-smothered and ecstatic with shredded clothing and blackened eyes. Perhaps it was an unforgivable intrusion into her world but, being curious to obtain a wimp's eye-view of gig-going, I attended a recent concert. Because Sham 69 are very big with my daughter and because lead singer Jimmy Pursey is at the pinnacle of her pubescent fantasies I chose Sham 69's farewell concert for my initiation.

In the ticket queue outside the Rainbow Theatre I was jostled by hundreds of bristle-headed, braces-wearing boys and girls whose ebullience boiled over spasmodically into jungle chants and a pounding of fists, piston-like, above their heads. Fans from Scotland kept clapping their hands and shouting 'SHUM, SHUM, We Want SHUM', and, standing there in my T-shirt dress, I felt more conspicuous than a hairy-legged woman in a Miss World contest.

A girl with a pink crew-cut nudged her friend on the shin with a laced-up boot and hissed: 'What's that nosey old bag staring at?' 'She's the fuzz ain't she?' sniffed her friend.

Feigning mateyness I offered them cigarettes. 'Bit old entcha?' observed pink crew-cut.

'What for?'

'Sham.'

'Why?'

'Well Jimmy sings about the 'assles of youth don't he? Them sort of 'assles are over by the time you reach your age ain't they?' Jimmy, it transpired, is a Messianic punk with a message: 'He wants city kids to get together. What Elvis done for Memphis, Jimmy's done for Hersham.'

Ankle-deep in beer cans, an army of thuggish youths, tattooed with swastikas, marched the pavements spitting and chanting, 'There's only one Hitler.' The girls explained: 'That's the British Movement mob, they go round all the gigs making trouble, they've had it in for Sham ever since Jimmy joined Rock Against Racism,' and suddenly a BM lunatic hurled a bottle into the path of a speeding juggernaut. The Sham fan whose cheek was cut by splinters of flying glass merely shrugged: 'Not to worry, bleedin' thugs, you get used to it . . .' I was feeling sick and definitely jumpy.

Jimmy Pursey, apparelled in stroboscopic lights, leaps through the swirls of dry ice and, in a voice like a pneumatic drill, he howls about dead end jobs and being united, until the fillings in your teeth rattle. From the balcony, peering nervously down upon several thousand bouncing skinheads, I saw a faction of BM toughs (exclusively male) marshal themselves into procession, chanting, thumping and shouting 'Sieg Heil'. By Sham's fifth song they had clambered on stage and halted the show.

In the ensuing imbroglio beer cans were hurled and bottles

flung. A girl received a cigarette end in her eye, another had her glasses smashed and in the general stampede some were knocked unconscious. After 20 minutes the thugs who came to create deliberate, mindless violence caused Sham's Last Stand to end and I felt extremely sad for Jimmy Pursey who attempted, in vain, to calm things down.

In the balcony kids clambered across seats and punched each other. I have not experienced such panic since being in a throng of CND protestors trapped beneath the flailing hooves of mounted police in Grosvenor Square. Turning faint I was rescued by a calm young man from Polydor records who led me to a private room behind stage where anxious 'friends of the band' sipped gin-and-limes; there, wearing a Sham 69 badge on her white polyester two-piece was Jimmy's mum, all het up, telling everyone: 'My boy will be in a right state after this fiasco, he's been rehearsing for weeks, we always say his fans are like a crown of barbed wire.'

Beatles concerts were never like that. I once advocated letting everything hang out. Now I am of the opinion that if this is the contemporary rock scene then it's time I put my plimsoled foot down. I have told my daughter, 'No more gigs.'

SCENES

8 October 1963

RAVERS' REQUIEM

Stanley Reynolds

If Jazz is a lightweight then the Liverpool Sound is a flyweight, and a punch-drunk one at that. Now, after a solid year of exposure, with the Liverpool scene so crowded with reporters from journals of all brows that they sometimes have to interview each other, the Merseyside Sound is going at the knees. The boxing metaphor is, perhaps, no longer apt; rather it is becoming more and more like those television wrestlers; it is flabby, not hard, muscle that is flexed at the Cavern Club today.

With Mr Harold Wilson plugging for a go-ahead Britain and the first Ford rolling off the lines at Halewood, perhaps the time is coming when the rockers will switch from electric guitars to electronics. Or at least get jobs. Mr Robert Wooler, resident disc jockey at the Cavern mecca of the Liverpool Scene, would be the last to say that Liverpool has sung itself out, but he does say: 'Perhaps if they were engaged in some back-breaking work they would be unable to expend so much of this sort of energy.' So, if times are getting better, as Mr Wilson and Mr Macmillan promise, then the Scene will perhaps shortly be tied up and filed away with the rest of 1963.

But before the Beatles, Gerry, the Searchers, and Billy J. fade away from the charts, to the Helen Shapiro hinterland of the 12-month wonders, it is only fair to wake the dead, like the Irish do, in the hope that the corpse may rise.

After all, it was a good exciting sound while it lasted. It revolutionised and monopolised the top 10, that poll of best-selling gramophone records; it revitalised the entertainment business all over the country. And in the depths of a workless year, when the bulge of the war babies were standing with their hands in their pockets outside labour exchanges, it put a smile, albeit like a row of condemned houses, on the face of Merseyside, that weather-beaten old Queen of Scouse. In fact, it made the old tart fashionable; put expressions like 'it's the gear' into the mouths of debs. Semantically it has been something of a breakthrough. How long has it been since a native expression ousted a transatlantic jargon import like gear did to crazy and judy to chick? It even gave birth to a newspaper, the flourishing *Mersey Beat*, devoted exclusively to the Scene with modishly deadpan photographs of the groups.

Now, after saying why the deceased should be of interest, the good obit writer, ruffling through the yellowed cuttings from the newspaper morgue, must begin at the beginning. The date is supplied by Mr Wooler, a close relative.

Mr Wooler, 31, pinpoints the date of birth as 27 December 1960, at the Litherland Town Hall, Liverpool. 'Before that,' he said, 'I had been visiting dancehalls all round Merseyside for a few years as a part-time compère. I couldn't get over the fact that there were all these teenagers out there every night wanting to scream. Early in December 1960, I jacked in my job as a British Transport Commission clerk at the Garston docks and took on compèring fulltime. One afternoon I was sitting in the Jacaranda Club in Slater Street, when two long-haired, leather jacketed boys came in. They said they had just come back from Hamburg. They were the advance party of the Beatles.'

After asking the manager of the show at Litherland for £8 for the whole Beatle group and being offered £4, Mr Wooler settled for £6. 'When they came out they sang "Long Tall Sally" and the place went mad. I've never experienced anything like it,' he said. Later, as we have been told so often, the Beatles were discovered by Mr Brian Epstein, a smooth young executive in a Liverpool retail music shop, and they started making records and selling them nationally. Before the Beatles there had been plenty of rock music on Merseyside: Rory Storm and the Hurricanes, Cass and the Casanovas, Derry and the Seniors. The list goes into the hundreds. What the Beatles did was to adapt the more sophisticated rhythm and blues of the American Negro singers, like Chuck Berry.

But Liverpool isn't just a bunch of disembodied voices and expensively amplified guitars, it is a whole new look: Polo-neck sweaters, button-to-the-neck collarless jackets, bell-bottom jeans,

Cuban-heeled boots, black leather everything – a complete break with the Italian-Ivy League, a kind of rush into everything prewar German, ultra-kooky and slightly kinky even to the long Brecht-brushed hairstyles. And the girls assert their self-assured sexuality with extravagantly coloured back-combed hair, heavily kohled eyes, and corpse-pale mouths.

These mouths are never smiling. 'I asked one of them once why they didn't smile.' Mr Wooler said. '"It's tougher not to smile," she told me. "The thing is you don't smile. Maybe it's the escape from the gymslips."' Mr Wooler calls the girls 'revolutionaries' – he has a gift for that kind of linguistics. He claimed that the girls have a profound knowledge of sex.

'They like to go to what they call raves,' he said. A rave, someone explained, is when you live it up. 'You get as high as a steeple, one way or another. You go into the horizontal, which would be the fade-out if it were a film, but it isn't a film, so there's no censor. And in the morning you have the hangover and so you have a couple more pills and that is where the addiction comes in.'

The pills are Drynamit, nicknamed Purple Hearts, Preludin tablets, and what are called Bennies. The Drynamit and Preludin come in on ships from Hamburg. A young lad with a boyish grin, who said he had just spent the night in jail, explained that he sent his girlfriend down to the shop to collect Purple Hearts, £500 worth, because girls weren't searched. He said the pills were left in the left luggage and then picked up by someone, he didn't know who. He got 100 pills for his part, but the police were on to him.

'There is this connection with Germany,' Mr Wooler said. 'Unfortunately I've never been there. I'm going to go, at the end of November. I'm going to see if I can trace this thing. These groups come back from Hamburg and they tell me about the riotous things they see there. What intrigues me about it is that they are such a short time in Germany. It's sinister in a way, all this black leather. I'm not saying they should go all 1939 and remember the Huns, but sometimes it seems a little too much like an Isherwood novel.'

The raves and the Purple Hearts, the set faces and the

undercurrent of cruelty are disturbing, and, unlike prewar Germany, there is no side as positive as political satire. 'I don't think they bother about politics,' Mr Wooler said. 'It's what I call rhythm and booze music. They are afraid of sentiment. They are cruel to each other because they are trying to prove they have no hearts. They try to show that they are not affected by anything.'

But coming out of the Cavern, Mr Ray McFall, the owner, pointed out a group of smiling well-dressed girls. Perhaps, like Joan Littlewood's Theatre Workshop drawing Princess Margaret into the audience, this is the trouble with the Liverpool Scene. But even given the fickleness of fashion and the saturation press and television treatment, there is still a wealth of talent on Merseyside.

'The pattern,' Mr Wooler said, 'has been set by these Rock and Beat records from the States. Because they are really striving so hard to duplicate the sound they don't think of anything else. If the American song happens to tell a story, that's OK, but it is the sound they like. Why don't they write songs with more subtle lyrics, with more originality, that tell a story, and that are about Liverpool? I wish I knew. But, personally I don't think any of these R&B groups will produce a song that is about Liverpool. They would find it embarrassing. They don't see anything romantic here. Harry Warren and Mack Gorden could see their way to writing about Kalamazoo, Michigan, but these Liverpool boys are really embarrassed by their hometown. We have these folk singers here, like the Spinners, but where does one draw the line between something new and the old Maggie May stuff. I don't think a person like Lionel Bart can do it. When Lorenz Hart wrote about Manhattan he knew what he was talking about. I have my doubts about Lionel Bart, even working with Alun Owen. And I don't see any back street Bart's around. Unless John Lennon and Paul McCartney [the song-writing Beatles] can sort of forget the American influence for a while, nothing new will happen. They are the only two with enough talent to do something new.'

The problem with the Liverpool Scene is striking a balance between the publicity and overexposure that seems to plague any likely newcomer in sports, letters, or show business, nipping him neatly in the bud.

16 July 1977

ROCK-A-BYE PUNK

John Cunningham

Billy Idol cups his hand over his headphones as though he can't hear the sound he is making. Face death-pale, his cherry red hair tones purple in the studio lights.

'They had James Dean! They had the Stones! We had nobody! Now we got our own New Orders.' The lead guitarist does a scissors leap between chords and the take ends with a burp from Billy which the late night listeners to John Peel's record programme won't hear.

This is Punk Rock in the making, the latest pulp-music which, the myth already has it, the kids on the streets have themselves contrived. Anyone can play it, sing it, write it, wear it. You don't need Mr Artful Agent and Global Records Inc to show you the big-time at your own expense, say 20 per cent, as you stand up before the fans in your freaky finery, protected by strong-arms, limousined away after performances and have your blemishes lied away by press agents.

If you're a punk rock performer, star even, you can piss next to the fans in the loo and not get mobbed. Elvis couldn't have done that, nor the Beatles, nor the Stones nor anyone who has ever tenanted rock and roll's hall of fame. Maybe they wouldn't have wanted to. But punk rockers want to stay near their roots, near their fans. To play in small halls, to run the show themselves, not to wear fancy gear, and to call it a day when it's a day.

Take three: take four: take five: in the cavernous studios the industry moulds and manipulates the product. At the moment the group have a name, Generation X, but not a label – no record company has yet signed them up but they are being bid for.

The lot on offer is four young men, ages from 18 to 24; white sweatshirts, narrow jeans threadbare at the knee; a small sheaf of songs; a bank of equipment that hasn't been dented because so far it has had to groove along only with the fans.

There are other lots: the Clash, the Damned, Stranglers and, most shocking to the straight ear and eye, the Sex Pistols, who obligingly swore on Bill Grundy's Thames Television show; got themselves temporarily banned by the BBC and several recording companies on account of a punk celebration jubilee disc, 'God Save the Queen'. Two of the group's members, the self-styled Johnny Rotten, their lead singer, and drummer Paul Cook, have both been knifed in gang attacks in London.

Punk rock is nothing if not two-faced. Generation X are sexy on stage, and off stage they are polite and friendly to the point of wholesomeness. They even include a disclaimer about punch-ups in one of their songs: 'Might take a bit of violence/But violence ain't our only stance'.

The music is aggressive; old Elvis's pelvic thrust – and much more besides – is there, but violence is not part of it, though it has been associated with some other groups.

The punch-ups have unfairly made the headlines. What has made photographs, not so unfairly, are snaps of performers, most notably Johnny Rotten in a denim jacket, the seams of which have been ripped apart and studiously replaced with safety pins, a line of which carefully edges the collar. There is a Nazi cross above his breast pocket, though no one seems to have got close enough to ask him what, if anything, it signifies for him.

In suburban high streets, the fans out-parody the fashion: strings of multi-coloured razor blades dangle from ears; large safety pins are apparently stuck through noses. The style ranges up to high camp, with girls making up their eyes with elongated mascara feline flourishes, and bunching up side-tufts of hair into cats' ears, while dyeing the close-cropped centre a different colour.

A glass thrown here and there; a few chases along shopping streets – rockers in pursuit of punks; some tribal news-sheets with titles like *Live Wire* and *Sniffin' Glue*; a few songs, a few slogans and enough has happened to (a) stun the older generation yet again; (b) alert the bench in a dozen towns; (c) cause some promoters to ban punk; (d) make most record companies hedge their bets by signing up at least one band in case punk rock becomes the biggest thing since the last time they missed out on what became the biggest thing.

Enough, little enough actually, has happened to turn punk rock into a trend to be investigated by sociologists who label it 'access music' and 'dole queue rock.' The first is possibly true; the second less possibly.

Musicologists are noting what's happening, but it could be that the media is already writing a requiem for punk music and that, when the history of rock is brought up to date, it will deserve no more than the meanest footnote.

Meanwhile a trend that is generally reckoned to have started from obscure origins about two years ago in Britain is being played and picked over. Musically, it certainly had something to do with the wish of kids who could manage three chords and latch on to crude rhythms to participate. Certainly there was no need for musical perfection; even ability was a wavering factor; the thing was and is to get up and play for the sheer joy/hell/whatever of playing.

Bands came together tentatively, fragmented and were re-formed with slightly firmer identities. Their venues were small; some played only a few gigs before breaking up. But by summer 1976, the first batch of leaders had emerged. Sex Pistols, the Damned and the Clash led in London; a few others in the provinces, but in the beginning no big link up by way of tours or airwaves.

The kids who played – many in their late teens – had set their hearts on the small time. The Beatles' record revival, and to a lesser extent that of the Stones, of the last two years appealed not to them but nostalgically to the 30s age group. Their own stars could be seen only at a distance in expensive concerts; and the great free and almost-free pop festivals of the late Sixties and early Seventies had been stamped out or else petered out.

And most of all, in the way that trends begin, nothing much new was happening and the music industry, which likes mid-decade elixir to keep the mogul alive, was wondering why its fix was late.

Along came punk rock: happily suspicious of almost everything; had to be coaxed into record studios; sometimes got on best with small record companies; wanted to speak with its own voice, mostly not quite sure what it wanted to say. But knowing this, that it wanted to speak for itself. And to look like itself, as Teds, Greasers, Mods and Rockers have each done in their turn.

Punk rock had now got, or been given, another name – New Wave – which suggests that someone is tampering with it. It is said to express a view that is nihilistic; anarchistic; anti-Establishment; violent; factional; aggressive; divisive; mindless; frustrated; crude. In fact, any permutation of the adjectives which have been stuck on rock and roll practitioners, with the exception of how nice and clean, which is how we labelled the Beatles in their early days.

Unlike everybody from Eddie Cochran and Buddy Holly, Bill Hayley, Elvis Presley, the Stones and the Who, there are few love songs in punk rock. It is self-centred, distrustful, unsure, believing in not much more than rock and roll itself.

Punk isn't entirely protesting. Its songs are certainly not in the same league, lyrically and compassionately, as Dylan or Baez. Nor are they as good even as the early Who, which summed up some of the frustrations of the Mod generation in the allegedly affluent Sixties.

It is something of a fiction also to classify punk music as dole queue rock. It is a fair trendspotter's hunch to try to align teen unemployment with an outpouring of anti-establishment feeling: to surmise that rock music has become the inheritance of kids from low-income families who have suddenly woken up to the fact that it's one short step from a pointless school career to apparently open-ended unemployment as a teenager. However, there seem to be as many fans and practitioners from middle-income as low-income homes.

But teenage unemployment is a very new phenomenon; even the Beatles with their lean postwar childhoods and the ability of Lennon/McCartney as songwriters did not cash in on it. It takes a dustbowl famine or an arrow to produce songs about joblessness. Teenage restlessness, on the other hand, is something everyone else has lived through before and some, like Mr Artful Agent and Global Records Inc, and fashion designers, and pop stars, have even got rich on it.

Generation X have blown the gaff on the unemployment kick anyway. One of their songs says, 'Don't want what a steady job brings/Can't spend my life saving up for things.' Their songs, so far, are mostly about uncertainties rather than brash defiance, so, 'You're too personal/Too too too too too personal.' Or 'What's it like to play a part? What's it like to have wooden heart?' They have all the conviction of minds being made up slowly.

Until they came together a few months ago in the present group, life had not treated them too badly. Billy Idol was at a further education college in Bromley doing his O-levels. Now he's the lead vocalist.

The oldest, Tony James, is 24, ex-Grammar school, office jobs, worked for a car auction firm, was on the dole for a year, while he worked with groups. The music kept them going: the belief that they loved playing and could play.

Their view of the world isn't especially sour. Tony James, who has seen most of it, says, 'I used to see my friends married with a kid and the telly. They looked bored to me. I always want to have that youthful feeling.' And Billy Idol, growing up in suburban Bromley, 'I always believed there was something else to have. The only thing that means anything to me is rock and roll.'

Well, for Billy Idol or Mark Laff, the drummer, the first job they've enjoyed is not highly paid. At the moment, they each draw £8 a week. They have a manager, John Ingham (who won't say what his cut is, but it is between 10 and 20 per cent), and an agent. They are about to be signed, after playing together for about six months, into the business. The thin end of it, as they see it, with a modest jump to £25 per week.

Their brand of music keeps itself close to its fans. They are suspicious of the apparently instant, massive successes of the Sixties, and the way, it seemed, that the Beatles took over half the world in a week. There are two extremes, Billy explains: 'We used to play in cellars and nobody knew. I went to see Bowie in concert last summer, and it was like a film.' They want to operate in the space between.

19 July 1980

THE LUSTRE OF HEAVY METAL

Mary Harron

The Wappentake is a modern pub in the centre of Sheffield, as anonymous as any other, but in the evenings it is like a secret clubhouse. The regulars are nearly all in their late teens or early twenties, and they come for one reason: to hear the heavy metal records that the resident DJ plays all night at ear-shattering volume.

Subtlety has no place in heavy metal. Critics have called it the worst form of rock music ever invented, but no form inspires such passionately devoted fans; the success of heavy metal is the phenomenon of the year in British rock.

On a recent Friday night the Wappentake regulars were jammed back to back in a haze of cigarette smoke. The DJ announced a single by Iron Maiden, and, as the music pounded, three teenage boys entered what looked like a slow-motion epileptic fit. Eyes closed in ecstasy, they jerked their heads back and forth in time, fingers strumming imaginary electric guitars. No one in the room batted an eyelid. It is a common ritual: at live concerts whole sections of the audience can be seen shaking their heads over phantom guitars.

There are girls at the Wappentake, but heavy metal is still boys' music, and the fashion style that is its trademark is exclusively male. This style is almost a uniform. The fans wear leather or denim jackets, decorated with badges and metal studs. Their denims are often embroidered with the names of their favourite bands: Saxon, Whitesnake, Sabs (short for Black Sabbath), Judas Priest. Their hair is long and flowing and their denim trousers are flared.

The reason these teenagers are adopting a dress style of seven years ago belongs to heavy metal's peculiar history. What is happening now is the resurgence of a style that flourished in the early Seventies under the name of 'heavy rock.' In an age of rock heroics, this music was the most grandiose: it had the biggest amplifiers, the longest solos, the most melodramatic vocals.

Then in 1976 punk arrived bringing a new ideology and a new fashion. Punk attacked the very idea that rock musicians should be heroes (although it created its own); it scorned the blissed-out passivity of the mass festivals and it declared the guitar solo self-indulgent.

In the late Seventies, heavy metal was as unfashionable in Britain as it is possible for any music to be. But it never died, particularly in the North, and a handful of groups kept playing to their loyal followers around the country. Long after everyone else had narrowed their trousers and cropped their hair, they clung tenaciously to their old music and their old style of dressing.

Astonishingly, about 18 months ago heavy metal began to attract a whole new audience. Perhaps it was because when punk lost energy it left a vacuum that needed to be filled. Or perhaps there were thousands of fans who were never comfortable with punk in the first place, the conservatives in rock, the ones who didn't want to be challenged or disrupted. They longed for the days when you could sit in passive reverence in a concert hall and listen to a 20-minute guitar solo.

The diehard bands like Black Sabbath and Judas Priest began attracting new young fans. The fans formed their own groups and the music press dubbed the movement the New Wave of British Heavy Metal. The new music does have more vitality than the old wave, although to an unsympathetic ear it sounds as if every cliché in Seventies' rock had been blended together and speeded up.

In many ways the new heavy metal is a regression to the old rock values, but the years spent in the cold have given this movement quite a different character. The clothes are illustrative. Heavy metal bands were losers for so long that the style they clung to developed into a losers' style. The new fans are no early Seventies dandies: their denims look faded and grubby. Their hair is lank.

Drugs also seem to play little part in this culture. At concerts you can often see fans stretched out, quite comatose, on the floor, but it is either due to alcohol or the decibel level. Indeed, there is something masochistic about the fans search for mystic obliteration through noise – they refer to themselves as headbangers. At concerts some will rush forward like lemmings to place their ears against the amplifiers, in search of certain aural damage.

Some aspects of heavy metal's appeal remain an impenetrable mystery, but anyone would be impressed by the bond of love between the bands and their audience. On stage the musicians seem as thrilled and delighted with their own solos as the boys imitating them in the front row. Brian Harrigan, who covers heavy metal for *New Music News* says, 'The fans expect loyalty, and they get it. Where else in music do you find a group with an album in the charts who will slip out to the local pub before a gig to spend an hour talking to their fans?'

Heavy metal has been, and probably always will be, strongest in the bleak industrial towns. Sheffield is one of the places where it never really went away: the Wappentake has been playing the same music since 1973. Now Sheffield has its local heavy metal heroes. A group of teenagers formed a group called Def Leppard there two years ago, and ended up in the charts. But, among the group of Wappentake regulars I spoke to, Def Leppard have fallen into disfavour.

'They're a Sheffield band, but they've just grown too big,' said a 19-year-old hospital porter called Martin. 'They've sold out. Well, they've gone to America, haven't they?'

What did he mean, that they'd left Sheffield?

'Yeah, for the big time. But heavy metal is for the people. It's something to live for. I mean, five days a week at work, what you got to look forward to, other than a night down here Friday or Saturday? But Def Leppard wouldn't think of playing down here again.'

Martin asked me why I wanted to write an article about heavy metal. I muttered something about it being a phenomenon. He grinned and said, 'What did you think when you came down here – "Oooh, I'm going to talk to a bunch of long-haired idiots"?'

Alison, a smartly dressed girl who works in a boutique, said, 'What annoys me is they always put heavy metal along with trouble and fights, and there isn't.'

She's right there. Heavy metal fans may dress tough, but most of them are gentle, headbanging lambs. As for the Wappentake, Mrs Jackson, the assistant manageress, says there has been scarcely any trouble there in seven years.

'They know you see, that is they get into trouble, they'll get banned. And they'd rather do anything than get banned. This place is like home to them. They'll come religiously whether it rains, hails or snows. They'll come when the buses are on strike. They always come at the same time, and they stand in one certain place and they drink one certain kind of beer.'

Heavy metal would never have survived if these fans weren't set in their ways. And for the next year or so their music will dominate the charts: a year of triumph over all the London poseurs who laughed at the headbangers for so long. But will it last? 'It'll probably die out,' said a boy with lank brown hair. 'But people like us, we'll never die out.'

7 March 2008

HOW TO LOSE THREE MILLION FANS IN ONE EASY STEP

Bob Stanley

Guy Hands wouldn't allow it these days – what are these 'artists' trying to do? Bankrupt the company? – but in 1983, no one batted an eyelid when a major chart band followed a multimillion selling pop album with something extremely obtuse. An album, even, that contained no obvious hits and soundtracked the cold war at its coldest. No one bought it, mind you, so Orchestral Manoeuvres in the Dark's *Dazzle Ships* came to be viewed as a heroic failure – the ultimate commercial suicide.

'Every year we'd visit American Forces Network [the broadcaster for US troops] in Germany,' remembers OMD's Andy McCluskey. 'There were almost a million people at [the US] Frankfurt base, it was like a colony. And we'd see the same guy every year when we went there to do an interview. So we gave him *Dazzle Ships* and he said, "Wow! Gee, what a weird album. Radio Prague? Let's play it! They'll think the commies have invaded!"'

Architecture and Morality, OMD's third album, had been a monster hit following its release in 1981, with any number of potential singles. 'Souvenir' was first out of the block and made No 3. When 'Joan of Arc' got rave reviews ahead of the album's release, McCluskey told *Smash Hits*: 'That's nothing. Wait until you hear the next single – it's our "Mull of Kintyre".' 'Maid of Orleans' duly became another huge hit in the UK, and Germany's best-selling single of 1982.

'It sounds strange, I know, but we had been trying to change the world,' says McCluskey. 'It was the naive confidence of youth, the idea that music is that important. The music we made had to be interesting and different. And somehow we believed that would change the world, the way people think. So when we sold three million albums and the world didn't change, we were scared.'

The result was a bout of writers' block. It wasn't as though OMD wrote conventional love songs to start with – 'Enola Gay' was famously about Hiroshima, 'Stanlow' about a power station – yet *Dazzle Ships* took off what McCluskey calls 'the sweet wrapper'. For starters, the first single was called 'Genetic Engineering'. 'I was very positive about the subject! I didn't expect someone like Monsanto to come along and say, "Fuck it, we can make money out of cross-pollination."'

However, when Dave Lee Travis played the single on Radio 1, he said – with some gravitas – that it was about time someone in the music world stood up to the evils of tinkering with nature. 'People didn't listen to the lyrics,' McCluskey recalls. 'I think they automatically assumed it would be anti. Generally, I was pretty dark and pessimistic. Very precious and strong-minded.'

The song is still one of *Dazzle Ships*' more overtly commercial moments. Disembodied voices from the eastern bloc sit over recordings of time signal pips, speak-and-spell machines, wartime submarines. 'It all made sense to us. We wanted to be Abba and Stockhausen. The machinery, bones and humanity were juxtaposed.'

Dazzle Ships entered the charts at No 5, then dropped like a stone. *Architecture and Morality* sold three million; *Dazzle Ships* sold 300,000. With one record, Orchestral Manoeuvres lost 90 per cent of their audience.

'I was the ideas man, Paul Humphreys made it happen. It was a symbiotic relationship. But I'm the one who took us right to the edge of the plank. When people heard *Dazzle Ships*, they obviously preferred our music with the sweet wrapper on. Not a song about someone's hand being cut off by a totalitarian regime. After that, there was a conscious and unconscious reeling-in of our experimental side. We got more . . . conservative.'

As, of course, did the whole country. *Dazzle Ships*, falling between the Falklands war and the Tories' emphatic re-election, sounded the bell for the new pop playground that the charts had become. An almost forgotten era, now lumped in with the ephemera that succeeded it – the likes of Johnny Hates Jazz – new pop was an attempt in 1981 and 1982 to marry chart music to the avant-garde. Incredibly, it succeeded. There was no manifesto, but the new generation – OMD, ABC, Soft Cell, the Teardrop Explodes,

Dexys Midnight Runners – had lived through punk, understood its situationist leanings, and understood the real value of music. While OMD name-dropped 'Dancing Queen', Ian Curtis and Mies van der Rohe, ABC claimed they existed to write 'a soundtrack for the 80s'.

At the turn of the decade, ABC had been Vice Versa, a Sheffield post-punk unit who leaned more towards the atonal than to Abba. They were interviewed for a fanzine called *Modern Drugs* by Martin Fry, and got on with him so well they asked him to become their singer. After changing their name to the perfectly minimalist ABC, they sat down to write some perfectly modernist love songs: 'Tears Are Not Enough', 'Poison Arrow', 'The Look of Love', 'All of My Heart'. All top 20 hits; all soulful, well-dressed pop. Their parent album, *The Lexicon of Love*, defined the charts of 1982.

ABC predated OMD in their attempt to take on the preconceptions of their fanbase, and their second album, *Beauty Stab*, did not define the charts of 1983. The strings were gone, replaced by some tough guitars that sounded weirdly dated – sometimes like Low-era Bowie, sometimes closer to Led Zeppelin. Had it been released two years later, when guitars were voguish once more, it would have kept the ABC boat afloat. Instead, it just sounded confusing.

Like 'Genetic Engineering', the first single from *Beauty Stab* – 'That Was Then But This Is Now' – was exhilarating and shrill, and made the top 20. The cause wouldn't have been entirely hopeless but for one line: 'Can't complain, mustn't grumble, help yourself to another piece of crumble.' It had perhaps been meant as a joke – it was followed by a cheesy sax break – but Roddy Frame of Aztec Camera lambasted it in an interview as embodying all that was bad in modern pop. Suddenly, the emperor's new pop clothes were revealed. The line has been a fixture in 'worst lyrics' polls for 25 years, attaining the top slot in one conducted last year by BBC 6 Music. *Beauty Stab*, like *Dazzle Ships*, died a quick death.

Which leads you to wonder what the hell happened in 1983. It was almost as if the country was tired of mavericks, had heard enough about unemployment figures and ghost towns and nuclear threat. They wanted glamour, in a Seaside Special way.

Duran Duran had their first No 1 in 1983. Paul Young, Wham! and Howard Jones – considerably more pliable and predictable than OMD or ABC – were the year's new stars. Waiting around the corner, jacket sleeves already rolled up, was Nik Kershaw.

According to Kevin Rowland of Dexys Midnight Runners, the music industry had started to become 'incredibly conservative. I was dealing with people who were much more careerist. At Mercury, by 1985, there were loads of public-school people – millions of them.'

Dexys had already crashed once when, following the No 1 hit 'Geno', they recorded the super-intense single 'Keep It Part Two (Inferiority Part One)'. It received no airplay and failed to crack even the top 75. 'I just had something to say,' says Rowland. 'I was disappointed with success – we were still cramped in a minibus on hot summer days. I did not think, in any way, that "Keep It" was difficult. It was truthful, 100 per cent truthful. "Geno" had been a No 1; I thought, if you like that amount of emotion, try this amount of emotion.'

Dexys, though, had a second wind, and fought back with the million-selling Celtic soul of *Too-Rye-Ay* in 1982. 'Come On Eileen' became an international No 1. They had survived and prospered. *Too-Rye-Ay*'s follow-up, *Don't Stand Me Down*, was an astonishingly personal and beautiful record, but it became Dexys' equivalent of *Dazzle Ships*. The problem was it came out three years after *Too-Rye-Ay*.

Rowland is understandably proud. 'I don't want to think about it too much because I want to think about what I'm doing now, but I remember coming out of the studio thinking, "That's the best I can do."'

Don't Stand Me Down emerged in a far less adventurous era than the one *Too-Rye-Ay* was released into. New mavericks on the block such as the Smiths and the Jesus and Mary Chain were entirely ignored by Radio 1. The same happened to Dexys, though it was their own fault – no single was released from the album.

'It was a stupid mistake,' Rowland says. 'I wanted "This Is What She's Like" to be the single, a 10-minute single. The manager said, "Good idea . . . or no single at all." It was a chance to be like the groups of the early 1970s, like Led Zeppelin. I thought that would be great, but I wasn't sure. There was a new guy at Mercury and he was like, "What?" That was it. I said, we're definitely not releasing one. They [the label] went with *Don't Stand Me Down* for about a fortnight. Then they moved on to something else.'

British eccentricity may well play a role in these crash-and-burn albums – a willingness to be contrary. Some Americans have followed gold albums with zero-sellers, but not many. Harry Nilsson's *Nilsson Schmilsson* contained the original lung-busting power ballad, 'Without You', and made him a rich man. Never one for the obvious, he gave its sequel the misleading title *Son of Schmilsson* and filled it with raggedly sung novelties. It contained no obvious hits, though 'You're Breaking My Heart', a song for his ex-wife, did stand out: ABC's 'apple crumble' line hardly holds a candle to: 'You're breaking my heart, you're tearing it apart, so fuck you.'

That was calculated self-destruction. Neil Young, having tasted fame and fortune with *After the Goldrush* and *Harvest*, famously said he would rather head for the ditch than stay in the middle of the road. And that's just what he did with *Time Fades Away*. Young recorded the stoned, muddy, hard-rocking album on a stadium tour to confused audiences who had never heard the songs before. No atmosphere, no acoustic balladry, just memories of getting a kicking in the schoolyard and an extended moan about LA. Young's profile duly plummeted.

Fleetwood Mac's *Rumours* had been recorded in trying circumstances. The sequel had the even more onerous task of following what was then the bestselling American album ever. Lindsey Buckingham assumed control of 1979's *Tusk*. Though it cost £1 million to make – a figure that even today seems barely plausible – much of it sounded clattery, half-formed, with strange rhythmic leaps and offbeat tics. *Hotel California* it wasn't.

It later emerged in his girlfriend's memoirs that Buckingham had become obsessed with Talking Heads, and was desperate to make Mac relevant to a post-punk world. The problem was that even though *Rumours* had been all about break-ups and unfaithful lovers, it still sounded as though the roof was down and you were heading up the highway in the sunshine. *Tusk* was unleavened weirdness, as close to its predecessor as the Beach Boys' lo-fi *Smiley Smile* had been to *Pet Sounds*. It simply didn't cut the midwest mustard. However, like *Dazzle Ships*, *Tusk* makes a lot more sense to 2008 ears.

'The album that almost completely killed our career seems to have become a work of dysfunctional genius,' says Andy McCluskey with a grin. 'The reality is that it's taken Paul [Humphreys] 25 years to forgive me for *Dazzle Ships*. But some people always hold it up as what we were all about, why they thought we were great.'

31 January 1997

THE SOUND OF ACID

Jon Savage

'Turn off your mind, relax and float downstream.' There are few commands more simple and evocative. They came to John Lennon after an LSD trip at the turn of 1965/66, during which he'd used a book as a guide. Edited by Timothy Leary, Ralph Metzner and Richard Alpert, *The Psychedelic Experience: A Manual Based on the Tibetan Book of the Dead* aimed to give a framework to the explicitly experimental use of this new drug, LSD.

At the end of the Beatles' album *Revolver*, 'Tomorrow Never Knows' made public what had been, until then, the preserve of a few CIA spooks, academics and bohemian West Coast musicians. The genie was out of the bottle: psychedelia had arrived.

In 1966, 'Tomorrow Never Knows' sounded like nothing the Beatles had ever recorded: not for nothing was its working title The Void. Beginning with a tamboura drone, the track resolves into a manically pumping Paul McCartney bassline and a Ringo Starr drum loop so massive that, as Ian McDonald notes in *Revolution in the Head*, it sounds like 'a cosmic tabla played by a Vedic deity riding in a storm cloud'.

Then comes the first of five endlessly repeating tape loops, a seagull-like swoop, seguing into a Lennon vocal pitched to sound like a massed choir of Tibetan monks. Unlike most pop records of the time, 'Tomorrow Never Knows' did not follow a linear pattern but twisted and turned like a Moebius strip, creating its own time: 'Play the game existence to the end . . . of the beginning.'

An explicit assault on contemporary perception, a manifesto for a different kind of consciousness, the track is timeless. Thirty years later, its influence is everywhere in rock: there are echoes in Oasis's 'Morning Glory' ('listening to the sound of my favourite tune'), the accented drum loops of the Chemical Brothers' 'Setting Sun', the Eastern sonorities and psychic propaganda of Kula Shaker's album *K*.

In its equation of drugs + aural loops = transcendence,

'Tomorrow Never Knows' also prefigures today's dance culture, where trance, drum 'n' bass and new acid recombine psychedelic ideas and sounds. Dance shops display flyers with computer psycho-imagery and records with titles like 'Retrodelica: Back from the Future', 'Phantasm III: Future Psychedelic Trance', 'Feed Your Head', 'Endemic Void', or, most explicitly, 'LSD' by Hallucinogen.

Nearly 30 years after 1967's Summer of Love – a phrase now trademarked by the Bill Graham Organisation – psychedelia is back . . . if it ever went away. Apart from its continued pop resurgence, it is the subject of several new books: Jim De Rogatis's 30-year overview, *Kaleidoscope Eyes*, Matthew Collins's landmark history of ecstasy culture, *Altered States*, and Sarah Champion's collection of 'new fiction from the chemical generation' *Disco Biscuits*, with short stories by Jeff Noon, Martin Millar and Irvine Welsh.

Advertising, design and contemporary art are infused with the style's op swirls; it continues to fuel the computer industry: games, the net and virtual reality. And the high Sixties are still being mined: in the release of the first 'Tomorrow Never Knows' on the Beatles' *Anthology 2*, in the spoken-word CD histories of Paul Kantner (Jefferson Airplane) and Ray Manzarek (the Doors), and in a major show, I Can Take You Higher, opening in Cleveland's Rock and Roll Hall of Fame this May.

If psychedelia is back, what is it and what does it want? The word is a postwar coinage, reflecting a CIA experiment in mind colonisation – the search for Aldous Huxley's somatic agent of social control in *Brave New World*. As Martin Lee and Bruce Swain write in *Acid Dreams*: 'Nearly every drug that appeared on the black market during the 1960s – marijuana, cocaine, heroin, PCP, amylnitrate, mushrooms, DMT, barbituarites, laughing gas, speed – had previously been scrutinised, tested and, in some cases, refined by the CIA and army scientists. But . . . none received as much attention or was embraced with such enthusiasm as LSD-25.'

Dr Humphrey Osmond was part of the small academic clique which clinically experimented with LSD in the early Fifties: he is also renowned as the person who, in 1953, gave Aldous Huxley a similarly psychotropic drug, mescalin. For the novelist, the experience was so profound that he sought to give it a new name: in their subsequent correspondence, Osmond came up with a term derived from the Greek psyche (soul) and delein (to make manifest); hence psychedelic.

In *The Doors of Perception*, published in 1956, Huxley wrote: 'I was . . . in a world where everything shone with the Inner Light, and was infinite in its significance.' He saw the drug's effects in terms of a major realignment of perception: 'something more than, above all something different from, the carefully selected utilitarian material which our narrowed, individual minds regard as a complete, or at least sufficient, picture of reality'.

If you take this experience out of the clinical or spiritual enclave and put it in pop culture, you are going to have a serious clash of values, and this is what happened in the Sixties. As Terence McKenna writes in *Food of the Gods*, between 1947 and 1960 the major indole hallucinogens were characterised, purified and investigated. It is no coincidence that the subsequent decade was the most turbulent in America for a hundred years.

Already prevalent on the West Coast, LSD arrived in the UK during 1965, and was adopted by pop stars like the Yardbirds, the Beatles and Donovan, who sought to turn the Inner Light into sound. Despite the fact that the main locus of the emerging psychedelic style was San Francisco, particularly the bohemian Haight Ashbury enclave, London also had a strong scene, based around bookshops like Indica and groups like Pink Floyd, whose 1966 light show can only be described as obliterating.

Whereas the San Francisco style was folk and blues based, increasingly messianic and politicised against the Vietnam war, the British added a pop spin in records like 'Strawberry Fields Forever' and 'The Piper at the Gates of Dawn': studio-based, inner-directed, but above all concentrating on the child.

This is a perennial romantic fallacy, but a powerful, and often useful, one. The combined use of cannabis, LSD and mescalin in the Sixties unlocked a surge of pop creativity. Coinciding with the rise of stereo hardware and software (hi-fi systems and long-playing records) and a moment when youth seemed to have total power, the psychedelic style, enshrined in the Beatles' 1967 *Sgt Pepper's Lonely Hearts Club Band*, marks pop at a moment of great ambition and outreach.

People tend to think of that period as the age of love and flowers, but just beneath the inclusiveness and warmth is another side: the trauma beneath the childhood wonder – expressed for all time by Syd Barrett and John Lennon; the anger behind the wish for peace and love – just listen to 'I Am the Walrus' and the Rolling Stones' 'We Love You'; the sense that you had undertaken a journey from which you might never return.

There are many risks in experimenting with your consciousness. If you're going to take a drug which makes the soul manifest, you may get more than you bargained for. You may be confronted by personal demons you didn't know existed or externally hostile situations which tip you into madness which, while temporary, is nonetheless real. You have seen God through a drug rather than the discipline of spiritual thought: this can leave a serious hole in your reality.

Not the least cause of these problems is the reaction of government and its instruments – the police, the army and the judiciary. It is a hallmark of psychedelic culture that it is visionary, and that this vision is implicitly questioning of, if not hostile to, established systems and perceptions. As Irvine Welsh writes in *The Undefeated*: 'Just do it now, just change your life in the space of a heartbeat, do it now . . .'

This is where we enter contemporary time. There is a line, only partially delineated in *Kaleidoscope Eyes*, from Sixties psychedelia to its contemporary mutations. It runs from the gay origins of disco, through late Seventies Euro synth-pop like Donna Summer and Giorgio Moroder's still unrivalled 'I Feel Love', to mid-Eighties black dance music, Chicago house and Detroit techno, whose earliest exponents, like Larry Heard, Derrick May and Juan Atkins, saw their function in visionary, psychedelic terms.

In adapting the possibilities of digital technology – sequencers and synthesisers – to what had previously been a perception expressed in rock, they created the style and approach that now dominates dance music. And when those early house and techno records – fabulous, minimal, spacey songs like Fingers Inc's 'Mystery of Love' – impacted with the increasing spread of ecstasy throughout British clubland from 1986 onwards, psychedelia again became a social phenomenon, only this time it was called acid house, then Madchester, raves, and now ecstasy culture.

During the past 10 years, a generation barely born in the Sixties has gone down a similar path to find that the questions posed by the hippes all those years ago have not been answered: not at all. The story of ecstasy culture echoes the Sixties. Although the composition and effects of LSD and ecstasy are quite specific, there are strong similarities: loss of ego, communal visions, altered perception.

There is also a similar trajectory of official reaction which is much more severe now than it was then. Chapter six of *Altered States* is an excellent summary of the growth of a 'techno traveller' culture from the free Stonehenge festivals of the Fifties, Sixties and Seventies through successive flash points to its peak moment of cultural visibility (the political vibrancy remains in the anti-road protest movement): the illegal party at Castlemorton Common in May 1992, attended by upwards of 25,000 people.

This was the event that accelerated the progress of the 1994 Criminal Justice and Public Order Bill, which, for the first time in living memory, legislated against a particular form of music: the 'repetitive beats' of techno and house.

In many ways, Britain is a society divided in perception as never before: between those who use drugs which are illegal and those who don't. The extraordinary success of Irvine Welsh, who, courageously, has not shied away from its implications, indicates a strong need to be heard from the part of those who do. While columnists and politicians on the New Right continue to demonise the Sixties, a significant section of the British population has voted with their feet: illegal drug use and altered perceptions are pandemic.

As in Prohibition-era America, the consequences are profound: flouted every day by hundreds of thousands, the whole institution of the law is brought into disrepute. Then there are the unpleasant social consequences of handing over a huge economy to the black market: a situation where large metropolitan areas resemble the Wild West. These serious issues are hardly being discussed, let alone addressed. Prohibition has failed.

The continued resurgence of psychedelia also throws up perceptual insights. For all their cheesiness, tunes like Hallucinogen's 'LSD' and Kula Shaker's 'Tattva' speak of a spiritual hunger on the part of young musicians through which to transcend a perceived crisis of materialist consumerism.

Indeed, in its very sonic wildness, psychedelia offers a valid alternative to hundreds of thousands living within a conservative body politic. The Right hasn't succeeded in eradicating the strong traces of the Sixties: the law doesn't seem to stop anyone taking mind-expanding drugs, nor do the risks. Psychedelia can be a form, it can be a marketing tool, it can be babyboomer nostalgia, but it also speaks of nothing less than the human wish to try things differently, to time-travel from the past and the future into the present. That nagging itch: Why not? What if? Why do things have to be this way?

At the core of psychedelia is a concentration on the *now* – the total intensity of the moment – that is the hallmark of youth and its culture. But psychedelia did something extra: it made the *now* into a god, and thus squared that curious circle between the pop experience (the now as frenzy) and Eastern religion (the now as eternal stillness). As Ian MacDonald writes about Richard Alpert's famous book *Be Here Now*, the slogan paraphrases the Vedic teaching that to dwell on past or future is to be dead to the present. Enlightenment consists of living continuously in the present – a philosophical paradox in that to do so requires will, yet will is time-bound, depending on memory and anticipation (consciousness of the past and future).

It is within this paradox that the endless fascination of psychedelia lies, as successive generations fumble with the doors of perception in the dark, trying to grasp the shafts of light as they appear through the murk.

5 May 1998

THE MYTH OF COOL

Andy Beckett

The inventor of Cool Britannia works in a narrow back office in London, between the Panamanian embassy and an old brothel. She is American. Most of the time, Sarah Moynihan-Williams is just another Mayfair solicitor, with clients from Hong Kong and Australia to plan taxes and form companies for. She is jolly but discreet. She has a jug of water on her desk for the tiny gaps between telephone calls.

Three years ago, though, Mrs Moynihan-Williams made a minor but decisive intervention in the life of the nation. On her way back from a tax seminar in Croydon, she was walking through Victoria station when she saw a stand selling ice cream. The brand was Ben & Jerry's, which she used to eat in America, and alongside the tubs and scoops was a pile of leaflets announcing a competition to name a new flavour. Moynihan-Williams likes entering competitions – 'Free stuff is good,' she says with her New York crispness, 'and it's like being their ad person' – so she took a leaflet home, bothered her husband about it for a week and then sent off her suggestion. Months later, in the spring of 1996, Ben & Jerry's chose Cool Britannia. Its creator was thrilled: she got a free trip to America, coupons for 100 tubs and satisfaction 'of seeing my ice cream in the supermarkets'. When the brand was launched that summer, she agreed to dress up as Britannia and ride a chariot around the Royal Albert Hall, dragging a 10ft (3m) inflatable ice cream tub. 'I'm a good sport,' she says, by way of explanation.

Then the madness started. At first, it was just a few newspaper cuttings sent by friends: Cool Britannia as a headline, as a fashion-page phrase, as a usefully flexible pun for articles about anything modern and British. Moynihan-Williams found the spread of her catchphrase interesting and mildly amusing, 'an ego trip'. Then the sub-editors' little secret became an editor's craze, a magazine cover concept, a commonplace on *News at Ten*.

By 1997, Cool Britannia meant rock bands and restaurants,

football managers and fashion designers, Union Jacks on everything by the beginning of this year, it was shorthand for the government's entire arts policy this spring, it has virtually become shorthand for the government itself. Moynihan-Williams, who stayed up all night cheering for Labour last 1 May, is horrified: 'Cool Britannia has become so exploited. It's been used as a stick to beat the government.' Perhaps they had it coming. Tony Blair, after all, has written articles for newspapers about a 'second industrial revolution'. Demos, his favoured think-tank, has talked about 'rebranding Britain'. And Robin Cook, not a foreign secretary noted for his interest in speed garage or combat trousers, launched something last month called Panel 2000, a 'task force' of cultural achievers to lead a 'full frontal attack on the myth of a tired Britain'. Nearly everyone on the panel was over 40.

Even John Major, the great recent misreader of the national mood, is beginning to snigger at this uneasy mixing of government and grooviness. 'Whenever I hear ministers speak that utter claptrap [about Cool Britannia], I am blushing for them,' he said in Parliament three weeks ago. 'It is rather undignified . . . It is actually doing no good to this government either.' When Labour-supporting comedian Ben Elton expanded on these sentiments, Blair interrupted a visit to Saudi Arabia to answer back: the government's interest in the British culture industry was not about being fashionable but about creating 'real jobs' and 'real investment'. Cool Britannia, it was reported, was 'a phrase he has come to detest'. Sarah Moynihan-Williams, it would seem, has a lot to answer for.

But there is more to Cool Britannia than a cute phrase becoming sickly. Moynihan-Williams was not quite the first to use it. In 1967, just as the last British cultural boom was starting to overreach itself, a bunch of student satirists named the Bonzo Dog Doo Dah Band recorded a twist version of 'Rule Britannia'. It ran: 'Cool Britannia, Britannia you are cool/Britons ever, ever, ever shall be hip . . .' Twenty-five years later, another American living in London, a waspish journalist called Cosmo Landesman, picked up the phrase again. His use of it, however, also lacked a certain something: 'Once, Cool Britannia ruled all the waves of youth culture,' he wrote in this newspaper. 'Alas, no more.' In the early Nineties, in Landesman's articles and in the odd piece elsewhere, this was the meaning attached to Cool Britannia. It was a pun poking fun at Britain's pretensions to a vigorous popular culture – when the country's fashions and musical fads were actually in decline, viewed from abroad, like everything else. On the covers of the pop music papers – always a sensitive cultural barometer – were a succession of white American rock musicians, week after week: Soundgarden, Mudhoney, Ministry, Faith No More and, most relentlessly of all, Nirvana. Their music and image owed almost nothing to the British pop traditions of flounce and outrage, instead the grunge bands were grindingly loud and masculine, made for Midwest stadiums and desert-suburb radio. Teenagers in Oxford and Oldham bought their albums regardless.

Meanwhile, in pop music, British symbols and subjects were close to forbidden. 'It was a long time since the Union Jack had been used on a front cover,' says Andrew Harrison, who was editor of the magazine *Select* in 1992. 'It was equivalent to the swastika.' Writing songs about Britain was scarcely more fashionable. The London sunsets and local parks that had entranced Sixties bands such as the Kinks and Small Faces looked quaint, pointless settings for modern pop. As Harrison puts it, they seemed to have been 'written out' of the art form. Yet all this was slightly deceptive. Whole cultures rarely develop in a single direction and in Britain, by 1992, despite the seemingly endless recession and the entrenched rule of the Tories, the wave of fashionable nationalism that would become Blair's Cool Britannia was quietly starting to form.

The first surges came from raves and football. 'The late Eighties dance culture brought back a notion that British people could make a difference,' says Harrison. 'Our innovators could go to the top.' That may seem a great weight to place on a few hundred warehouse parties and bleary dawns beside the M25, but the Acid House craze of 1988 and 1989, for all its lurid briefness, established a network of dance music entrepreneurs and customers and attitudes that only existed in Britain.

Nobody was waving Union Jacks, of course, yet when part of the rave culture mutated into a movement based in Manchester during 1989 and 1990, a more overt kind of pride appeared. 'Madchester', as it quickly called itself, was really just a few sharp bands (the Stone Roses, the Happy Mondays) and a nightclub (the Hacienda) but it marketed the scene and the city with an inventive fervour: T-shirts printed with Lancastrian boasts and the Manchester dialling code were ubiquitous at 1990's summer music festivals.

Then there was that year's World Cup. For the first time in a decade, for many, supporting England stopped being an embarrassment. And thousands of the cheerers for Lineker and Gazza were the same people who went to raves in Essex or clubs in Manchester. A distinctively British set of leisure loyalties was becoming available.

In April 1993, Harrison put a Union Jack on the cover of *Select*. 'It's the job of the music press to create fictitious movements, but we knew what was happening was real.' The special issue had 'Yanks go home!' as its cover line and Made in Britain as its logo, its graphics were borrowed from *Dad's Army* and the war and its interviews, with a new cluster of self-consciously British bands such as Pulp and Suede, lingered lovingly over the musicians' favourite pubs and cul-de-sacs. The *Mirror*'s 'Achtung Surrender!' headline against Germany's footballers during Euro 96 was only three summers away. In 1993, though, not everyone was ready for this. *Select*'s rivals claimed outrage. In September, when *Melody Maker* published a patriotic cover of its own, with Damon Albarn of Blur (a middle-class band who had taken to dressing – almost – like skinheads) declaring that 'our culture is under siege', the whole edition had to be hedged around with denials of sympathy for the National Front. The letters pages steamed for months.

But 'Britpop', as it was now called, had momentum. In April 1994, Kurt Cobain, Nirvana's singer and guiding spirit, committed suicide – the vogue for US bands was over. The British music industry saw its opportunity. 'Grunge had moved profits back to the US,' says Andy Blake, director of cultural studies at King Alfred's College in Winchester, 'but once British record labels could market guys playing guitars again, they could make people think of the Sixties and start reinventing the decade all over again.' By the end of 1994, Blur, Pulp and Suede were all selling heavily. Oasis, who had been part of the Madchester scene as locals, were also growing into stars. The 'Brit' prefix began to be used to enliven some other, slower-off-the-marks bits of the national culture: films, literature, fashion. For the first time in three decades, there seemed to be a national brand. It was a matter of time before a politician noticed.

It was John Redwood. In March 1996, he wrote a curious article for this newspaper claiming Britpop for Conservatism. From a few scraps of lyrics about English skies and tentative optimism, he suggested an entire national revival was there for the government's taking. His argument was threadbare – all the Britpop bands were melancholy in their view of Britain, and Labour-voting – yet the ambition of it was prescient. 'Margaret Thatcher saw popular culture as an irritant,' says Blake. 'John Major went to Stamford Bridge to watch Chelsea. The prime minister was taking on board popular culture.' In May 1996, Virginia Bottomley grinned her way through a showing of *Trainspotting*; its story about Edinburgh heroin addicts was Britain's representative at the Cannes Film Festival. 'I think I should see a film that's been so successful,' she said.

In November, after Ben & Jerry's had launched Cool Britannia, and *Newsweek* and *Vanity Fair* and all the other American tastemakers had granted the whole British phenomenon their approval, Major joined in. His speech to the lord mayor's banquet abandoned all his trademark talk of morning mist and cricket grounds. 'Our pop culture rules the airwaves,' he announced, in language that these days he might call 'rather undignified'. He described Britain under the Conservatives as bustling, rudely inventive: 'Our pubs, clubs and restaurants are packed. Our television programmes are in demand worldwide . . . Our theatre gives the lead . . . Our country has taken over the fashion catwalks of Paris.' Five months later, he had lost the election. But this idea, like many of the Tories', found a happy new home with Labour. Within weeks of taking office, the Government renamed the deliberately fusty-sounding Department of National Heritage as the dynamic-sounding Department of Culture, Media and Sport. 'Cool Britannia is here to stay,' wrote Chris Smith, the ministry's new controller.

Nowadays, this judgement looks a little reckless. Like most fashions and coinages, Cool Britannia has spread faster and faster across its particular pond, like algae, until it has coated the whole surface of British culture. Over the last few weeks, references to the phrase in newspapers have run at dozens every day. And now there is the backlash: the whole colony is suffocating and dying.

There may be other reasons for Cool Britannia's demise, besides this lifecycle. For one thing, it was always a heavily self-conscious phenomenon, reliant on the past. 'Cool Britannia was framed by "Swinging London" in 1966,' says the cultural critic Jon Savage, 'and "Swinging London" was a media construct too.' American recognition has been crucial to Cool Britannia as well: Oasis and Blur, for all their patriotism, have made frequent and nervous transatlantic forays to 'crack America'.

Meanwhile, the actual products of Cool Britannia have seemed less and less interesting or fun. Britpop, which originally was meant to unite dance music and literate songwriting alike, has narrowed into what Savage calls 'Britrock' – guitar-dominated, macho and trapped in the sounds and poses of the Sixties. The participants in Cool Britannia, similarly, seem less diverse in class or race than its inclusive rhetoric first suggested. 'Middle England wasn't included,' says Blake. Nor, with the glossy magazines preferring to write about new restaurants than drum and bass on council estates, was much of the culture of the less wealthy in Britain.

The government, it seems, has bought into a fashionable line just as the clearance sale is imminent. And Labour has done so unconvincingly: 'There's an obvious mismatch,' says Blake, 'between puritanism, which the government represents, and hedonism, which the arts represent.' Next month, Ben & Jerry's is withdrawing Cool Britannia from the British market. This decision is only 'for the time being', the company says, and the flavour will still be sold in America. But the symbolism seems clear enough. The words ‘Cool Britannia’ should very soon stop appearing in newspapers.

Then again, the culture they were coined for is unlikely to disappear. Jarvis Cocker and his imitators will keep singing about bus stops. There will be people in the government, for the first time, who actually listen to the words and, quite rightly, take them seriously as export earners. And Sarah Moynihan-Williams will find it all secretly gratifying. She even says ‘ta’ and ‘chuffed’ these days.

16 August 2002

MUSIC TO DRIVE CARS BY

Dorian Lynskey

If they were asked to create a compilation tape featuring 2002's key records, selective music-lovers might be tempted to fill it with hip crossover acts such as the Hives, the Streets and Doves. Like previous generations of tasteful hipsters, those music-lovers would be sadly mistaken. Any honest attempt to assess the year's soundtrack would have to include two far more ubiquitous songs: Nickelback's 'How You Remind Me' and Pink's 'Don't Let Me Get Me'.

The former is a Nirvana-lite grunge ballad by a bunch of hirsute Canadians, which, since its US release last December, has broken US Billboard airplay records with an official listenership of 131 million. The latter is faux-angsty powerhouse soft-rock performed by a former R&B singer and co-written by Linda Perry, erstwhile frontwoman of post-grunge one-hit wonders 4 Non Blondes. Both singles have helped their host albums, *Silver Side Up* and *M!ssundaztood* respectively, achieve multiple platinum status. And both are representative of a genre that has defied fashion for three decades; a genre that has reinvented itself to accommodate every musical sea-change; a genre adored by Alan Partridge, Homer Simpson and *American Psycho*'s Patrick Bateman; a genre that will never die: drivetime.

A recent survey into US driving habits revealed that 87 per cent of drivers listen to music in the car, and 71 per cent sing along. Given that most listen to the radio, the potential exposure for records that sound good with the accelerator pedal down is enormous. In a radio context, drivetime simply refers to the late afternoon slot when homebound commuters are a captive audience – the eclectic Radio 2 show of that name recently spawned the *Drivin' with Johnnie Walker* album – but it also defines a specific kind of music apparently designed with motorised transport in mind.

Since, unlike punk or acid house, it has no reverently

researched and well-defined family tree, drivetime is hard to define but the perfect specimen should have a chorus twice as loud as its verse and contain no ambiguity or irony whatsoever. As a quick test, imagine you're in a convertible shooting down some west coast highway (as in California, not Wales), one hand on an illusory steering wheel. If, when the chorus kicks in, you feel your foot involuntarily twitching where the accelerator should be, it's drivetime.

As teen-pop and dance music fall on hard times and guitar bands hog the airwaves, drivetime is resurgent. Toploader, whose biggest hit remains their cover of King Harvest's 1972 drivetime stalwart 'Dancing in the Moonlight', release their second album, *Magic Hotel*, this week. Meanwhile, Avril Lavigne, a 17-year-old Alanis Morissette mini-me, leads a clutch of starlets being pitched as anti-Britneys, armed with artfully distressed clothes and inoffensive guitar riffs. Christina Aguilera has hired Linda Perry to give her a Pink-style rock makeover. And nu-metal has moved away from rap crossover into the post-grunge balladeering of Staind and Puddle of Mudd. Even Eminem samples 'Dream On', Aerosmith's deathless 1970s drivetime hit, on his current album. After nu-metal, please welcome nu-drivetime.

Like sex and dancing, driving has always been at the core of rock's lexicon. Blues pioneer Robert Johnson's 1930s hit 'Terraplane Blues', an innuendo-stuffed homage to a particular brand of sedan, was probably the first, while the Beach Boys devoted an entire album, 1963's ropey *Little Deuce Coupe*, to the joys of motoring around southern California looking for girls. In fact, before the advent of FM radio many pop records were specifically mixed to suit the tinny acoustics of the AM car radios on which they would most often be heard.

Drivetime, however, aspires to something more than teenage kicks, and its Year Zero is Steppenwolf's 1968 hit 'Born to Be Wild'. Originally a counter-culture anthem immortalised in *Easy Rider*, it was transformed by relentless airplay into an all-purpose, ain't-driving-grand paean that enabled any listener to feel like a hard-rocking outlaw even while en route to a sales conference in Iowa. These days, its imperious command to 'get your motor runnin'' is most likely to be heard waggishly introducing a local news item on traffic restrictions.

'Born to Be Wild' heralded drivetime's early 1970s heyday. 1973 alone saw the release of Lynyrd Skynyrd's 'Free Bird', King Harvest's 'Dancing in the Moonlight' and the Doobie Brothers' 'Long Train Running'. This was a mixture of rock bands showing their sensitive side (Aerosmith's 'Dream On' remains the apotheosis) and blue-collar, everyman rock beloved of long-distance truck drivers. Bachman Turner Overdrive, creators of the Smashie and Nicey favourite 'You Ain't Seen Nothin' Yet', even went so far as dressing like long-distance truck drivers, while Lynyrd Skynyrd doffed their baseball caps on 'Truck Drivin' Man', a shameless appeal to their fanbase equivalent to Travis recording Mondeo Drivin' Man. The soundtrack to many an American adolescence, as reflected in such nostalgic coming-of-age movies as Richard Linklater's *Dazed and Confused*, these records have since entered an eternal afterlife on classic rock radio stations. Even as you read this, somewhere in America a DJ is no doubt playing 'All Right Now' by Free and a motorist is punching his fist in the air as he sings along.

In Britain, however, few of them even grazed the charts. Drivetime is a uniquely American phenomenon, born of a country where roads symbolise freedom and romance rather than tailbacks and Little Chefs, a difference wryly noted on Billy Bragg's adaptation of 'Route 66', entitled 'A13 Trunk Road to the Sea'. If drivetime in 1970s America meant listening to Aerosmith as you sped along uncluttered desert highways, in Britain it meant watching your dad pulling into Heston services while humming along to Mike Oldfield's 'Moonlight Shadow'. European records such as David Bowie's 'Always Crashing in the Same Car', Gary Numan's 'Cars' or Kraftwerk's 'Autobahn' tended to equate driving with alienation and death, and that wouldn't do at all.

Drivetime waned in the late 1970s as heavy rock became too heavy and soft rock too soft. Its renaissance in the mid-1980s can be attributed largely to the influence of movie producers Don Simpson and Jerry Bruckheimer. Simpson commissioned songs with the same preposterously overblown high-gloss melodrama as the movies they soundtracked. Hence *Beverly Hills Cop* launched Glenn Frey's 'The Heat Is On' and *Top Gun* begat Kenny Loggins's 'Danger Zone'. The songs' staple ingredients were thunderous drums, bright, clean power chords and cheesy 1980s synthesizers, and the typical video was shot either on an airfield or atop a windswept desert peak. Basically, the music playing inside Simpson's head while he snorted cocaine off a call girl's chest.

In fact, most 1980s drivetime carried traces of white powder. One of the most accurate scenes in *Boogie Nights* features a drug dealer reaching a fever pitch of coked-up hysteria to the deafening sound of Night Ranger's grotesque power ballad 'Sister Christian'. In this music, every emotion – I love you, I'm the best, I really like rock 'n' roll – is writ bullyingly large. It's no wonder many of the biggest hits went arm-in-arm with a blockbuster. Think Peter Cetera's 'Glory of Love' (*The Karate Kid II*), John Parr's 'St Elmo's Fire' or Starship's 'Nothing's Gonna Stop Us Now' (*Mannequin*), which was co-written by the father of Strokes guitarist Albert Hammond Jr.

Nirvana's *Nevermind* brought that period of drivetime to a decisive close, but it died only to reappear in a new incarnation, like Dr Who with power chords. By making angst voguish, Nirvana inadvertently inspired a squad of AOR approximations of the Seattle sound. Hence, 4 Non Blondes' insufferable 'What's Up' (the band name's suggestion that hair colour somehow signals authenticity is very nu-drivetime) and Soul Asylum's 'Runaway Train', a blustery power ballad clad in plaid instead of spandex. Those two songs have proved remarkably prescient in their bogus rebellion and ersatz torment. Take Pink's 'Don't Let Me Get Me', on which she snaps: 'Tired of being compared to damn Britney Spears/She's so pretty, that just ain't me.' Fair enough if you look like Janis Joplin, but rather disingenuous if, with your midriff-baring and videos set in high school, you're angling for precisely the demographic which three years ago was listening to your alleged nemesis.

So for the next year or two be prepared for a legion of faux-mavericks, peddling freeway-friendly AOR under the guise of leftfield rock. How long will it be before a *Pop Idol*-style talent show casts its net in the direction of long-haired pretty boys with guitars? Of course, tastes will change eventually but then drivetime will simply retreat from the Top Ten and return to its lairs – the classic rock airwaves, VH1 and digital TV adverts for mail order CDs – to bide its time until yet another comeback. Drive safely now.

Drivetime 'classics'

• 'How You Remind Me' by Nickelback (Roadrunner, 2002). Canadians channel Nirvana's sore-throated angst into lighter-waving power ballad. In case you're wondering: no, Kurt Cobain did not die for this.

• 'Don't Let Me Get Me' by Pink (Arista, 2002). Singalong self-hate from R&B B-lister turned surly soft-rocker. Could have been sung by Ally Sheedy in 1980s brat-pack flick *The Breakfast Club*.

• 'Hero' by Chad Kroeger & Josey Scott (Roadrunner, 2002). Brick-subtle balladeering from Mr Nickelback and his portly chum on the *Spider-Man* soundtrack. Video shot, inevitably, atop a skyscraper.

• 'Wherever You Will Go' by the Calling (RCA, 2002). Glossy boy-band soft rock on the Jerry Bruckheimer-produced *Coyote Ugly* soundtrack, along with LeAnn Rimes's über-drivetime 'Can't Fight the Moonlight'.

• 'Blurry' by Puddle of Mudd (Interscope, 2002). Unfortunately named Limp Bizkit protégés share their post-grunge pain. In a previous decade, they would have been Whitesnake.

• 'Born to Be Wild' by Steppenwolf (MCA, 1968). From Dennis Hopper in *Easy Rider* to Jeremy Clarkson in *Top Gear*, the fate of the pioneering, definitive drivetime record symbolises the whole genre.

• 'Free Bird' by Lynyrd Skynyrd (MCA, 1973). Flighty cad hits the road, telling hapless girlfriend: 'This bird you cannot change.' The soundtrack to many a back-seat seduction in 1970s America.

• 'Broken Wings' by Mr Mister (RCA, 1985). Reagan-era emotional melodrama in excelsis, courtesy of briefly popular LA session musicians. Sampled on no fewer than two rap records last year.

• 'We Built This City' by Starship (RCA, 1985). Epically disingenuous hymn to the outlaw joys of Californian rock radio. 'Someone's always playing corporation games,' they protest. Yes, Starship. It's you.

• 'I Drove All Night' by Cyndi Lauper (Epic, 1989). Driving all night 'to make love to you' reaffirms the time-honoured cars-equals-sex equation. Still a regular on Johnnie Walker's Radio 2 Drivetime show.

18 May 2007

THE COPYCATS WHO GOT THE CREAM

Alexis Petridis

For some people, it was the Beatles on *The Ed Sullivan Show*, or the Sex Pistols at the 100 Club. For others, the world was never the same again after catching sight of Nirvana on *The Word*, or hearing Oasis's *Definitely Maybe*. But for Patrick Haveron, the Damascene musical moment was seeing Björn Again at Roehampton University in the early 1990s. 'It was their first UK tour,' he says. 'They were amazing.' There's a pause. 'This was the original Australian lineup,' he adds, with the casual one-upmanship of someone telling you they saw the Velvet Underground with Nico singing and Andy Warhol doing the lights.

Scoff if you will at an Aussie tribute band being placed among such exalted company, but Björn Again at Roehampton University really did change Haveron's life. He decided to set up a company and start putting together his own tribute bands: he struck lucky early with Utter Madness and Rob Lamberti, 'a roofer from Scunthorpe who's a fantastic George Michael'. A decade on, the website for Haverson's company, Psycho Management, lists 213 tribute acts on its books. At one stage in the late 1990s, he had 32 Abba impersonators alone: 'It was almost like Abba football cards or something, where people from different bands would ring up and go, "Have you got a Frida for tonight?" or "I'll swap you an Agnetha for a Benny".' Today, he prides himself on the breadth of tribute acts he can offer, which even he seems to find a bit ridiculous. 'I think we had the slogan "From Abba to Zappa" before the *Observer Music Monthly* did. I'm a bit pissed off about that, to tell you the truth. You can have a Frank Zappa tribute band, Pirate Radiohead, a Steely Dan tribute,' he says, with mounting incredulity. 'I mean, there's two or three UB40 tribute bands . . .' His voice trails off in disbelief.

But, if nothing else, the existence of two or three UB40 tribute acts, doggedly informing the denizens of Britain's pubs and Chicago Rock cafés about the presence of a rat in their kitchen, proves how vast the tribute act market has become. A decade ago, there was a handful of musicians making a living impersonating legendary, usually unattainable figures – the Bootleg Beatles, the Counterfeit Stones, Björn Again, No Way Sis. Today, as Haveron points out, 'If you're doing well and you've got two albums' worth of material, then there'll be a tribute band to follow you.' It has mushroomed into a kind of alternative musical universe, which occasionally and uncomfortably collides with the 'real' rock world – as when Ian Brown performed a set of Stone Roses hits live, backed by a Stone Roses tribute band called Fools Gold, or the Jam's Bruce Foxton and Rick Buckler announced their decision to tour as From the Jam, with a Paul Weller impersonator filling in for their reluctant former frontman. But usually it keeps a discreet distance.

In tribute world, things look and sound similar, but you're constantly reminded that normal rules do not apply. The tribute world has its own svengalis, but they are of a noticeably more pragmatic bent than larger-than-life rock managers of popular myth: at the moment, a fair proportion of Patrick Haveron's time seems to be taken up gently suggesting to various Darkness tribute acts that they might now be better served paying tribute to someone more popular ('a lot of them have invested in good quality equipment, a van, that sort of stuff – if you're running it properly as a business, you have to keep it going').

This world has its own stars, including Gavin Munn, a former actor with a passion for karaoke, who worked for eight years as a Robbie Williams tribute called Probably Robbie, and then, in a musical volte-face that would have confused David Bowie at his chameleonic peak, decided he wanted to be Billie Joe Armstrong of Green Day instead. 'He had musical differences with himself,' chuckles Haveron. 'Then he split himself up.'

En route to a gig in Aberystwyth – where his band Green Dayz will support, of all people, fading R&B starlet Jamelia – Gavin Munn offers a more prosaic description of his change of heart: 'Robbie was never really my kind of music anyway, I was always more into punk and rock stuff. And then when the *Rudebox* album came out, of course, I thought, I can't do any of this because it's rubbish. I was at a gig in the North and a girl said I looked a bit like Billie Joe. I thought, hang on, I play guitar, Green Day are absolutely massive . . .'

This world also has its own hotly-tipped newcomers, like Ben Ferrari, a former schoolmate of the Feeling, currently awaiting delivery of a specially made guitar from America that will enable him to take to the stages of student unions fronting a Muse tribute group called B-Muse. It even has its own festival, Glastonbudget, which takes place this weekend in Leicester: 22 tribute bands over three days. It's in its third year, and the organisers are expecting 5,000 people.

And it has its own arena-filling global superstars, among them Jason Sawford. Sawford is in his early 40s and looks not unlike the comedian Bill Bailey. He is in the middle of a tour of the kind of huge venues that most musicians dream about – the Royal Albert Hall, the Manchester Evening News Arena, two nights at Glasgow's SECC – and yet, while friendly and polite, has the unmistakable, slightly baffled reserve of a man who is not entirely certain why a journalist is talking to him. It's less like interviewing a rock star than it is a guy who works in IT or admin.

By his own admission, Sawford wasn't the greatest Pink Floyd fan when he applied for the job of keyboard player in the Australian Pink Floyd Show – 'I didn't know much about Pink Floyd, I'd only just started to get into them because my brother's girlfriend was really a Pink Floyd fanatic, she'd play it all the time and I'd think, "I quite like that."' But events over the past 20 years have rather forced his hand. 'You've got to have respect for the music,' he says, equivocally, 'because you have to listen to it all the time and study it.'

The Australian Pink Floyd Show started out in 1988, playing pubs around Adelaide, part of a wave of Antipodean tribute acts – including Björn Again and the Australian Doors – that Sawford thinks emerged because 'not that many bands toured in Australia and when they did, it was logistically difficult to play all over the country'. They moved to England in 1993, and lived 'on the breadline for quite a number of years'. Today, they are huge in Canada and the US, while in Liverpool, an area of the UK where being obsessed with the Floyd seems to be less of a lifestyle choice than a legal requirement, tickets for their show at July's Summer Pops festival are apparently selling faster than those for Amy Winehouse's appearance at the same event. They have even received Pink Floyd's seal of approval, playing at David Gilmour's 50th birthday party.

Chas Cole, their manager, has a tendency to describe the Australian Pink Floyd Show in evangelical terms. 'It's almost like a religion. I'd say they feel they have a mission, they're almost on a crusade, a crusade for Pink Floyd's music around the world.'

Given that Pink Floyd have sold 250 million albums worldwide, you do wonder precisely how badly their music requires a global crusade on its behalf, but you can understand Cole's excitement: you would be hard-pushed to call the Australian Pink Floyd Show's success anything less than phenomenal. It's fairly obvious why more musicians than ever are willing to spend their lives pretending to be someone else. It's apparently not an easy life, whether you're playing pubs or arenas. Haveron is full of tales of dispiriting gigs in holiday camps or 'playing to the chicken-in-a-basket circuit', while Cole colourfully notes that the Aussie Floyd's punishing schedule – 'They're doing 150 shows a year whereas a normal band with an album out might do 50' – means that 'over the years we've had as many inter-band relationship problems as the real Pink Floyd'. But there's a definite financial incentive. Even at the bottom end of the business, says Haveron, 'there's Jimi Hendrix or ZZ Top tribute acts playing in a music pub for £300, but that's still better than the £150 you'd get if you were a three-piece blues band. You can double your money by putting on a silly wig.' In the admittedly unlikely event that you reach the level of the Australian Pink Floyd Show, you're going to be doing very nicely indeed. Not, as Chas Cole is quick to point out, as well as a 'proper' band playing the same venues, but 'the individual musicians get paid well. Let's say they're making a senior politician's wage out of it.'

The question of why more people than ever are willing to go to see tribute bands is a more thorny one. Ten years ago, you could argue that the vast majority of tribute bands were offering something you couldn't get anywhere else: they mimicked artists who had died or bands that had split up. Today, British venues are awash with tributes to current bands: Arctic Monkeys, the Killers. Among the delights at Glastonbudget, there's a tribute to Feeder. Perhaps it's indicative of the current resurgence of live music, and people just aren't particularly troubled by who's actually playing it. Patrick Haveron notes that the rise of the tribute act coincided with the rise of the 'firework band', catapulted from obscurity to ubiquity and back in a matter of months by an overheated media. 'There's a real problem in the live music scene that bands will jump straight from a tiny venue to a massive one. Quite a lot of them miss out the small circuit, the student venues can't get them, but there's still a demand for that kind of music played live by a young, enthusiastic band, so they book the Kaiser Killers or the Antarctic Monkeys.'

'I've been in Kansas at Australian Pink Floyd gigs and you realise that Pink Floyd is almost like a brand, it's like a Hoover,' says Cole. 'Whether it's actually a Hoover or a Dyson, it doesn't really matter as far as the guys in Kansas are concerned.' Nor does it matter to the guys – and they are mostly guys, and mostly of a certain age – who fill the Brighton Centre for the Australian Pink Floyd Show. There is an argument that says the proliferation of tribute bands is testament to the way rock music has increasingly become less an art form than a branch of light entertainment, that it makes a mockery of notions of authenticity, or artistic intent. But it's not an argument anyone here is interested in. No one seems worried that 'Shine On You Crazy Diamond' might be sapped of some of its power since the people performing it didn't actually witness Syd Barrett's disintegration at first hand, nor concerned by the unlikely application of a wacky sense of humour to Pink Floyd's gloomy oeuvre: instead of an inflatable pig, they have an inflatable kangaroo, while 'Wish You Were Here' is introduced with a snatch of the theme tune from *Neighbours*. It's clearly more important that the musicianship is faultless, and the lightshow impressive, which both are.

Afterwards they mob the merchandise stall, which sells T-shirts and a double CD of the band performing the albums *Wish You Were*

Here and *Animals* in their entirety. As I watch money change hands for the latter, I feel genuinely baffled. These people are Pink Floyd fans, which presumably means they already have copies of the original *Wish You Were Here* and *Animals* at home. And if that's the case, why on earth would you ever choose to listen to a perfect note-for-note facsimile of those albums by a bunch of anonymous Australian musicians, rather than the albums themselves? It makes no sense. Then I remember I'm in the alternative universe of tribute bands. Normal rules do not apply.

QUESTS

20 April 2001

JOEY RAMONE CAN SHOW WILLIAM THE WAY TO VICTORY

David Cameron

As he awaits the start of the election David Cameron, Conservative PPC for Witney, sets out a unique path for the Tories to follow. He explains why the rock legend Joey Ramone, who died this week, could provide the inspiration for a Tory revival.

There is an iconic figure from the 1970s and 80s that should inspire the Conservative party this week. I am of course referring to the hairy godfather of punk rock who recently died of cancer, Joey Ramone.

What? Has another Conservative candidate flipped his lid? Before you metaphorically cart me off to the funny farm let me explain why the lead singer of the Ramones holds the key to success for the Tories in this phoney election period.

I am not suggesting that the party's law and order stance should be toughened along the lines of the lyric much quoted in obituaries this week: 'Beat on the brat, beat on the brat, beat on the brat with a baseball bat.' Neither am I proposing that the only response to the current state of the opinion polls is to be found in the Ramones' memorable track 'I Wanna Be Sedated'. Nor am I suggesting compulsory shoulder length hair and leather jackets for members of the shadow cabinet.

The genius of the Ramones was that their songs, like 'Rockaway Beach' or 'Sheena is a Punk Rocker', were incredibly short and almost unbelievably repetitive. Verses were out, perpetual choruses were in. In most tracks three chords were seen as unnecessary; two would do. Once you could hum one tune (if tune is the right word, which it isn't), you could hum them all.

Similarly, the secret of effective political communication is to find the right tune and then repeat it endlessly until the message is driven home. I once worked for a cabinet minister who used to reject press releases because, as he put it: 'I've said all this before.' Eventually he agreed to persevere. It was only when he came back from one event and said that people had started repeating his own message back to him that I said it was almost time to move on to something new.

The Conservatives have more than enough messages for a Ramone-style, election-winning album. There is no need for William Hague to finish all his campaign speeches with Joey's meaningless wind-up to (virtually) every Ramones song 'gabba, gabba hey', but I am yet to find a voter in Witney who dissents from the two-chord riff: 'Your taxes are up but public services have got worse.'

Some commentators complain that the Conservatives have not developed enough detailed policies. This is nonsense: the party's superb Campaign Guide for Candidates is so long that you have to read it off the intranet or a CD-ROM, as printing it would clog your ageing laserjet printer for about a week.

But the key to success is in the big picture policy statements, not the fine detail. In every area of policy the Conservatives have a clear and attractive message. On Europe, keeping the pound and opposing further transfers of sovereignty from Westminster to Brussels. On crime, 3,000 more police officers on our streets. On the economy, leaving hardworking families with more of their own money to spend. On health, treating patients in line with clinical priorities rather than centrally set waiting list targets. On education, giving head teachers wide ranging powers to run their schools. Every time a coconut.

In Oxfordshire, for example, one the biggest local issues is housing. In a county with clogged roads, overcrowded schools and public services under severe pressure, there is almost universal opposition to Labour's centrally imposed plans for 40,000 more houses. People are rightly worried that the countryside could be swallowed up in a new tide of concrete, yet they are concerned about the lack of affordable housing for local people. What is the Conservatives' answer to this puzzling conundrum? Scrap the centrally imposed national targets and let local authorities decide how many and what sort of houses should be built. Then priority can be given to affordable housing schemes and protecting the countryside.

The problem isn't the policy, which is spot on. The real difficulty is ensuring that, in spite of all the background noise of an election campaign, the message gets home to Witney's 70,000 voters over the next six weeks. So, Ramone style – with just a few chords and catchy titles in my head – I am ready to go. Gabba gabba hey.

25 July 2003

DESPERATELY SEEKING KRAFTWERK

Alexis Petridis

The bar at London's Institute of Contemporary Arts is swamped. The crowd are an uneasy alliance of asymmetric-haired trendies and what may be their polar opposite: nervous, bespectacled thirtysomething men who look like they regularly won the maths prize at school. Regrettably, some of the latter are wearing Gary Numan T-shirts.

The crowd's appearance may be odd, but it's nothing compared to their conversation. Queuing for a pint, I overhear two men enthusiastically discussing computerised hi-hat patterns. 'It's sort of a tsk-ch-ch-tsk,' suggests one. 'No,' counters his friend, 'it's more ch-ch-ch-tsk.' Ask people why they are here, and they have a tendency to fix you with a gaze somewhere between pity and total incomprehension: 'It's Kraftwerk, innit?' Well, not quite.

In fact, the ICA is packed for a rare live appearance by Karl Bartos, who was once Kraftwerk's percussionist, but left the Düsseldorf quartet a decade ago. Even the ICA's organisers seem slightly overwhelmed by the public response to the concert. One tells me that there were 200 applications for a guest list of 40. People unable to make the gig sent money and pleading letters asking for posters. 'Not a lot of women here, are there?' she frowns. 'I feel like I'm going to grow a beard if I stay here much longer.' It's certainly a peculiar evening, testament to Kraftwerk's continued appeal: days later, the sight of a large group of maths prize winners literally squealing with delight when Bartos played Kraftwerk's celebrated song 'Computerworld' is still proving difficult to eradicate from the memory.

But then Kraftwerk are a peculiar and unique band. The remaining members – Florian Schneider and Ralf Hütter, who formed the band in 1969, plus two hired hands called Fritz Hilpert and Henning Schmidt – are about to release the first new Kraftwerk album in 17 years.

Tour de France Soundtracks, a musical celebration of the famous cycle race, was intended to coincide with this year's event, but Kraftwerk's endless perfectionism meant that the album's release date has been repeatedly pushed back. It will now come out next month, weeks after the race itself has finished. In the ICA bar, this news is greeted with a sort of doleful resignation: it's Kraftwerk, innit?

Most people had given up on Kraftwerk ever releasing any new music years ago. After all, Schneider and Hütter have spent the last two decades gradually cutting themselves off from the outside world. They rarely give interviews, and when they do, they come with strings attached: one magazine which secured an audience with Hütter was informed that he would only discuss his collection of bicycles and that they were not allowed even to mention that he was a member of Kraftwerk. Their legendary Düsseldorf studio, KlingKlang, has no telephone, no fax, no reception and returns all post unopened. They have not attended a photoshoot since 1978: their record label has had to make do with blurry shots from their highly infrequent live appearances and pictures of the band's painstakingly constructed robot doubles. No band has shunned publicity with such dedication.

And I should know. I have spent the few weeks since the announcement of *Tour de France Soundtracks*' release attempting to penetrate Kraftwerk's enigma. It seems a worthwhile task. After all, Kraftwerk are one of the few bands in history who genuinely bear comparison to the Beatles. Not because of their sound or their image, but because, like the Beatles, it is impossible to overstate their influence on modern music. It's the five albums they made between 1974 and 1981 that really matter: *Autobahn*, *Radioactivity*, *Trans Europe Express*, *The Man Machine* and *Computerworld*. In their clipped, weirdly funky rhythms, simple melodies and futuristic technology, you can hear whole new areas of popular music being mapped out. Kraftwerk were so far ahead of their time that the rest of the world has spent 25 years inventing new musical genres in an attempt to catch up. House, techno, hip-hop, trip-hop, synthpop, trance, electroclash: Kraftwerk's influence looms over all of them. It's difficult to imagine what rock and pop music would sound like today if Kraftwerk had never existed.

In addition to their artistic importance, there's certainly plenty to talk about. In lieu of actual publicity, bizarre rumours about Kraftwerk began to abound during the 1980s. Ralf Hütter was said to have suffered a minor heart attack, not due to stress – in fairness, overwork was hardly likely to be a factor – but as a result of obsessively drinking coffee. There were also allegations of a kind of cultural Stalinism: after Bartos and fellow percussionist Wolfgang Flür left the band, not only were their names removed from some covers, but their faces were removed as well. Less troublingly, someone once solemnly swore to me that the Düsseldorf accent in which Kraftwerk sing was a Teutonic equivalent of the Brummie drawl, which would certainly add a whole new layer of humour to their deadpan lyrics: 'Oi prowgramme me howme compewter, bring meself into the fewcher' etc.

With this and other burning topics running through my mind, I attempt to go through the official channels, pestering their record company for an interview. A tentative maybe swiftly becomes a definite no. So I decide to take matters into my own hands. If Kraftwerk won't come to me, I'll go to Kraftwerk: I resolve to go to Düsseldorf in an attempt to track them down. Even if I can't find them, perhaps the city itself will shed some light on their oeuvre.

Few bands have ever seemed as rooted in their environment as Kraftwerk. While their German peers – Can, Faust, Tangerine Dream – muddied their cultural identity with a liberal dose of commune-dwelling, acid-munching hippy idealism, it's hard to see how Kraftwerk could have appeared more German without taking to the stage clad in lederhosen. While everyone else was letting it all hang out, they sported suits, ties and short haircuts. Their sound was precise, efficient, emotionally cold and technologically advanced. It was music that had bagged the sun loungers while everyone else was still snoozing.

Occasionally, their image even led Kraftwerk into slightly sinister waters. In 1975, Ralf Hütter told one gobsmacked music journalist that 'the German mentality' was 'more advanced' than anyone else's and that German was 'the mother language'. The night before I leave, a telephone call comes from Kraftwerk's

British press officer. Somehow, the band have got wind of my scheme. Ralf Hütter, it is intimated, will give me an interview on condition that I abandon any plans to go to Düsseldorf. This has rather the opposite effect from the one intended. Why are they so keen to keep me away from Düsseldorf? What am I going to find there? I think of Wolfgang Flür's memoir, *I Was A Robot*. Less an autobiography than an extended treatise on Flür's virility, *I Was A Robot* paints Kraftwerk not as emotionless 'man-machines', but shameless groupie hounds. Perhaps Düsseldorf is filled with evidence of their youthful indiscretions, populated by children who bear a startling resemblance to members of Kraftwerk. In the case of Schneider, whom the late rock critic Lester Bangs once described as looking like a man who could push a button and blow up half the world without blinking, this is a disturbing thought indeed.

The next morning, there's another flurry of communication between EMI and the *Guardian*. Hütter is now asking for the arts editor's written assurance that any article will not paint Kraftwerk as part of a German music scene, nor will it contain any jokes at the expense of Germans. This seems a bit rich coming from someone whose public image has involved the deft manipulation of a Teutonic caricature, but nevertheless we agree. I glumly consign a notebook packed full of rib-ticklers about bratwurst and square-headed men with no sense of humour to the bin.

Next, we get sent a list of pre-interview conditions stringent enough to make your average Hollywood superstar baulk. Hütter will not discuss Kraftwerk's history, their KlingKlang studio or indeed anything other than the new album. This poses a problem, as nobody in England has actually heard the new album yet. You suspect the end result will bear an uncanny resemblance to Kraftwerk's most recent German interview, in which Hütter and a fearless correspondent from *Der Spiegel* spend two pages attempting to bore each other to death. Its gripping highlight comes when Hütter is forced to admit that computers are smaller nowadays than they were in the early 1970s. We tactfully decline their kind offer and I head for Heathrow.

After an abortive attempt to garner some support for my

expedition from an organisation called Düsseldorf Marketing And Tourismus (no, they don't know anything about Kraftwerk; no, they never get tourist enquiries about this subject; they would recommend I visit the Rhineburn instead – 'it's the largest decimal clock in the world!'), I meet up with Dirk, who is going to be both photographer and de facto interpreter for my trip. Dirk is a nice man, but he regards me with deep suspicion. Unlike Düsseldorf Marketing And Tourismus, he's heard of Kraftwerk, but can't believe that I have just turned up in Düsseldorf with no leads at all. He seems to think I'm making it up about the veil of secrecy around the band. 'You have looked on the internet?' he asks, triumphantly double-clicking on a website called Kraftwerk FAQ. 'The band does not encourage active correspondence,' it reads. 'There is no official fan club and no way of making contact has been announced.'

Indeed, the only solid information we have to hand is a series of hints to the whereabouts of KlingKlang studios, dropped in Pascal Bussy's *Kraftwerk: Man, Machine and Music*. According to Bussy, KlingKlang is near the station, it is a 'yellowish' building, it overlooks a cheap hotel and there is a Turkish grocers nearby. Dirk is confident – 'we will find this!' – and leads the way to his car.

It quickly becomes apparent that you could never accuse Bussy of giving too much away. Every street adjacent to Düsseldorf station features a yellow-ish building, a Turkish grocers and a cheap hotel, frequently blessed with an appetising name such as Hotel Wurms. Every street also seems to feature a table-dancing club, something called a Sexy-Kino and a lot of furtive-looking men. Perhaps realising that driving very slowly up and down the streets of Düsseldorf's red light district while staring out of the car window is liable to attract the attentions of the polizei, Dirk suggests we continue our quest on foot. After an hour of tramping around Düsseldorf's least salubrious area ('This is junkies' corner,' sniffs Dirk, becoming more nonplussed by the minute), we come across a building that certainly might be KlingKlang. Not only does it fit Bussy's description, it also houses an electronic instrument manufacturers. Parked in its courtyard, there is a vintage Mercedes, of the kind Hütter and Schneider used to collect. One of its buzzers is left tantalisingly blank. Pushing it is no use, but inside the courtyard, we find an unlocked door.

Is this it? Are we about to walk into the world's most mysterious recording studio unchallenged? Will we be confronted with the sight of Hütter and Schneider furiously working to complete their latest opus? Perhaps they'll be impressed by our tenacity – not to mention our disregard for the law – and grant us an interview on the spot. Perhaps not. The door leads only to a series of empty rooms. We leave crestfallen, unsure of whether or not we have just stumbled upon the world's most mysterious recording studio. Dirk, in particular, takes this news rather badly. He begins a lengthy monologue, delivered to no one in particular, in which the word '*Scheisse*' seems to crop up with alarming regularity and considerable emphasis.

Either he's angry at me, or he's remembering the last time Kraftwerk made the news in Germany, thanks to their involvement in the technological festival Expo 2000. Hütter and Schneider were paid DM400,000 (around £145,000) to come up with a four-second jingle. Snappy financial thinking like that eventually caused Expo 2000 to lose a staggering DM2.4bn (£700m) – £10 for every man, woman and child in Germany – and the media deemed Kraftwerk guilty by association. As Dirk's assistant confirms, Kraftwerk's image at home could do with a wash and brush up. 'I think in Germany people today prefer Robbie Williams,' she says, sadly. 'All the girls like him so much he had to play two concerts in Düsseldorf.'

Her opinion appears to be confirmed as we head to the old town, a square kilometre containing a staggering 260 pubs. According to Wolfgang Flür's book, Kraftwerk used to come here of an evening in order to ogle local models, an experience recalled in their most famous song, 'The Model'. It's also home to Düsseldorf's techno record shops. Surely here we will find traces of the local boys who in effect started it all? Initially, however, we meet only indifference. In one shop our timid enquiries are dismissed with a non-committal wave of the hand.

Finally, we strike gold. Wilfried Belz, proprietor of a shop called Sounds Good Records, claims Florian Schneider is both an old friend and a customer. In the early '80s, he ran a club called Peppermint, at which Schneider was a regular. Would it be worth us trying to track him down in one of the nightclubs on Düsseldorf's famous Monkey Island? Wilfried shakes his head: 'He's always interested in new music, but he doesn't go out to clubs any more, so he stops by here, I tell him what music is great or fabulous and he listens to them. He was last in here three weeks ago.'

This information sets Dirk off again, but his increasingly threatening demands for the whereabouts of KlingKlang fall on deaf ears. 'They are very private people,' says Wilfried, lifting his index finger to his lips. Nevertheless, he insists that some Düsseldorfers still prefer Kraftwerk to Robbie Williams. 'We have sold out of their last single, "Tour De France 2003", long ago,' he smiles. 'They're a cult. Do we get many tourists asking about them? No. Nobody knows where they are, nobody will tell you where they are, so why would you come here?' With this final remark ringing in our ears, we leave.

Over a glass of Altbier, a remarkable local brew that smells of bacon, we weigh up our options. We have failed to find KlingKlang. Record companies and music shops have proved no use. The largest decimal clock in the world aside, Düsseldorf itself has proved not to be the sort of futuristic technopolis that would inspire Kraftwerk's music, but a slightly dull German city where people like Robbie Williams. We have got nowhere.

There is one last option. As evidenced by the title of their new album, Hütter and Schneider are obsessive fans of cycling. Indeed, Bartos once claimed that their love of racing bikes was a decisive factor in his departure from Kraftwerk: 'Every day we would meet and have dinner. Ralf always talked about how he rode 200km that day. That would bore me to death.' Maybe Düsseldorf's cycling shops hold the answer.

Rosso Sport certainly looks like a very Kraftwerk kind of shop. A converted industrial warehouse next to a disused railway line, it is staffed by rather stern-looking men with lycra shorts and shaved heads. One drags himself away from the giant television screen showing the Tour de France long enough to answer my queries. Yes, he says, Florian Schneider sometimes comes in here. He has two bikes. A racing model and a small collapsible bike. And with that, he curtly turns away, like a man who has suddenly remembered some kind of Kraftwerk confidentiality agreement. Perhaps he thinks that the whole carefully constructed edifice of secrecy surrounding Kraftwerk is in jeopardy now that a foreign reporter knows that Florian Schneider owns a collapsible bike.

I start to giggle, before a troubling thought strikes me. I have flown from England to Düsseldorf, made innumerable telephone calls, wandered around its streets for a day, illegally entered a building, and really annoyed one of the city's top photographers. And what is the sum total of knowledge gleaned from this experience? Have I gained any insight into the fascistic overtones of some of their early statements? Have I discovered the key to an appeal so vast that people will fill a venue just to see the band's former percussionist play live, a decade after his departure? Have I even found out whether or not the Düsseldorf accent is a Teutonic equivalent of Brummie? No.

My investigations have exclusively revealed that one of Kraftwerk's members owns a collapsible bike. Dirk appears at my rapidly-sagging shoulder. 'I don't think we win the Pulitzer prize here, huh?' he says softly, a master of understatement.

5 January 2006

EXCUSE ME, WEREN'T YOU IN THE FALL?

Dave Simpson

It's a Tuesday morning in December, and I'm ringing people called Brown in Rotherham. 'Hello,' I begin again. 'I'm trying to trace Jonnie Brown who used to play in the Fall. He came from Rotherham and I wondered if you might be a relative.' 'The Who?' asks the latest Mr Brown. 'No. The Fall – the band from Salford. He played bass for three weeks in 1978.' 'Is this some kind of joke?'

This has been my life for weeks. I've become an Internet stalker and a telephone pest, all because of an obsessive drive to track down everyone who has ever played in the Fall. That's 40-odd people, including drummers abandoned at motorway services, guitarists left in foreign hotels and various wives and girlfriends of the band's provocateur-ringmaster, Mark E. Smith.

The Fall lend themselves to obsession. In John Peel's record box – which contained the late DJ's favourite records – Fall records had an entire section to themselves. Peel called them the Mighty Fall: 'the band against which all others are judged'. More than 25 years after the band first formed, their audiences still include fans who don't follow other bands. Smith's inspired, social sci-fi songs are revered by everyone from comedians Frank Skinner and Stewart Lee to the designer Calvin Klein, artist Grayson Perry, and authors Irvine Welsh and Philip K. Dick. Musicians and music critics love them, too: David Bowie, Bo Diddley, Thom Yorke and Alex Kapranos all claim to be fans, and the band's latest album (their 26th), *Fall Heads Roll*, won a five-star review in the *Guardian* for its 'paint-stripping riffs, hail of one-liners, withering put-downs and bewildering images'.

My own obsession with the band has been a long time in gestation. I first saw them play at Leeds' Riley Smith Hall in 1981: the fact that the singer was called Smith and the guitarist (Marc) Riley seemed to give this some weird significance. As the band approached their 30th year, I began to wonder if the Fall's continued relevance could be attributed not only to Smith's genius way with splenetic observations, but to the trail of havoc left by the revolving line-up. At the very least, I wondered where all these people were. As Peel had said, noting that most former Fallers simply disappear: 'I don't know if he's killing them or what.' So I resolved to track them down, not realising that this would involve afternoons writing letters to defunct addresses in Doncaster and eight-hour sessions searching for a single person.

I started with Smith, who sank pints of lager in a Manchester hotel as he explained his policy of successively 'freshening up' the band. 'It's a bit like a football team,' he said. 'Every so often you have to get rid of the centre-forward.' Smith has based his career on looking forward, so he was unlikely to give me numbers for clarinet players who left in 1981. The numerous record companies the Fall have had over the years had only ever dealt with Smith. The Musicians Union claimed to have 'no information relating to anybody who was ever in the Fall'.

I did have another lead, however. Sixteen years ago I interviewed a man called Grant Showbiz, and remembered that he sometimes produced the Fall. He gave me some numbers, though sadly, most of them were dead – the numbers, not the ex-members. But I did reach former guitarist/sleeves man Tommy Crooks, now an artist in East Lothian. He'd been a part of the Fall's most notorious implosion, when the band (bar Smith) had disintegrated following a punch-up on stage in New York in 1998.

Over a crackling phone line, Crooks recounted what was to become a familiar theme. He describes being in the Fall as 'the pinnacle of creativity' but with 'a lot of madness'. His first day in the band was spent rehearsing in a room where the lights kept going out; Smith would 'unplug my amplifier and hold the microphone up to the strings, just to freak me out'. The New York punch-up kicked off, Crooks recalls, after Smith had arrived in a particularly bad mood, having just been held at gunpoint by a taxi driver. Things were said on stage and 'everything just went apeshit'. Crooks saw Smith being bundled into a police car, and hasn't heard from him since. 'I remember the band's bus driver asking, "So what are this lot like, then?" The soundman said, "This is as weird as it gets."'

After a few days of trying to track down 43 former members of the Fall, things were getting pretty weird for me, too. Searching on the internet for 'Mike Leigh', the band's 1980 jazz-cabaret drummer, was a nightmare: Google offered me 4,500,000 entries relating to the film director. I sent an email to Manchester University asking: 'Are you the Ruth Daniel who used to play in the Fall?' and discovered a keyboard player who lasted a day in 2002. She revealed that Smith liked to warm up for gigs by 'barking like a dog'.

The more people I found, the more punch-ups I heard about. Marc Riley – now a DJ but a Fall guitarist from 1978–82 – says he was sacked for hitting Smith back after the singer punished the band for an 'average' gig by slapping each musician in turn.

'Smith doesn't do average,' says bassist Steve Hanley, who met me in a Manchester pub. 'He'd rather do 10 great gigs and 10 rubbish gigs than anything in the middle.' Hanley's fearsome bass defined the Fall from 1979 until he, too, exited following the New York rumpus. After taking 'two years to calm down', he became a school caretaker. He remembers post-gig inquests that would go on for hours as Smith – seeking a reaction – accused his bandmates of '"playing like a fuckin' pub band". Chairs would fly. It was like guerrilla warfare.'

Some of this was tongue-in-cheek. Smith confessed to me that he used to fine drummers £5 each time they hit the tom-tom, and that on tour in Europe he would employ the 'European phrasebook', sending guitarists to say things like 'I am a flower' in German. Hanley's brother Paul, a drummer, remembers how one of Smith's favourite jokes was to 'take new members abroad just so he could send them home'. Another was to dismantle the band's equipment in the middle of a gig. 'When you're playing five or six nights a week the group get slick,' Smith said in his defence. For him, routine is 'the enemy of music'.

For all that he can be surreally funny, Smith's intent is deadly serious. As a man called Eric the Ferret – the band's bassist in 1978, and one of the people at whom Smith threw a chair – comments, sagely: 'The Fall don't cruise.' Among Smith's tactics for instilling the required creative tension, the trump card is threatening the sack.

I was curious to discover how long the Fall had been in Smith's control, so I met Tony Friel, who founded the band with Smith, Martin Bramah, Una Baines and a drummer usually called 'Dave', whose surname no one can remember and who was sacked for being a Tory. Now living in a terraced house in Buxton, Friel, about three years ago, played in the Woodbank Street Band; it was thanks to their website that I tracked him down.

Friel had been 'best mates' with Smith and even coined the band's name (from the novel by Camus), but hadn't lasted long, quitting over Smith's decision to bring in then-girlfriend Kay Carroll on management and backing vocals. 'I thought she muscled in,' he says, 'although Mark asked me to stay.'

I found Carroll, too, in Portland, Oregon. After emailing to ask if I was 'a stalker', she mailed me an hour of taped Mancunian vitriol. 'I knew that Mark got me in to fuck off Friel, and it worked,' she says. She believes Smith is a natural manipulator who knows when people have outlived their usefulness. Carroll – who masterminded the early Fall's hardline approach to the music industry – left the band during a US tour in 1983.

The more people I found, the more I'd hear how they were recruited from the road crew (Riley, Hanley) or from support bands. Smith told me how once, when the rhythm section was late for a gig, he brought on players from the support band and was delighted when the errant pair walked in to see their replacements. In 2001 he drafted in the whole of Trigger Happy to be the Fall, giving them only eight hours' notice before they had to play a gig.

Brix Smith joined the Fall – and became the first Mrs Smith – after she met Smith in America. Remarried, and with the name Smith-Start, she now runs Start fashion boutique in London. She tells how, the night they met, she played Smith a demo of her band. 'He just said, "I like your songs. Can we use them? Can you play on them?" He's so fucking smart I can't tell you,' she sighs. 'He wasn't educated, but he was extremely well-read. The way he looked at the world was so different. Because he wouldn't see things the same way, he wouldn't speak the same way.'

A bizarre number of Fall members seem to have come from the

same 500 square yards in Prestwich/Salford, or Smith's local, the George, before it was knocked down. Guitarist Adrian Flanagan recalls how, when he was 15, he would 'put notes through Mark's door saying: "You're my hero. Everyone else is rubbish. Maybe when I'm of legal drinking age, we could go for a drink?"' He soon ended up in the band – 'He'd always give local kids a break.'

One of the strangest entrances is that of Nick Dewey, who attended the 1999 Reading festival as the manager of the Chemical Brothers and ended up on stage with the Fall. 'This drunk man [guitarist Neville Wilding] came backstage asking if anyone played drums,' he says. 'The band had had a fight and left the drummer at motorway services.' Dewey hadn't played for 10 years, but once a Chemical Brother put his name forward, Wilding refused to take no for an answer. Dewey was led to a darkened tour bus to meet Smith, 'passed out with his shirt off. The guitarist had to punch him in the face to wake him up. Then they began fighting over whether or not they should teach me the songs. Mark said no!' With a blood-covered Smith offering occasional prompts, Dewey pulled it off.

I tried to ask Wilding about this incident but his neighbour said he was 'in Guadalajara'. The neighbour is Adam Helal, who also appeared in the Fall, playing bass from 1998 to 2001. Perhaps Smith really can take any member of the public and 'mould them'.

'I was a terrible guitarist when I joined aged 17,' agrees Ben Pritchard, who has survived in the guitar hot seat for the past five years. 'Maybe that's why Mark wanted me in the group. The challenge is to take someone wrong for the group and make them right.' He compares the Fall frame of mind to that at 'Boot Camp'. He has been abandoned at airports to make his own way to gigs; the band's last tour was so stressful that, at 22, he is losing his hair. Why do it? 'The Fall are making history,' he says. 'I have nightmares, but it's never boring. It's not Coldplay.'

As the search continued, ex-Fallers started suggesting there should be 'some sort of support group', while others asked to be put back in touch with people dumped in foreign climes, making me wonder if I should set up a Fall Reunited website. Equally, I was worried by the fates of the disappeared. In particular, Karl Burns – who was hired and fired nine times between 1977 and 1998 – seemed to have vanished after punching Smith on stage in the New York meltdown. Several former members worried that he was dead. Some suggested he had 'moved to the hills' in Rossendale, Lancashire, but appeals to the area's local papers produced nothing. Riley suggested I 'try the prisons', which led me to Ed Blaney, who indeed left the Fall because he was sent to prison ('Dangerous driving,' he says). He hadn't seen Burns either.

When I caught up with former Fall/Elastica keyboard player Dave Bush (now studying web design in Wiltshire), he told how Burns once turned up for a US tour armed only with sticks and a hat, was fired, spent two months riding around on a motorcycle before taking the same flight home as the band. Bush cleared up one of the Fall's biggest mysteries, the fate of founding drummer 'Dave'. Bush knew him on the Manchester party circuit as Steve, and says he became schizophrenic before throwing himself under a train.

Original keyboard player Una Baines had a lead for Burns – 'My friend Barbara says she thinks she saw him a year ago. I'll ask around' – and her own moving story. Over herbal tea in a Chorlton café, she recalled how her time in the Fall ended in two drug-induced nervous breakdowns and hospitalisation as a result of 'wanting to break down every barrier. Musical. Personal. Mental. But contrary to what Mark says, he never sacked me. I was just too ill.' She recovered to make a classic album in Blue Orchids' *The Greatest Hit* (with former husband and ex-Faller Martin Bramah) and is now a singer with the Procrastinators.

There were just two names left. Guitarist Craig Scanlon – Fall fans' favourite – hadn't given an interview since being sacked in 1995 and was rumoured to work in the dole office. Contacting him involved negotiations with a mysterious go-between called 'Moey' before an email, claiming Scanlon is in 'top secret government work', arrived from the Department for Work and Pensions.

'Steve [Hanley] rang and said Mark had sacked the whole band,' Scanlon says. 'Then it was just me.' According to Scanlon, Smith – who revealed in a 2001 interview that firing the veteran guitarist was his 'biggest mistake' – later invited him to a gig, something of an olive branch, but 'after three hours in the pub with him I realised I was better out of it'. Tantalisingly, Scanlon had actually seen Burns, a 'while back', when he'd been 'scruffy, big beard . . . I thought he was a tramp.'

It reminded me of something Hanley said a month before: 'Mark's had all these talented people in the band, but not many have done anything without him. He must have something . . .'

4 August 2006

MISSION: UNLISTENABLE

John Harris

In the 1980s, American researchers found that the average album was played 1.6 times. Given the new practice of impatiently scouring a CD for one or two highlights and then discarding it, the iPod age has presumably seen that figure tumble, but the basic point remains: most of the music we buy lies pretty much unplayed – either because it is rubbish, or because it says a lot more about our vanity than what we actually like.

On the latter score, history's most shining example may be *Trout Mask Replica* by Captain Beefheart and His Magic Band, an allegedly classic album that must surely sit undisturbed in thousands of households. Playing it – or rather, attempting to – is a bit like being in one of those cartoons in which the principal characters cagily open a door, only to find all hell – elephants, possibly, or a speeding train – breaking loose behind it, whereupon they slam it shut again. Its opening moments let you know what you're in for: a discordant racket, all biscuit-tin drums and guitars that alternately clang and squall, eventually joined – apparently by accident – by a growling man complaining that he 'cannot go back to your land of gloom'. Skipping through the remaining 27 tracks does not throw up anything much more uplifting. Indeed, one song finds the same voice rather distastefully evoking the Holocaust: 'Dachau blues, those poor Jews/ Dachau blues, those poor Jews/One mad man, six million lose.'

When this kind of experience happens to a rock critic, it can easily bring on a chill feeling of inadequacy. After all, Beefheart – those in the know rarely use the 'Captain' – remains a gigantic influence on so much rock music that has claimed to stand as something more than mere entertainment, from the post-punk likes of Pere Ubu, Talking Heads, Gang of Four and Public Image Limited, through names as varied as Tom Waits and Happy Mondays, and on to such talents as P.J. Harvey, Franz Ferdinand and the White Stripes. Equally importantly, he is a crucial part of the gnomic culture through which those people (men, mostly) whose lives have been hopelessly afflicted by music commune with one another. It's not in the film, but the Jack Black character in *High Fidelity* was surely a Beefheart obsessive.

A quick bit of history, then. Captain Beefheart was/is the stage-name of Don Van Vliet, a Californian born in 1941. In the wake of his relatively straight 1967 album *Safe as Milk*, he set out on a quest to combine (and this is crude, but bear with me) his Howlin' Wolf-esque vocals with rock music that drew on the spirit of free jazz. *Trout Mask Replica* – produced by Frank Zappa, and supposedly made with the assistance of musicians who were 1) subject to psychological warfare, and 2) on a lot of drugs – remains his most loved album, though it was succeeded by eight more, two of which formed a rum mid-1970s interlude when he attempted to go mainstream and singularly failed.

Having rediscovered his brand of bluesy avant-gardery, Van Vliet ceased his musical work in 1982 and began a new life as a painter. Since the mid-1990s, he has gone very quiet; his ex-colleagues seem to be united in the impression that he is ill, and he is rumoured to be suffering from multiple sclerosis. This month sees an upsurge in his profile, though he is not directly involved in the rerelease of his extremely variable last run of records, from 1974's famously hopeless *Unconditionally Guaranteed* to 1982's much better *Ice Cream for Crow*.

Charged with the job of going back to my handful of unplayed Beefheart CDs and navigating through his music anew, I start off by contacting Gary Lucas, the New York-based musician latterly famed for his work with Jeff Buckley, but also noted for his stint as Beefheart's guitar player and manager.

I explain my serial problems with Beefheart's music, and he responds with a torrent of tributes to his former boss, drawing my attention to his 'Dionysiac qualities' and the fact that his art amounts 'to the roots of music deconstructed and flung back at you like an action painting'. *Trout Mask Replica*, he tells me, is 'like *Finnegans Wake* or *Ulysses*'.

My next move is to renew my acquaintance with Andy Partridge, the sometime chief of XTC, songwriter, and major

Beefheart fan. The idea is to leaven Lucas's florid adjectives and grand claims with the more straightforward counsel of a man still resident in his native Swindon. Amazingly, this works: I am quickly transported to Wiltshire circa 1969, where the young Partridge had become dimly aware of an American act a friend mistakenly termed 'Captain Beefy and his Beefs'.

'I had another friend called Spud,' Partridge recalls, 'and he used to send off, via mail order, for the most out-there, avant-garde records you could get. I liked quite straight pop music, but he was listening to [free jazz legends] Albert Ayler and Sun Ra. He had this crusade to kind of force them on me. At some point, he said, "You've got to try *Trout Mask Replica*." And I put it on and just thought, "What the fuck is this? They're mucking about! They can't even play their instruments: they're all out of tune, the drummer can't drum in time, the singer's not even singing, he's just growling." But Spud said, "No, no – stick with it. You will get it." And I eventually had a road-to-Damascus experience: this sudden revelation. It just clicked.'

That sounds very simple, I tell him. The problem is, after six plays, *Trout Mask Replica* still sounds fucking awful.

'Oh, it sounds like a ball of rusty barbed wire,' he says. 'It sounds like a piece of the Somme, lifted up and put in an art gallery.'

Partridge's analogies at least start to whet my appetite. A song called 'Ella Guru', he tells me, is akin to a 'metal sock', while the experience of getting lost in *Trout Mask* is described as follows: 'You're running around stairs and gangways and gantries – things are swinging across, and you've got to grab them to get to the next level. It's like being trapped in a mad, giant watch. Do you know what I mean?'

Thus far, I don't. But going back through my interview with Gary Lucas, I find one promising bit of advice. 'The way in, I think, is via *Clear Spot*,' he tells me. 'That's the most commercial album that still retains the essence of Beefheart's humour and weirdness. There are groove songs that really rock, and a bit of the old polyrhythm and dissonance, but generally it's hot playing and singing, with really funny lyrics – it's all there.'

The next day, I am driving along a rural backroad with a double-play CD on the stereo. It is split between Beefheart's 1972 album *The Spotlight Kid*, which combines jerky blues-rock with the plonking sound of a marimba and rather does my head in, and the album Lucas has recommended. And lo! Just as I am passing a disused service station outside Leominster, something happens: the title track, an opaque tale of spending the night close to a swamp, reveals itself to be impossibly great: a groove somehow being turned inside-out, with twin guitar parts that lock together like two sets of teeth. Soon enough, the entire album has me in its spell, and for the next three days, I go back to it time and again.

Now, I think, I may be ready for the difficult stuff. I play *Trout Mask* three more times, but its wonders stubbornly fail to reveal themselves, though I am more comforted by the arrival of the aforementioned reissues – replete, bizarrely, with adverts for Beefheart ringtones. I have also received an email from Franz Ferdinand's Alex Kapranos, who has tapped out his Beefheart thoughts while on tour in Japan. He is particularly keen to extol the wonders of 1980's *Doc at the Radar Station*, which was apparently a big influence on FF's last album (and you can tell: for proof, play its opening track, 'Hothead', next to FF's 'Do You Want To').

Kapranos tells me that he and his colleagues have been in the habit of playing a 'bootleg DVD with various live performances on it. It was so exciting, we watched it on repeat. He was locked-in and dangerous – he does a weird thing with his hand, like a medicine man casting a spell. That record is the antithesis of his other rambling LPs after *Clear Spot*. The riffs are all rhythm and jerk; hypnotic and lean.' By way of a route-map into Beefheart's music, Kapranos cuts to the quick: '1) "Hothead". 2) "Electricity" [from *Safe As Milk*]. 3) Some good grass. 4) *Trout Mask Replica*.'

The next day, I set off for London, where I hope I might find a copy of the 1971 album *Lick My Decals Off, Baby*, suggested by Gary Lucas as the logical next step after *Clear Spot*, but unavailable on CD. At Notting Hill's Record & Tape Exchange, I meet Michael, a Beefheart enthusiast who is very knowledgeable and helpful, though – perhaps because he works in a shop like this – his advice comes with the whiff of gentle one-upmanship, particularly when I ask him how many plays it took him to crack *Trout Mask*. 'I got it the first time,' he says. 'I like free jazz, you see.' This makes me feel like a member of McFly. On the train home, I defiantly keep my Beefheart CDs in their cases and listen instead to Wings.

But fair play to Michael. As it turns out, the LP he sold me is in the same prickly vein as *Trout Mask*, but it's a little bit more bass-heavy, and free of the air of desperation that puts me off some of Beefheart's supposedly seminal work. Listening to a song called 'Wow-Is-Uh-Me-Bop', everything coheres, and I actually start to get it. I thus go back to *Trout Mask*, and despite the fact that the really difficult stuff is still vexing me, it palpably begins to open up. I now understand: it is not about verse-chorus-verse or any of that prosaic nonsense. At its most extreme, I am not sure I even like it as music. What matters is the fact that it pulses with energy and ideas, the strange way the spluttering instruments meld together, and those lyrics.

So, everything is moving in the right direction. By next week, perhaps I will be jumping around the lounge to such hitherto unlistenable songs as 'Neon Meate Dream of a Octafish' and 'Hobo Chang Ba'. On a whim, I put in one more call to Andy Partridge and ask him a question, this time out of genuine curiosity rather than journalistic duty: has he ever met the great god himself?

'I nearly met him once,' he tells me. 'XTC were staying at the Gramercy Park Hotel in New York, and I was drinking at the bar, and somebody came in and said, "Beefheart's staying here." I said, "I've got to do radio interviews in the morning, so I can't wait around to see if he comes in. I'll go to bed, but if you see him, tell him I'm a huge fan and give him my room number." Apparently he did come in, very drunk, and they sent him up, but he forgot the number, wandered around for a while and went to bed. And then Colin Moulding, our bass player, saw him the next morning buying porn from the little concession stand in the hotel. I quite liked that. It's good to know he has earthly needs.'

18 November 2006

BUY IT NOW!

Peter Robinson

Pop merchandise is brilliant. Dolls, lunchboxes and ironing board covers, and that's usually just the Thom Yorke solo 'oeuvre'. But even better than the official items – those trinkets painstakingly conceptualised via endless approval sessions with artists concerned about 'brand values' and 'value for the fans while still raking it in' – are the pieces of absolute, unarguable crap which still make their way into fans' homes, usually via eBay. Right now the site is offering items like a Bob Dylan personalised pillowcase (the photo shows a pillowcase with a pic of the chirpy minstrel alongside the actual words 'YOUR NAME DREAMS OF BOB DYLAN EVERY NIGHT') and a Billy Joel CD clock (which is a compact disc with a clock mechanism stuffed through the middle).

And even better than all those items are the absolute, unarguable pieces of crap based around popstars who aren't even famous which, these days, means *X Factor* contestants. Certainly, it is hard not to feel that, behind the brazen opportunism and fly-by-night shoddiness of the whole thing, there's something fabulously postmodern about someone bidding on an item called 'Shayne Ward, Mug'. This season's *X Factor* has thrown up a brilliant selection of hopeless tat that, amazingly, people have been happy to buy. Particular highlights have been a Louis Walsh T-shirt (which in keeping with the *X Factor* vernacular was presumably '110%' cotton), a MacDonald Brothers drinks coaster and a Christmas stocking decorated with a photograph of Eton Road.

At the time of writing there's an Ashley fridge magnet. It's a photo of Ashley which looks like it's been taken off the telly, then stuck into a cheapo plastic case with a magnet on the back. The item description is straight out of a marketing masterclass: 'QUALITY FRIDGE MAGNETS, CHEAPEST AROUND.' It is clearly both robust and affordable. Why, then, has nobody placed a single bid on this item? In business terms the terrifying thing is that 11 people have looked at this item without bidding. This would not impress them on *Dragons' Den*, because it means that eleven – possibly many more – people out there are interested in the idea of an Ashley from *X Factor* fridge magnet, but feel that this specific Ashley from *X Factor* fridge magnet, straight outta Spalding, Lincolnshire, United Kingdom, does not meet their needs. Does it fail as a fridge magnet? How can it fail? What more do these people want?

Clearly the *X Factor* merchandise on offer at eBay is not up to scratch and the *Guardian* must intervene. It is time, with the aid of some pictures nicked off the internet, a printer, some scissors and some Sellotape, to give the punters what they really need. I opt for four items. First, to commemorate the recently booted-out Kerry McGregor, I cut out a little circle and stick it to the bottom of a glass pot that could, at a push, double as an ashtray. I really make the ashtray my own. It's a potential fire hazard, so I'm forced to add the disclaimer: 'Do not use near naked flames. For decorative use only.'

Eton Road are represented in my auctions by a beautiful candle (which I list with the phrase 'keep the flame burning for Eton Road!'). With Ashley, meanwhile, I sidestep the already-established fridge magnet problem and instead stick a photo on to a hairbrush I find down the back of the office sofa. Finally, I go for the eBay slam dunk: yes, it's a fridge magnet, but this one's got Ray on it. Ray, he with the voice of an angel and the face of pure evil. I add a simple 'GO RAY!' message to the picture which, I feel, vaults this item on to a whole different plateau of *X Factor* fridge magnets. Learning from the mistakes of the Ashley 'cheapest around' listing, I even suggest a practical use for the item. 'Think of Ray every time you make something to eat!' This, undoubtedly, will swing it, and I sit back and wait for the bids to roll in.

Things get off to a slow start. It seems for a terrifying few hours as if I have been wasting my time, not to mention a lot of creativity. The *Guardian* will be made to look like a fool in front of everyone. Self-doubt creeps in. Am I no better than that fat old man outside Sugababes concerts festooned with whistles, hopelessly waving £5 flags with Mutya still on them? But things begin to turn around and, by Monday, there's a veritable bidding *frenzy* on the Ray Quinn fridge magnet, with three people battling it out for a piece of the action. The candle, too, has received one bid.

Ten minutes before the four items close, two of them – the hairbrush and ashtray, both items featuring contestants to have already left *X Factor* – still have no bids. Is this a damning reflection of the modern, totally transitory nature of the fame system? No! With five minutes to go the highest bidder on the candle storms in and scoops both the hairbrush and the ashtray. Having looked at my other items, she has clearly been in complete awe of this top-quality pop merchandise. I email to ask her what thoughts were buzzing around in her head when she placed the bids. She doesn't email back, but she does get PayPal to send me the cash. At the end of the auctions, I have made a total of £4.74 – the most valuable item of booty being the Ray fridge magnet, which goes for £3.20, suggesting that I may have discovered the key to *X Factor* fridge magnet success.

The tragedy is that while researching this feature I have also started bidding on other eBay items – and, in a modern eBay-centred twist on getting high on your own supply, I am also now the highest bidder on someone else's Eton Road poster. The description tells me it is a ONE DAY LISTING!!!!!!!!!!, so I can't hang around, you see.

30 March 2007

UKRAINE IN THE MEMBRANE

Michael Hann

Six CDs of everything the Wedding Present recorded for John Peel's radio show? Including 13 numbers in which the Leeds band eschewed their muscular guitar pop for Ukrainian folk? Why, Castle records, you are spoiling us. Well, you're spoiling me.

When I was in my teens, the Wedding Present were my band, the one of whom I could bear to hear no evil spoken. A mutual interest in matters Ukrainian led me to befriend their then guitarist, Peter Solowka (I had an unrequited crush on a girl with Ukrainian parents; he actually had Ukrainian parents), and when I discovered his passion for the music of his forefathers, I supplied him with a couple of the Ukrainian songs the band eventually recorded.

Come autumn 1988 and I was working as an intern in the House of Representatives in Washington DC, for a congressman named Robert Matsui. The work was, at best, tedious: clipping newspapers, answering phones, running off to rightwing firebrand Newt Gingrich's office to get free cans of pop from a woman I knew who worked there (the Coke bottling plant was in Gingrich's district; he had a whole room full of complimentary cans). To perk things up, I started visiting the Congressional Research Service, which I milked ruthlessly for its files on Ukraine. Why I thought this would impress either the girl of my dreams or my favourite band, God only knows. In my defence, I was only 19. I know better now.

But what to do with this wealth of material? Then: a stunning idea! The US version of *Hansard*, *Congressional Record*, has a section called Extension of Remarks, which consists of undelivered speeches, printed under the congressmen's names, to show some moaning special interest group that, yes, we feel your pain and we take your problems seriously. So, I put it to my lackadaisical supervisor (a Republican who had somehow found himself in the office of a liberal Democrat), why not let me write some Extensions of Remarks about Ukrainian matters? Nothing too heavy, just praising the indomitable spirit of the Ukrainian people under the Soviet yoke in this, the 1,000th anniversary of Christianity in Ukraine. The kind of thing that the near non-existent Ukrainian community of Sacramento (Matsui's district) would surely cheer. He agreed. And my deathless prose on matters Ukrainian duly appeared in *Congressional Record*.

But was this enough to prove myself the Wedding Present's most devoted fan? Perhaps not. And so I hatched a plan to get a piece of legislation through Congress. I would persuade the world's most powerful legislative body to designate one day of the year as National Ukrainian American Day. Alright, it wasn't the introduction of a universal healthcare plan, but I refer you again to my age.

Getting Congress to approve a day of commemoration isn't that hard. You don't need a bill to pass both houses, you don't need a gruelling committee stage, you don't need presidential approval (leastways, you certainly didn't in 1988). All that was required was a small number of congressional signatories to get the proposal before the relevant committee, which would then wave it through (no one would bother questioning something that might win them a couple of votes).

Gingrich was on board early, making it truly bipartisan. (He thought I worked for him, I was in his office so often picking up pop. 'How you doing?' he'd say, clapping me on the shoulder as he strode through his foyer. 'Doing a great job here.') Though when I say 'on board', what I mean is one of his assistants forged his signature on my sheet. For weeks, I traipsed the corridors of the Rayburn, Longworth and Cannon buildings, where the representatives' staff work, getting friendly interns to persuade their supervisors to add their bosses' names to my list. Slowly, we were getting there – until disaster struck.

National Ukrainian American Day was a couple of signatories short of going to committee when the House rose for the 1988 presidential and congressional elections, and anything not already passed was scrapped. My legislative triumph, the one that would have put the Wedding Present on the US political map, was lost forever.

Six months later the Wedding Present released their album of Ukrainian folk songs, featuring the ones I'd sent them. And guess what? I didn't even get a thanks in the sleevenotes.

20 July 2007

THE CAR, THE RADIO, THE NIGHT – AND ROCK'S MOST THRILLING SONG

Laura Barton

Dusk in a supermarket car park in Natick, Massachusetts. Outside there is snow in the air and the wind is up. A shopping trolley whirls its way across the tarmac unaided and the cars of Route 9 rush by. I wind the window down. It's cold outside.

People make rock 'n' roll pilgrimages to Chuck Berry's Route 66, to Bruce Springsteen's New Jersey Turnpike and Bob Dylan's Highway 61. They flock to Robert Johnson's crossroads, to Graceland, to the Chelsea Hotel, hoping to glean some insight into the music that moves them. In January this year, I made my own rock pilgrimage to the suburbs of Boston, to drive the routes described by Jonathan Richman and the Modern Lovers in the song 'Roadrunner', a minor UK hit 30 years ago this week.

'Roadrunner' is one of the most magical songs in existence. It is a song about what it means to be young, and behind the wheel of an automobile, with the radio on and the night and the highway stretched out before you. It is a paean to the modern world, to the urban landscape, to the Plymouth Roadrunner car, to roadside restaurants, neon lights, suburbia, the highway, the darkness, pine trees and supermarkets. As Greil Marcus put it in his book *Lipstick Traces*: '"Roadrunner" was the most obvious song in the world, and the strangest.'

One version of 'Roadrunner' – 'Roadrunner (Twice)' – reached No 11 in the UK charts, but the song's influence would extend much further. Its first incarnation, 'Roadrunner (Once)', recorded in 1972 and produced by John Cale, but not released until 1976, was described by film director Richard Linklater as 'the first punk song'; he placed it on the soundtrack to his film *School of Rock*. As punk took shape in London, 'Roadrunner' was one of the songs the Sex Pistols covered at their early rehearsals. Another 20 years on and Cornershop would cite it as the inspiration behind their No 1 single 'Brimful of Asha', and a few years later, *Rolling Stone* put it at 269 on their list of the 500 greatest songs of all time. Its impact would be felt in other ways, too: musicians playing on this song included keyboard player Jerry Harrison, who would later join Talking Heads, and drummer David Robinson, who went on to join the Cars. Its power was in the simplicity both of its music – a drone of guitar, organ, bass and drums around a simple two-chord structure – and of its message that it's great to be alive.

Maybe you don't know much about Jonathan Richman. Maybe you've heard the instrumental 'Egyptian Reggae', which hit No 5 in 1977 and earned him an appearance on *Top of the Pops*. Or perhaps you recall his cameo as the chorus in *There's Something About Mary* (the Farrelly brothers are dedicated fans). But if you want to know what Jonathan Richman was about, first think of the Velvet Underground, and then turn it inside out; imagine the Velvets cooked sunny side up. Imagine them singing not about drugs and darkness, but about all the simple beauty in the world.

What characterises Richman's work, and 'Roadrunner' especially, is its unblighted optimism. 'Richman's music did not sound quite sane,' Greil Marcus wrote. 'When I went to see him play in 1972, his band – the Modern Lovers, which is what he's always called whatever band he's played with – was on stage; nothing was happening. For some reason I noticed a pudgy boy with short hair wandering through the sparse crowd, dressed in blue jeans and a white T-shirt on which was printed, in pencil, "I LOVE MY LIFE." Then he climbed up and played the most shattering guitar I'd ever heard. "I think this is great," said the person next to me. "Or is it terrible?"'

There are plenty of versions of 'Roadrunner'. The Unofficial Jonathan Richman Chords website lists 10 discernibly different versions: seven given an official release and three bootlegs. Richman apparently wrote the song in around 1970. The 1972 John Cale version was a demo for Warner Brothers, and only saw the light when the Beserkley label in California collected the Modern Lovers' demos and put them out as the *Modern Lovers* album in 1976. Two more 1972 demo versions, produced by the notorious LA music svengali Kim Fowley, would be released in 1981 on a patchy album called *The Original Modern Lovers*, and a live version from 1973 would appear a quarter of a century later on the live record *Precise Modern Lovers Order*. In late 1974, Richman recorded a stripped-down version of the song for the Beserkley, which apparently took a little over two hours. This would be 'Roadrunner (Twice)', the most successful version. A further take, extended beyond eight minutes, and recorded live, was titled 'Roadrunner (Thrice)' and released as a single B-side in 1977.

While every version of 'Roadrunner' begins with the bawl of 'One-two-three-four-five-six' and ends with the cry of 'Bye bye!', each contains lyrical variations and deviations in the car journey Richman undertakes during the song's narrative, though it always begins on Route 128, the Boston ringroad that Richman uses to embody the wonders of existence. In one, he's heading out to western Massachusetts, and in another he's cruising around 'where White City used to be' and to Grafton Street, to check out an old sporting store, observing: 'Well they made many renovations in that part of town/My grandpa used to be a dentist there.' Over the course of the various recordings he refers to the Turnpike, the Industrial Park, the Howard Johnson, the North Shore, the South Shore, the Mass Pike, Interstate 90, Route 3, the Prudential Tower, Quincy, Deer Island, Boston harbour, Amherst, South Greenfield, the 'college out there that rises up outta nuthin'', Needham, Ashland, Palmerston, Lake Champlain, Route 495, the Sheraton Tower, Route 9, and the Stop & Shop.

My pilgrimage will take me to all of these places. For authenticity's sake I have chosen to make the trip in January, because, as Richman observes in 'Roadrunner (Thrice)' on winding down his car window, 'it's 20 degrees outside'. Having consulted a weather website listing average temperatures for Boston and its environs, I find it is most likely to be 20 degrees at nighttime in January. And, as in 'Roadrunner', I will drive these roads only at night, because 'I'm in love with modern moonlight, 128 when it's dark outside.'

Richman was born in the suburb of Natick in the May of 1951. It was there that he learned to play clarinet and guitar, where he met some of his Modern Lovers. But that is not where I begin my journey. If you want to find out where Richman was really born, musically speaking, you have to head to a redbrick building in central Boston. On my first afternoon, as I prepare for my inaugural night drive, I pull up on Berkeley Street, within spitting distance of the Mass Pike, trying to find the original site of the Boston Tea Party, the venue where Richman first saw the Velvet Underground as a teenager.

Richman was infatuated with the Velvets, from the first moment he heard them on the radio in 1967. He met the band many times in his native Boston, opened for them in Springfield, and in 1969 even moved to New York, sleeping on their manager's sofa. 'Roadrunner' owes its existence to the Velvet Underground's 'Sister Ray', though the three-chord riff has been pared back to two, just D and A.

A live recording from the Middle East Café in Cambridge, Massachusetts, made in October 1995, has Richman introducing his song 'Velvet Underground' with the recollection that he must have seen the band 'about 60 times at the Boston Tea Party down there at 53 Berkeley Street'. So along Berkeley Street I walk, counting down to number 53, the cold from the pavement soaking up through my boots, the air before me hanging in frosty white wreaths. The venue is gone now, and today it is a civilised-looking apartment block with no hint of the rock 'n' roll about it save for a plaque announcing that Led Zeppelin and the Velvets, B.B. King and the J. Geils Band all played here. It does not mention Jonathan Richman.

That evening I drive along Route 128 for the first time. I head up towards Gloucester, as the night drifts from rain to sleet to snow. All the way there, the road is quiet; the rush-hour traffic has thinned, and I drive behind a minibus emblazoned with the words Greater Boston Chinese Golden Age Center. The street lights peter out and at times I can barely see the road markings; by the time I reach the North Shore I am hunched over the steering wheel squinting at the road. In Gloucester, I draw into the car park of Dunkin' Donuts. Cars swish by on Eastern Avenue, rain falls heavily. Inside, one lone figure in an anorak is buying Thursday night doughnuts. This is the very end of Route 128.

It feels exhilarating, alone out here in the darkness. I peer through the windscreen at the cosy houses of Gloucester, a seaside resort and home to 30,000 people. Televisions blink behind drawn curtains, and I think how cold and late it is and how by rights I should be indoors. But what matters right now is out here: the radio and the dark and the night and this glorious strip of tarmac before me.

Route 128 was opened in 1951, and is also known as the Yankee Division Highway. It runs from Canton on the South Shore up here to Gloucester. At times it intertwines with I-95, the interstate highway that runs from Florida to the Canadian border. Route 128, and what it represents, is an important element in 'Roadrunner'. Between 1953 and 1961, many businesses, employing thousands of people, moved to lie alongside Route 128, and the road became known as America's Technology Highway. During the 1950s and 1960s, Boston's suburbs spread along the road, and the businesses were joined by people, the residential population quadrupling in the 1950s and then doubling again in the '60s. This was the world in which Richman grew up, a world that rejoiced in technology, that celebrated the suburbs and the opportunities offered by the highway.

In Tim Mitchell's biography *There's Something About Jonathan*, Richman's former next-door neighbour and founder member of the Modern Lovers, John Felice, recalls the excitement of driving that route with his buddy: 'We used to get in the car and we would just drive up and down Route 128 and the turnpike. We'd come up over a hill and he'd see the radio towers, the beacons flashing, and he would get almost teary-eyed . . . He'd see all this beauty in things where other people just wouldn't see it. We'd drive past an electric plant, a big power plant, with all kinds of electric wire and generators, and he'd get all choked up, he'd almost start crying. He found a lot of beauty in those things, and that was something he taught me. There was a real stark beauty to them and he put it into words in his songs.'

Driving back towards Boston, past factories and blinking red lights, I head down to the South Shore, to Canton, where Route 128 becomes I-95, heading off towards Providence, Rhode Island, and way on down to Miami. Canton is the home of Reebok and

Baskin Robbins, and I drive aimlessly through its dark streets before scooping back up to Quincy, where Howard Johnson's and Dunkin' Donuts began, and out along Quincy Shore Drive. I put on 'Roadrunner (Thrice)', my favourite version of 'Roadrunner'. 'Well I can see Boston now,' it goes. 'I can see the whole Boston harbour from where I am, out on the rocks by Cohasset/In the night.'

The next day I head out to Natick. My mission is to see the suburban streets where Richman grew up, and to visit the Super Stop & Shop, on Worcester Street. The Stop & Shop is a supermarket chain founded in 1914 and which now boasts 360 stores, most of them in New England. The Stop & Shop is one of the key locations in 'Roadrunner', for it is where Richman makes a discovery about the power of rock 'n' roll radio: 'I walked by the Stop & Shop/Then I drove by the Stop & Shop/I like that much better than walking by the Stop & Shop/'Cause I had the radio on.'

The experiment is important. Richman states that having the radio on makes him feel both 'in touch' and 'in love' with 'the modern world', and the presiding connection with modernity throughout 'Roadrunner' – with the highway, with the car, with rock 'n' roll, conveys Richman's delight at living entirely in the moment.

Natick Stop & Shop looks too modern to be the same store Richman walked past, then drove past. 'How long has this Stop & Shop been here?' I ask the cashier. He is young and slightly built, a faint brush of hair on his top lip. 'Uh, I dunno . . .' he frowns. 'Did you know there's a famous song that mentions the Stop & Shop?' I press on. 'No.' He looks at me, hairs twitching, and his colleague interrupts as she packs my bags: 'Can I take my break?' she demands, squarely. Outside, I walk slowly past the Stop & Shop. Then I climb into my silver Saturn with its New Jersey plates and drive past the Stop & Shop, with the radio on for company. I feel in touch with the modern world.

Some hours later, having driven out along Interstate 90 – the Mass Pike – and down the 495, past Framingham and Ashland and Milford, I find myself in the Franklin Stop & Shop, standing at the Dunkin' Donuts counter. 'Oh my gawd! We've almost run out of glazed!' cries one of the attendants. 'The other day we sold one glazed all day!' 'Mm-hmm,' replies her colleague, in a world-weary tone. 'Some day you sell none at all, other days they all just go.' They are playing Paula Abdul's 'Opposites Attract' in the café, and I sit there with my doughnut and my coffee and my map of Massachusetts, plotting my route out towards Amherst and the University of Massachusetts, and up to Greenfield, about two hours west. I love to think of Richman making this drive, about the 'college out there that just rises up in the middle of nuthin''. There is the glorious feeling of driving for driving's sake, away from the draw of Boston, away from the ocean, and delving deep into the heart of Massachusetts.

It is late when I get home. After staying a couple of nights at a hotel overlooking the harbour I have moved to the Howard Johnson, out by Fenway Park, home of the Red Sox. It is a low-rise hotel across from a McDonald's; inside it is filled with a weary light and the stale smells of the Chinese restaurant attached. In its heyday, Howard Johnson's was a hugely successful chain of motor hotels and restaurants, famous for its 28 flavours of ice cream. Richman loved the Howard Johnson's chain, devoting an entire song to it in his early days, in which he declared happily: 'I see the restaurant/It is my friend.' At one point, Tim Mitchell writes, Richman personalised his Stratocaster guitar by cutting out a piece of it, spraying it the recognisable greeny-blue of the Howard Johnson logo and then reinserting it. Today, there are only a couple of Howard Johnson's restaurants in existence, none of them in Massachusetts, and the logo lives on only as part of a budget hotel chain.

Outside the hotel tonight the snow is deep; it piles up around wheel arches and lies thickly across bonnets and windscreens. I haven't really spoken to anyone for days, and my firmest friend has become the radio. I'm tuned to AM, in homage to 'Roadrunner', with its gleeful shouts of: 'I got the AM!/Got the power!/Got the radio on!' Tonight in the neon glow of the car park, I flick through stations broadcasting only in Spanish, music shows, adverts for dating websites, custom replacement windows, car loans, Dr Kennedy's prayer show, until they blur into one long rush of song and speech and advertisement. 'Truththattransforms.org, for $29.99 you get one free, You wouldn't stay away as much as you do/ I know that I wouldn't be this blue/ If you would only love me half as much as I love you.'

For my final night's drive it is snowing heavily. I decide to cover every single geographical point on the 'Roadrunner' map in one long drive, setting out shortly after nine o'clock for Gloucester. It is a beautiful night, the roads empty, the snow falling onto my windscreen in great beautiful plumes; I put my hand outside the window and the flakes float gently, coldly on to my fingers. I drive past the Stop & Shop, I drive out towards Amherst, to south Greenfield. I take in Route 128, the Mass Pike, Route 3; from R9 I loop down to R495, down towards Quincy; I head out to Cohasset, to the rocks. And as I spiral about the snowy landscape I feel like a skater, pirouetting across the ice.

I drive for hours. 'But I'm hypnotised,' as 'Roadrunner (Thrice)' puts it. And it is a funny thing, driving alone, late at night; pretty soon you come to feel at one with the car, with the road, with the dark and the landscape. This is one of the themes that rise up out of 'Roadrunner', that feeling that 'the highway is my only girlfriend', that, here, loneliness is a thing to be cherished. 'Now I'm in love with my own loneliness,' he sings.

These are the early hours of the morning. I am tired. My mouth is thick with coffee and my throat dry from the car heater. As I loop back towards Route 128 for the final time I turn off the radio and put on 'Roadrunner (Thrice)': 'One-two-three-four-five-six!' Suddenly there is a lump in my throat. I pull over and wind the window down, let the cold night air rush in, and through the falling snow I watch all the lights of the modern world, blinking out over Boston.

BUY, BUY, BUY

30 November 1956

THE TOP TWENTY COME TO THE PUBLIC BAR ROOM

by our own reporter

In a hotel at Portmeirion, North Wales, there is a coin-operated music box, believed to date from the turn of the century, which plays lesser-known melodies of the Victorian musical comedies. The owners keep it as a curiosity, although the only tune on its aged metal records that they recognise is 'Rule, Britannia'. Proprietors of the more sophisticated modern jukeboxes, on the other hand, pride themselves on keeping several weeks in advance of the top 20 list of 'pops.' The contrast emphasises how remorselessly 'canned music' is pressing forward.

A few years ago, the jukebox was the plaything of youth alone. 'The kid who handled the music box' with a threepenny bit was as alien to the life of the adult Englishman as Service's original. But now, its advocates claim, the jukebox is becoming a part of our social life. It has graduated from a corner of the amusement arcade, through the milk and snack bars, chip shops and transport cafés to some pubs and clubs. There is even one in an unnamed grocer's shop in the area of the Wash; fugitives from *Housewives' Choice* have apparently accepted it without complaint.

Indeed, the most unlikely places have surrendered their immunity. A London journalist reports finding a little inn in a North Country market town, full of pewter and sporting prints, which seemed just the place to take his ease early after a long day's driving. His head had barely touched the pillow when the notes of the latest rock 'n' roll tune floated up from the bar – the prelude to a performance which lasted till closing time. The morning disclosed a jukebox standing unashamedly beneath the polished horse-brasses, and lunch-time brought its best customers, two local youths, back for more music.

Opinions differ as to whether its widening field will make the musical range of the jukebox more catholic. One operator reports that publicans at first demanded Gilbert and Sullivan or the

'Merry Widow' for their more mature patrons, but within a fortnight were begging for 'Elvis the Pelvis' and Johnnie Ray with the most 'square'-abhorring milk bar. 'Juke', the record reviewer in *The World's Fair*, an organ of the show business, offers an interesting guide to what the customers want. He says a record combining 'Rock around the Clock' with 'See You Later Alligator' and 'The Saints' Rock 'n' Roll,' is guaranteed to make even the squarest listener start tapping his or her feet – a confirmation of the theory that a distinctive rhythm is the essential feature for jukebox popularity.

This is certainly the faith of those who have nailed their standard firmly on the Hit Parade. With advance information from the record companies, an encyclopaedic knowledge of the respective sales of recent tunes and a feel for the nuances of Afro-beat, 'Rock' and the rest, they tell you knowingly that 'Green Door' – 'Frankie Vaughan's, not the Jim Lowe version' – now ranked fifth, is sure to succeed. Some machines have 'popularity counters' which allow a 'post-mortem' on such judgements. Changes of the records in a machine once a fortnight keep the clients at the most lucrative sites satisfied.

Other operators are less confident that they can mould musical tastes. They offer older people, particularly their public-house clientele, a discreet mixture of André Kostelanetz, the piano music of Winifred Attwell, Scottish accordion melodies by Jimmy Shand, with occasional contributions from Gigli and Mario Lanza. (Rock 'n' roll houses are not 'tied,' and Mario Lanza is persona grata there also.)

What siren lures the average café or public-house proprietor, long past his frantic youth, to install a jukebox? Probably the answer, as one advertisement lyrically puts it, is 'sheer, beautiful earning power.' The machines cost between £400 and £650, but many are not bought by the caterers; they are 'placed' by operators, who service them, change the records, and give the owner of the premises a proportion of the earnings. This varies, but it is usually of the order of a quarter or a third. The average jukebox may earn £7 or £8 a week, and even on a good selling position would rarely take more than £15, thus giving the café owner a maximum profit of £5.

The real advantage, however, is in the catering business which the machine attracts. Mr Stanley Morris, a Manchester manufacturer, who, with his brother, took seven years to perfect what they claim is the first all-British machine, has a revealing story about his first 'placing'. He selected a small milk bar which was clearly suffering from the competition of three more imposing establishments near by, and lent its owner a jukebox on specially favourable financial terms. Within a few months the rivals had all asked for a machine to win back some of their lost customers.

A keen struggle is now going on for the developing market. Debates about the types of record suitable for each make are carried on in the trade press. Office walls bear maps of Britain with little flags to show the farthest flung jukeboxes. Makers sell most of their machines to operators and some direct to café owners, but they maintain a few on a direct basis in order to know the pulse of the market. Technical standards seem high. A youth who acts as a tester in the Manchester factory spends his day dropping threepenny bits in each of the long row of machines. Their sound equipment has been removed to preserve his sanity.

The public-house jukebox movement is still in its early stages. It is said to appeal particularly to landlords who find difficulty in getting a regular and reliable band or pianist. Operators in the past have tended to favour the more lucrative milk bar trade, but the new market will not be neglected, and one firm has produced a smaller and cheaper machine suitable for the lower spending average bar.

There is one legal problem – the attitude taken by local licensing authorities. The justices' view of this music appears to vary from place to place. Some areas hold that a music licence is required for a jukebox, whether it is in a public house or a milk bar. As a result, Liverpool, for example, is thought to have no jukeboxes at all. The consensus of opinion is that the North is more old-fashioned – and therefore less accommodating – than the South.

The people most persistently affected by the jukebox are the staff of the establishment where it is placed. The dreamy look which goes with the service of some milk bar tea suggests that the young women regard Messrs Ray, Laine, Presley and Haley as part of the attraction of the job. Proprietors are not always so personally appreciative. A café owner in Manchester, while acknowledging that his new machine brought a crowd of extra customers later in the evening, watched with frank distaste when a customer set it off at tea-time. As the plaintive air of 'The Whiffenpoof Song' rose above the hiss of the geyser, he turned with determination to the sporting columns of his evening paper.

27 December 1956

ENCOURAGING CRITICISM OF 'POP MUSIC'

by our own reporter

The pupils rattled the classroom door in their eagerness to begin the lesson. In the quiet scholastic surroundings of Egerton Park Secondary Modern School, Denton, near Manchester, they were soon rocking gently in their desks to the rhythm of Bill Haley's 'Rocking through the Rye'. After listening to a record of 'Green Door' as sung by Frankie Vaughan, a boy on the back row explained enthusiastically that it 'sends me'. 'Oh, yes,' said the teacher patiently, 'and where does it send you?'

This exchange between teacher and pupil is typical of the school's experimental 'project in popular music', which in a few lessons each week aims to encourage the children to be more critical of 'pop' (or popular) music. Mrs M. de Mierre, head of the school's music department, was concerned at the apparent boredom with which the children listened to serious music in the school's record library and at the often wide gulf between her own taste in music and that of the majority of her pupils. She decided to meet them on their own ground.

The pupils bring their own records – the school library cannot afford to buy such 'ephemeral music' – and Mrs de Mierre plays them on the gramophone and then discusses them with the class. She encourages the children to react normally to the music, or to indulge in what the experts of 'rock 'n' roll' like to call 'audience participation', as long as they can explain why they like the music.

After a performance of 'See You Later, Alligator', only two boys (apart from Mrs de Mierre) admitted to not liking the music, and one of them had been seen to participate in the chorus of 'Ooooh' as if unable to help himself.

From the education point of view, the interest of the experiment lies in the fledgling attempts at criticism. At the end of 'Blue Suede Shoes' sung by Elvis Presley (also known as 'Elvis the Pelvis') Mrs de Mierre put it to the enthusiasts: 'I have heard this before but I can't make a good deal of it. Perhaps you can help me.'

The classroom was suddenly quiet with juvenile concentration. Then a girl ventured: 'I just like the rhythm. It makes me all funny inside.' When the male guffaws had died down, she admitted nevertheless that even the records of 'Elvis the Pelvis' grew 'stale' after about a month of steady playing.

The ephemeral nature of the 'pop records' was freely admitted by everyone. When one looks over the reports on the 'project' since its beginning a few weeks ago a definite improvement both in expression and sharpness of criticism can be detected. One record was dismissed by a critic simply as 'No more tune in it than a dog's bark', and another as 'A waste of 5s 7d retail'.

The pupils have even reached the stage of making a shy attempt to define what they had previously taken for granted. 'Rock 'n' roll music,' wrote a 14-year-old, 'does not need any special step. It seems just as though it is the old-fashioned step, the Charleston, hotted up.'

Mrs de Mierre hopes that in time her pupils may learn not to distinguish between serious music as 'school' and popular music as 'pleasure'. As a preliminary report on their progress, she has listed some 'typical individual reactions'. 'Dislikes' include long records (which causes some worries about their powers of concentration) and most records without a singer (the young people are great believers in the cult of personalities). The list of 'likes' is longer and includes 'noise, clear words, gimmicks (mild variety, not too clever, like Goons), religious slant, sincerity, story songs, singers who always run to type, American accents'.

But even since the list was made, there have clearly been some slight changes. The girls were reported to prefer simple tunes, men singers, and 'the romantic element', whereas the boys were more interested in clever orchestrations, 'gimmicks', and cowboy songs. But when a visitor attended a recent lesson of the 'project', he found that among the boys he met he was in a minority of one as an admirer of cowboy songs. One boy mentioned the name 'Beethoven' with slightly bated breath and dismissed 'Elvis the Pelvis' as 'a jerky singer'.

20 November 1999

POP STARS AS YOU'LL NEVER SEE THEM

Tom Cox

I have a certain contingent of friends who want to protect me from the music business because they think it's riddled with merciless charlatans and overprivileged spongers. They've arrived at this conclusion by pure intuition. I ask them if it's down to something I've told them or first-hand evidence, and they say no, it's just something they can sense.

And that's why I've made a strict mental note never, never, to offer them a spare invitation to a record company showcase. For those paranoid about the venal machinations of the pop industry, the showcase is the ultimate conspiracy theory, a one-way ticket to the horrific realisation that what you maintained was the truth, but secretly believed was not possible, is actually spot on.

You'll know you're at a showcase when you get a wave of that precise, oozing nausea normally held in reserve for jammed elevators inhabited by Mia Farrow, combined with the nagging suspicion that every eyeball in the room is activated by a celebrity-sensitive spring, and the overwhelming perception that no one knows quite why they're there, save for the limitless flow of free drinks and the infinitely resistible possibility of standing next to Keith Allen in the toilet queue.

You will wonder why the record company has squandered such largesse on such an occasion when it could have staged a strategically leaked 'secret' gig for half the price and twice the coverage. Confusion will be consolidated when you ask the PR involved what the showcase's function actually is, and they reply, 'Press', yet request that you don't write about it.

Clive Davis, president of Arista Records, also believes that the archetypal showcase doesn't work – too much ligging, with the music relegated to the status of sounds-to-rub-shoulders-to. For this week's launch party for The Artist's Arista debut album, *Rave Un2 the Joy Fantastic*, at London's Mermaid theatre, Davis thought he'd approach things differently, seating a few hundred journalists, record company employees and pop stars in a would-be lecture theatre and playing them the album start to finish, while they sat frozen in horror.

It was an exasperating juxtaposition of moods: the flashback to an evil maths teacher cackling as he informed us that the lesson would overrun well into our lunch-break, battling with the suspense and uncertainty as to whether we were ever going to see The Artist perform.

While we sat listening to a record that had already been out on the street for a week, Davis, a sixtysomething Frank Butcher look-alike, bopped, shimmied and, at the conclusion of each number, padded over to the mike to treat us to an irony-free 'Owww!' The more insecure members of the audience clapped – uncertain whether they were applauding Davis's dancing, the forced R&B of The Artist's so-called 'return-to-form' album, or the imposing twin speaker stacks. The rest of us fidgeted distractedly or nipped outside to breathe some tension-free air.

Two and a quarter hours after the doors opened, The Artist appeared, accompanied by possibly his funkiest band yet (including former Sly Stone guitarist Larry Graham), and played a set that slowly metamorphosed from electrifying (the hits medley) to tedious (the stodgy jam and audience participation) to tepid (the new single, 'The Greatest Romance Ever Sold'). Everything was geared towards total rave-up – Prince in his element, bouncing into the crowd, deconstructing his celebrity, confusing us as to whether he was The Artist masquerading as Prince or Prince masquerading as The Artist, but making sure we knew it was one of the two.

So why did I leave feeling so emotionally hollowed out? I put it down to guilt. I like Prince, 1978–90 inclusive (though I'm far from a completist); and here he was, in a relatively miniature venue, standing about three feet away from me, riffing on the stairs, goading us to join him on his expensively designed stage and bond with him. The performance ended with upwards of 30 crowd members invading his lectern, including a clearly disoriented Beck. But if this was a celebration, it was contaminated with insiders-only vanity and a bogus flavour of adventure.

Prince doesn't often come to Britain, and it's unjust that when he does, his fans should only find out about it after the event. I could have refrained from writing about it, of course, but that would just have meant that the truth was left festering in a clandestine hole. If you're a Prince fan outside the inner media circle, it's important that you know he played in a small London venue earlier this week, that the event didn't happen in a real world, where rock 'n' roll can be fully vital and exhilarating, and that the people who arranged it don't use their budget to cherish you like they should.

5 May 2000

PLUG AND PLAY

Licensing pop songs is bigger business than ever

Dave Simpson

Once upon a time, a good song, radio play and a television live appearance would be enough to guarantee a hit record. Nowadays, with more records being released and more competition than ever before, the music industry is moving into areas of 'subliminal marketing' to shift its products.

Consider Moby's *Play* album. In the last few months, the album's killer tracks have featured on countless television adverts and in television programme trailers. 'The Sky Is Broken', for example, advertises Galaxy; 'Everloving' plugs Thorntons; 'Bodyrock' sells, inevitably, Rolling Rock. *Play* even advertises rival products: 'Run On' – now also a hit single – features in a Renault Kangoo advert, while 'Find My Baby' memorably draws admirers towards the Nissan Almera.

There are numerous other tie-ins. Tracks from *Play* feature in no less than six movie soundtracks (including *The Next Best Thing* and *The Beach*, which uses 'Porcelain', soon to be another hit single) and simply acres of TV exposure. There's *Match of the Day* ('Bodyrock'), Sky football (numerous tracks), and Posh Spice's docu-soap, *Victoria's Secrets* (that's 'Run On' again). In fact, there are so many tie-ins that Moby's record label Mute has virtually lost track of them. 'There may have been something with adidas as well,' they say. All this before we even get out of England.

In Europe, Moby advertises the Volkswagen Polo ('Porcelain'), Maxwell House coffee ('Run On'), Bosch and France Telecom (both 'Porcelain' again), the Renault Scenic ('Run On') and several more within individual countries including, bizarrely, Bailey's Irish Cream, in Spain. Then there's America . . . Result? A year after release – it performed only moderately initially – Moby's *Play* album has sold over a million worldwide and spent the last three weeks as the British No 1.

There are countless other examples of subliminal marketing. Andreas Johnson's smash 'Glorious' enjoyed heavy rotation on Sky. The new Death In Vegas hit, 'Dirge', has a three-second loop of its hookline in a Levi ad. The Lightning Seeds' success was arguably built on adverts and *Match of the Day* exposure (and it fell away when this exposure dried up). But Moby is the most successful.

'Moby is very hot property at the moment,' confesses John McGrath, head of Mute Publishing, who handle the domeheaded danceman. 'The Nissan Almera ad has done wonders for him. Suddenly everyone else wants to use the music and the album has developed a whole new lease of life. I can't turn on the TV without hearing Moby. I just go ker-ching, it's Moby yet again . . .'

So is this 'subliminal advertising' on television adverts, programmes and incidental music a better way of selling records than Radio 1? The simple answer is no, but within this increasingly sophisticated and curiously secretive area of the music industry, nothing is quite so simple.

'TV isn't actually more effective than Radio 1, but it's an increasingly vital area of secondary exposure,' says Tony McGuinness, director of marketing at Warner Brothers, home of Andreas Johnson. 'If you list the reasons why people buy records, radio play is the most important. However, if you're hearing a track 10 times a day on TV – even if you're not consciously aware of that – and then turn on the radio and it's there, you can't help but register it. The DJ goes "That's so and so by Andreas Johnson . . ." The chances are quite a bit higher that you'll go out and buy it.' Ker-ching.

Nor is Moby the only astonishing career turnaround. When it was originally released, Babylon Zoo's 'Spaceman' flopped because it was ignored by radio. Once the song was chosen for a Levi ad, the result was an international number one.

There's nothing new about advertisements selling pop music. The practice boomed in the mid-80s. What has changed markedly, however, is the level of sophistication now involved. 'The song title itself is very important,' reveals McGuinness. 'A couple of years ago there was an ad using an old M People track, 'Search for the Hero'. Interestingly, the record company didn't rerelease it as a single, they just promoted a best-of album on the back of the inclusion in the ad. That's an incredibly smart move.'

Sometimes, it's hard to decide whether the record is selling the product, or the product/advert is selling the record. 'Sometimes, the music is so strong that it walks all over the product,' John McGrath agrees. 'You'll think, "Jesus that is amazing" – and then 10 minutes later you wouldn't be able to remember what the song was advertising.'

All sorts of Machiavellian practices proliferate. Moby's *Play* has been particularly successful because different songs (or even the same song with different visuals) fit different requirements, from a chocolate ad to *Match of the Day*. Interestingly, in the Nissan commercial, 'Run On' has been speeded up to match the car. The message is more urgent, faster: buy the car, buy the record. Ker-ching.

The other key switch has been away from old 'classics' and into new or unreleased music. Adverts generally used to use old soul standards. Now, with the enormous increase in disposable incomes available to the under-30s, advertising and TV companies are using more and more up-to-date music.

Part of the reasoning behind not using old tracks so much any more is that 'classic' artists (the Rolling Stones, say) are notoriously difficult to licence. However, it's far more about identification with a target audience. Sky Sports, for example, is aimed at male, slightly laddish under-35s. There's no point in playing some old new romantic music from the early 1980s; artists favoured are current, including Embrace and Oasis. Sky's music librarian Susie Pugh confirms that the company does look for 'certain styles of music or a certain word within the music. "Glorious" [by Andreas Johnson] is perfect because it has that uplifting, anthemic feel'. Anything to make Middlesbrough versus Derby seem exciting.

Sky and ITV have different target audiences, but they are equally desperate for our attention. 'Sky want to be siding with whatever's popular at any given moment,' explains Mute's McGrath. 'The TV companies want to be seen to be hip. I would imagine ITV's programme trailers work in the same way, but they have a captive audience. Sky is different, in your face. It's all "brilliant" and this music is really pounding into your head. Even the way Sky Sports edit everything, it's goal, goal, cheer, cheer: exhilaration all the time.'

Equally sophisticated are the ways in which the music industry targets television to market their new records. Publishers and record companies are investing in direct mailouts and marketing to TV production companies. Agencies known as 'song sourcers' specialise in supplying suitable music to TV and advertising agencies.

The links between television and the music business are closer than ever before. But experts are divided over whether Sky and the BBC, for example, are pluggable in the way that radio pluggers service Radio 1 producers. John McGrath at Mute explains that his publishing company doesn't actively plug TV, but that its own song sourcers have a 'very good relationship' with the broadcasting business. 'There's always somebody plugging something, somewhere,' he says.

Warner's TV plugger Sue Winter insists you can't directly plug Sky or the BBC. But Warner's marketing man McGuinness says you probably can. 'We send all our music to TV stations and the people picking music there tend to know people in record companies because we're plugging conventional TV shows. There are numerous contacts.'

Curiously, the TV companies themselves are reluctant even to acknowledge the existence of plugging. 'Whatever do you mean?' asks Sky's Susie Pugh, coyly. 'We don't play something purposely to make it a hit. Okay, we might do occasionally . . .' Other stations won't comment at all. One 'alternative' terrestrial broadcaster put my call on endless hold, accompanied by repetitive trance music – presumably something that hadn't been plugged.

In the advertising industry, which is composed of creative people, responsible for coming up with ideas, the ad agencies consider themselves unpluggable. The people picking pop for ads tend to be hip young dudes with strong opinions about music and unconventional tastes, who spent last year listening to Death In

Vegas and Moby. Any day now, perhaps another band will be plucked from total obscurity, Forrest Gump-like (as were Scotland's forgotten Bluebells, No 1 via Volkswagen in 1993), to worldwide exposure.

If we are to have our records chosen for us, perhaps they're better coming from a hip young ad exec or TV researcher than an industry-soaked Radio 1 producer. Daytime Radio 1 is dominated by R&B, boy bands and the business's hot projects. TV is less predictable. Sky, for example, have championed the Flaming Lips and Six By Seven. They haven't made them hits, but as Sky becomes more mainstream it might be just a matter of time. The more power that can be removed from Radio 1 and MTV, the better it will be for consumer choice.

At the end of the day, TV will always have a certain autonomy from the powers in the music industry because, unlike radio, the sound has to work with visuals. But could an artist deliberately tailor a song towards an ad, in the same way they used to tailor song titles to include the word 'radio'?

'"Glorious", the Andreas Johnson track, was just perfect for a pompous car ad,' muses Tony McGuinness. 'It's almost advertising copy. But songwriters are primarily artists. I don't think he wrote that song with an advert in mind.' However, McGuinness admits to being 'very interested' in the contents of the forthcoming Heather Small (M-People) album. Then there's the new single by the Bluetones: an ode to a car. It's crying out for use in an ad.

Cynical, maybe? The artists' views on these sorts of things have changed rapidly since the 1980s, when New Order refused to change the words to 'Blue Monday' to sell Sunkist. Now, Moby is said to refuse anything concerned with cosmetics, petrochemicals or involving cruelty. But aren't cars petrochemical? On the other hand, *Play* is a fantastic album. Is it really such a bad thing if it takes subliminal television advertising for the public to appreciate it?

'The key thing about music on TV is it bypasses all the industry bullshit and all the awkwardness and cool factors in buying music,' says McGuinness. 'A year ago dance people were saying Moby was old hat. But the people buying that album now are unaware of the difference between two-step and Chicago House. They just like the music. The beauty of these alternative routes is that – if you get a big marketing campaign – you're able to reach the great unwashed, and sometimes their tastes are refreshingly honest.'

And exceedingly profitable for all concerned. Ker-ching.

5 October 2002

PLUG AND PLAY

Product placement and pop

Peter Robinson

Bloody, bloody, bloody kids. You spend eight months spamming their mobile phones, devising elaborate viral marketing campaigns and unleashing hordes onto the streets with spray cans and stencils, and does mention of your oh-so-cool brand provoke even the slightest flicker of acknowledgement on their ungrateful little faces? Goddammit, they don't even recognise your logo!

Head to France, and those in the Cognac region have accidentally achieved blanket brand recognition without a single PowerPoint presentation. In the few months after Busta Rhymes released 'Pass the Courvoisier', US sales of the drink rose by 4.5 per cent, and since the single's worldwide release, that increase has run into double figures.

One media consultant whose work involves product placement and 'advertising opportunities beyond the conventional' says that the value of the endorsement is found 'specifically in its not having been paid for', as well as the associated benefits of cruising in the slipstream of established artists' credentials.

In the instance of 'Pass the Courvoisier', he estimates the achievements – recognition in a brand new market – as being worth millions of pounds of marketing cash. Daimler-Chrysler recently forced Stereophonics to remove the trademark Jeep from an album title but that, of course, was Stereophonics, so fair point.

Elsewhere, does the 'no such thing as bad publicity' theme really run completely true, even if games consoles are referenced on the same record as recreational drug abuse?

What about TV channels being namechecked only as a showcase for films of copulating beasts? All good, it seems . . .

Product: *GQ* Magazine

Song: 'What You Got' by Abs

An unexpected reworking of Uptown Top Ranking features ex-Five star Abs meeting a girl (as you do) with a 'body like nothin' I seen, she's telling me she's on the cover of *GQ* magazine'. We never find out whether she's telling the truth. Dylan Jones, editor, *GQ*: 'He was in Five? Not Blue? It's all very confusing. I heard the single and my reaction was that it was good to be mentioned, and if he's saying all the best girls are on the cover of *GQ* then that's very flattering. It's very odd to be namechecked by someone whom none of our readers would have anything to do with and I'd say that in terms of our readership his fans would be peripheral to say the least. Very strange. . . I don't know if he's the personification of the *GQ* man, but if the song's about blowing out your girlfriend in order to spend time with a model then he's probably perfectly in tune, although *GQ* man might contact his lawyer first. Anyway, the July and August issues were 15 per cent and 7 per cent above forecast, so Abs, boy, I take my hat off to you!'

Product: Cristal

Song: 'One Night Stand' by Mis-Teeq

Do Mis-Teeq act wild? Yes they do. But have they got style? Oh yes indeed. How do we know? Because, of course, they 'ain't sipping if it ain't Cristal'. Alongside 'And away we go!', the lyric for which Alesha and pals will always be remembered. Alison Dillon, marketing director, Louis Roederer UK (they make Cristal, don'tchaknow): 'With the Mis-Teeq track, it's more than just a namecheck – it's clearly aspirational and we're delighted people enjoy Cristal and choose to mention it in that way because we don't court publicity. We can't – we simply don't have enough product. It's a great endorsement of Cristal product and I think it works in a positive way because people who are fed up of being marketed at feel like they're discovering us all by themselves. Actually, Cristal has a little brother called Brut Première – that's really where the marketing should happen. I wish people would mention that a bit in songs. Cristal's getting so much press and its little brother is being ignored. But there you go!'

Product: The Discovery Channel
Song: 'The Bad Touch' by Bloodhound Gang
1999's out-of-character plunge into Euro disco found the Gang paying tribute to 'love, the kind you clean up with a mop and bucket' with the memorable couplet 'You and me baby ain't nothin' but mammals/So let's do it like they do on the Discovery Channel'. MTV altered the video at the request of gay rights campaigners. Alanna Carty, director of marketing and communications, Discovery Channel UK: 'I remember dancing to this one in Italy! In terms of advertising, you just can't put a value on this sort of thing because it's been voluntary – but we had no idea it was going to come out. We see it now as being positive for the channel. The target for the channel tends to be older men – upmarket, 28- to 34-year-olds – but combined with Eminem's namecheck in 'The Real Slim Shady' it was quite exciting that we'd got into popular culture with acts that were appealing to a young audience. If we could choose an ideal artist, it would probably be Sting. He's an environmentally aware kind of guy . . .'

Product: Sony PlayStation
Song: 'Has It Come to This?' by the Streets
Namechecks the games unit in various tracks on *Original Pirate Material*, including 'Has It Come to This?' with its talk of 'our zone – videos, televisions, 64s, PlayStations'. Carl Christopher, sponsorship and events manager, PlayStation/PlayStation2: 'In many ways, this is a dream ticket – the Streets is the perfect artist for the PlayStation generation and it's street-level marketing, for an audience that's quite difficult to get at. PlayStation is something that's obviously part of Mike Skinner's lifestyle – he's a gamer and it's an excellent endorsement. To say we were happy about the drugs references on the album would probably be something of an overstatement, but they're not mentioned alongside or in relation to PlayStation so we're OK about it. It's all about context. The value of the namechecks comes from the word-of-mouth it generates. Sales have increased whether coincidentally or not in the time *Original Pirate Material* has been available – and, as it happens, we recently agreed to support his forthcoming tour.'

Product: Holiday Inn
Song: 'Rapper's Delight' by the Sugarhill Gang

In hip-hop's answer to 'The Wasteland', the Sugarhill Gang get a 'fly girl', drive her off and 'go hotel, motel, Holiday Inn'. They also issue a word of advice: 'If your girl starts actin' up, then you take her friend.' More recently, the refrain has been revived by the likes of Tweet and TLC. Nick Barton, marketing director, Holiday Inn UK & Ireland: 'Holiday Inn is the world's most recognised hotel brand which makes it inevitable that it is sometimes used as a generic term for a hotel. To have such recognition and high awareness is a great asset. We would consider using songs that feature Holiday Inn in an advertising campaign, however they would obviously need to be relevant to our campaign theme and the target media. Our key target audience is the business traveller and rap songs are not usually their preferred choice of music; however, with regards to usage of the brand name in the song, we must remember that the youth of today could be our business guest of the future.'

Product: Mother's Pride
Song: 'One Love' by Blue

The band's new single – which is about city streets and the Darren Dayesque ghettos of the band's youth – includes the line 'One love for the Mother's Pride'. They also have 'one love' for 'the hip-hop beats'. But of course! Sarah Robertson, group brand manager, British Bakeries: 'It's all good news – bread's strange because there'd be an outcry without it, but nobody talks about it very much. The amount of girls being sent down the shops for bread and subliminally going for Mother's Pride will be pretty minimal, and they probably weren't intentionally discussing bread, to be honest. If they were going "Mother's Pride bread is the best bread" then perhaps it would be better. But it does trigger awareness among consumers. There's value in a positive association, but it could be negative, too. Someone like Eminem wouldn't be very positive for us because our brand is about goodness and having a relationship of trust between mothers and that brand. Given Eminem's relationship with his own mother, I doubt the association would be positive. Popstars going on wheat-free diets doesn't help things much, either.'

22 November 2002

HOLD TIGHT THE MASSIVE

Alexis Petridis

It has been described as a new studio, a nerve centre and the headquarters of Essex's top pirate radio station, and admittance has been granted only after a rigorous vetting procedure. I have been quizzed at length. ID has been demanded. The *Guardian*'s photographer has been accused of spying for the government: 'I'm sorry about that, mate,' says our guide, a 19-year-old who bears the fitting pseudonym of Stealth. 'But he looks exactly like an inspector from the DTI – he's even driving a Ford Mondeo.' Finally, though, Stealth has agreed to drive us to the secret location. On the way, the car stereo blares out Soundz FM. It plays chirpy UK garage topped not with patois-heavy rhymes about guns, 'haters' and inner-city violence, but rap of a distinctly Essex strain. 'Big shaaht aaht to the XR3i crew,' says the MC. 'Buzzing abaaht in the rain on a Sunday afternoon.'

The screening procedures are so exacting, it's difficult not to be slightly disappointed when you arrive. You can call this place a studio until you are blue in the face, but there is no getting around the fact that we are standing in the middle of someone's garage. The turntables nestle on a workbench amid cans of de-icer and Hammerite. The DJs and their friends sit on piles of stacked-up garden chairs, their baseball-capped heads nodding in time to the beats.

A DJ called Mr Y2K is hunched over the turntables, while his fellow DJ Softmix chatters into a microphone, taking requests and demands for 'shout outs', and reading text messages. The mobile phone rings. He hands it to Mr Y2K, and a brief, animated conversation takes place, just audible over the beats. A listener is criticising Y2K's choice of records. 'Yeah, I know, mum,' he mutters. 'I didn't really want to play it myself.' He pauses and looks momentarily pained. 'Will you stop interfering?' he asks, plaintively. 'Big up Mr Y2K's mummy!' cries Softmix. Stealth rolls his eyes. 'Sometimes his nan rings up as well,' he says.

Soundz FM is far removed from the popular image of a pirate radio station. For a start, we are not in a crumbling Hackney tower block, nor is the atmosphere fugged with marijuana smoke. Judging by the litter on the floor, Soundz runs on nothing stronger than junk food and cigarettes. The atmosphere is cheery, with the added frisson of illicit behaviour. It is somewhere between a youth club and a house party being held while parents are away. Everyone is friendly, if startled by the arrival of a national newspaper in their midst. 'Shout going out to the *Guardian* posse,' cries Softmix, by way of introduction. 'Checking out the studio, writing an article on Soundz FM!' He then decides to conduct an interview of his own. 'What do you make of it?' he asks, thrusting the microphone into my hands. But I have neither the voice nor the vocabulary for pirate radio. 'So far it seems very impressive,' I say, sounding like the winner of a competition to find Britain's most middle-class person. Aware that Soundz FM's street credibility is threatened, Softmix takes the microphone back. 'Wicked,' he says.

From Radio London in the 1960s to So Solid Crew's Battersea-based Delight FM, pirate radio has traditionally been a London phenomenon. Two years old, Soundz is one of a new breed of suburban pirates, uncomfortable with the gangster posturing and occasional bursts of violence that have become associated with illegal radio in the capital. Although Soundz reaches London, the majority of its audience comes from the suburbs: Essex, Surrey, Kent and Hertfordshire. The 'staff' of Soundz FM are curiously prudish. Swearing is banned on air. 'Some stations use filthy language, you know,' bridles one DJ indignantly. 'They're asking to be taken off the air, no question.'

'In London they want that rude boy attitude,' says Stealth. 'In certain parts of north-west London. . . well, there's a pirate station there that's actually based in a crack den, so that gives you an idea of some of them. But we're not all like that. We're referred to as polite people from Bexley. We're a friendly, community station. We're from the suburbs, we don't bother trying to get non-suburb listeners.'

There's a musical distinction as well, albeit one of those

infinitesimal sub-generic shifts that anyone not completely immersed in the dance music world has no hope of understanding. DJ L-Dubs attempts to explain it to me. 'Shady garage', he says, is to be avoided at all costs, whereas 'happy garage' attracts 'uplifting people who want to be uplifted'. The latter, he informs me, is what Soundz FM is all about. I nod knowledgeably, but have no idea what he is talking about.

Equally bewildering is the station's co-founder, Master Control. Portly and middle-aged, he cuts an incongruous figure amid the sportswear-clad teens. He was a teenager himself when he first got involved with pirate radio. Now it has completely taken over his life. During the week he makes 'rigs' – radio transmitters – that he sells to other stations. At the weekends he careers around the Essex countryside, checking Soundz's aerial, ensuring that the signal is not causing interference to television or the emergency services. Ask him what the appeal of pirate radio is and he looks completely mystified. 'I don't know. I find it . . . I don't know. I can't really do anything else. It's the only thing in my life that I can do. I make rigs that work, I do it properly. You get a sense of achievement, I suppose.'

He's not alone in his inability to explain the compulsion to break the law on a weekly basis, endure the endless hassle and expense of having your transmitter impounded by the Radiocommunications Agency (or stolen by a rival station) and risk unlimited fines and two years in prison. There's certainly no financial reward – the DJs pay a £10 weekly subscription to play on the station, which goes towards running costs – and little chance of celebrity. While some of the Soundz staff clearly see the station as a means of breaking through, circumventing the politburo of ageing celebrity DJs who control the dance scene, it is statistically unlikely that they will. For every So Solid Crew, who have converted their pirate notoriety into a more tangible form of celebrity, there are scores of DJs beavering away in semi-obscurity: Dom Da Bom, Miss Giggles, Lukozade, DJ Bangers, the hopefully named Aylesbury Allstars.

It's peculiar, but then pirate radio has always been a bit peculiar. By definition it exists outside the mainstream, attracting strange characters who don't really fit in anywhere else. As befits a criminal enterprise, it regularly changes its identity. It began in 1964, the brainchild of Irish businessman Ronan O'Rahilly, who noted that, in the heyday of Beatlemania, the BBC Light Programme was broadcasting only two hours of pop music a week. O'Rahilly's Radio Caroline and its competitor Radio London invented pop radio as we know it today. By 1967, however, the Marine Broadcasting Offences Act had made the seafaring stations illegal, and Radio 1 had swiped both the pirates' all-pop format and their biggest DJs: Tony Blackburn, Dave Lee Travis, Kenny Everett and John Peel.

Deprived of both legality and raison d'etre, pirate radio went into decline. By the 1970s, it was the domain of crackpots: Radio Nordsee featured a DJ called Spangles Muldoon and broadcast virulent Tory propaganda during the 1970 general election. Radio Enoch, meanwhile, offered military music and plummy voices denouncing immigration.

It took the rise of dance music to revive the pirates' fortunes. Britain's underground soul and reggae scenes grew throughout the Seventies, but were largely ignored by Radio 1 or the new commercial stations. Pirates stepped in to fill the void. Invicta, Radio Free London, Solar, Horizon and LWR eschewed fishing trawlers and set up in the centre of London, broadcasting urban music in an urban setting. When acid house was in effect banned from Radio 1 after 1988's tabloid drug exposés, a host of new pirates sprung up: Centreforce, Sunrise and Fantasy among them. It set a pattern that has repeated ever since, in which the pirate stations are the scourge of the authorities and a vital source of new music for the record industry.

When a new dance genre emerges – hardcore, drum'n'bass, and most recently UK garage – a new wave of pirates appear, devoted to the new sound. Virtually every garage or drum'n'bass tune that makes the national chart will have been played on a pirate station first. Occasionally, a pirate DJ finds himself at the helm of a hit. Flex FM's DJ Dee Kline went to No 11 in 2000 with 'I Don't Smoke', a garage record that sampled Jim Davidson doing his comedy West Indian voice.

Radio 1 repeated the trick it pulled off in 1967, luring DJs Pete Tong and Tim Westwood from LWR, Gilles Peterson from Horizon and the Dreem Teem from Blackbeard Radio. But this time the pirates, attracted by the relatively low cost of setting up a station (estimated by Stealth at around £2,500), won't die away. In 1991, the RA carried out 475 operations against pirate stations. Last year, it carried out 1,438. London's airwaves are currently jammed with a startling array of illicit stations. At the weekend, you can hear anything from the pre-pubescent children of So Solid's Dan Da Man spinning garage on Delight to Ghanaian gospel music courtesy of WBLS's improbably named DJ Rabbi.

Stations rise and fall with dizzying frequency – the victims of internal feuding, a lack of suitable studio locations and raids by the DTI's Radiocommunications Agency – but there is always someone to replace them. So far this year, the RA has raided 179 pirate stations in London. Most went straight back on the air. As the RA dolefully admits: 'There's no easy victory or cure for pirate radio. You take them down, they put them up again. You can't be sure people won't reoffend. You're just dealing with a specific complaint at a specific time.'

According to Stealth, central London's airwaves are so over-crowded that the suburbs are the best option for a new station. 'We're doing it as a hobby. There are too many stations in London and they're all doing it for money. When it turns into a money market, you get people using dodgy rigs, employing thick cement mixers to install the equipment.' Meanwhile, he says, pirate stations are springing up in locations that make Bexley look like a teeming metropolis: Weymouth, Newquay, Telford, Ludlow, Swindon.

To prove the point, Stealth suggests a visit to his friend's station, Y2K Kent, which broadcasts from Margate. The next weekend, we rendezvous in a lay-by near the Blackwall Tunnel. Stealth arrives in a small hatchback, with a large skull and crossbones flag sticking out of the sunroof.

In Margate I am introduced to Y2K's founder, a stocky 20-year-old who works for a drainage company by day and who calls himself Fraudster. Fraudster has been involved in pirate radio since he was 13. He originally DJed around London before realising the pirate scene was simply too crowded there. 'We realised we needed to go somewhere else,' he says, 'so we packed everything into the car and just started to drive out of London, through the Blackwall tunnel. This was the first place we got to.'

Fraudster says that in its year of existence, Y2K Kent has been successful enough to attract complaints from the local commercial radio station. 'They said we nicked 1,000 of their listeners, but they play music for over-30s, so I don't see how that works.' Nevertheless, it is a modest set-up, located in the box room of a student house. The room is so tiny that three people constitute a life-threatening crush. DJs and associates crowd outside, peering in. It is extremely hot, and the unmistakable stench of bloke wafts down the stairs. The windows must be kept shut, lest anyone notices the noise and contacts the RA. 'You have to be careful in Margate,' says Fraudster, 'because there's no crime, the police have got nothing to do. The front page of the local paper is "man steals pork pie from Tesco's".'

On the floor, an electric fan cools a tangle of wires and electronic boxes, apparently assembled to plans by Heath Robinson. On our arrival, it breaks down. 'Hold tight the massive,' says the MC, 'as we sort it out inside the place.'

Stealth immediately springs into action. 'You need a graphic on the mixer,' he suggests. 'I need another studio,' groans Fraudster, looking harassed. In fact, Fraudster spends most of my visit looking harassed. His mobile phone rings constantly, not with shout-outs or requests, but irate calls from his girlfriend, for whom the novelty of pirate radio has clearly long worn off. 'I sometimes wonder why I do this,' Fraudster admits. 'I spend my whole week cleaning out shitty drains, then spend all weekend doing this. I'm not in it to earn anything. I suppose it's for the joy of the music.'

The RA's spokesman argues that 'people suffer as a result of pirate radio. They tune into a station they want to listen to, and find something else blocking it. I take their calls, and they're absolutely furious. If you live nearby they create a noise nuisance. They're anti-social.'

You take his point – you wouldn't want to live next door to an illegal radio station, pumping out UK garage or drum'n'bass from Friday evening to Monday morning. However, it's hard not to be impressed by the determined attitude of the pirates. There is little fame and less cash in their world of box bedrooms and converted garages.

Yet still they doggedly carry on, buying new rigs, finding new studios, skulking about in search of suitable transmitter sites. Although most of them are far too young to remember the Sex Pistols, there's something resolutely punk about their attitude: confronted with a dance scene that has slid into mundane irrelevance, they have decided to do something for themselves. Their ambitions are not commercially driven, yet they extend far beyond anti-authoritarian posturing. At Soundz, there's a lot of talk about digital radio. When legal stations switch to digital transmission, they live in hope that the RA will leave the obsolete FM band to them. Soundz even has aspirations beyond playing music. 'We run a show between 8 p.m. and 12 a.m. where we do comedy,' says Stealth, proudly. 'It's absolute chaos. We had a bloke out with a microphone doing wind-ups on people in McDonald's in Lakeside shopping centre, and on drivers at the Dartford tunnel. You'd crease up if you heard it.' A little corner of pirate radio, it seems, will be forever DLT.

A few weeks after my visit, Stealth telephones. Both Soundz FM and Y2K Kent have gone off the air. Soundz has collapsed due to internal disagreements: Stealth and Master Control have fallen out over music policy. Y2K Kent, meanwhile, was raided by the RA, who found not only their rig, but two station staff standing next to it. For the first time, Stealth sounds bleak about the future of pirate radio: 'Fines are going up, more stations are getting raided, things are getting tighter all the time. They're really turning up the heat.'

But it's still not hot enough to discourage Stealth and Fraudster. Within weeks, both are back in business with new stations, Fraudster with a station called Essence 105.1 FM, Stealth with Impact 99.7 FM. He has moved out of the garage and set up a studio in an industrial estate. And he has finally nailed pirate radio's unique appeal. 'The buzz is when you're driving down your local high street and you hear it playing out of someone else's radio, or you hear people talking about it on the bus,' he says. 'You realise you're having an effect. If it was going nowhere, you'd soon lose interest.'

27 December 2003

FACE THE MUSIC

Peter Robinson

Where will you be in August 2004? Sir Cliff Richard knows where he'll be: on the beachfront steps of his Barbados mansion, wearing a black and pink sarong, cocking a seashell in the direction of his right ear. At least, that is how he has chosen to illustrate his August in the official 2004 Cliff calendar.

When most people hold a shell to their ear they hear the sea, but the waves splashing around in Cliff's own shell will be barely audible above the sounds of thousands of pounds emptying themselves into his bank account. Calendars can be big money-spinners for musicians seeking alternative revenue streams in the music industry's gloomy current climate.

They shift up to half a million units and net their subjects a healthy sum – certainly more than the average single release is likely to earn – for a day's work, or for a few hours' work, or in some cases for no work at all. (Tupac has been particularly lazy this year.)

But it's not all about the cash. With the turnover of new acts increasing every year, calendars reserve precious wall space for an entire year. For the likes of 50 Cent and Gareth Gates, whose futures seem uncertain for quite different reasons, a 2004 calendar is a statement that says, 'I will be around in 12 months'. Which is heartening news for Rachel Stevens, who entered the pop calendar charts at No 9 in the same week that her second single limped into the proper charts at a painful No 26.

It is, says Danilo calendar advisor Jennie Halsall, all about timing: having been pestered for months, rugby hero Jonny Wilkinson finally agreed to an official calendar earlier this month, and 100,000 copies sold out within seven days, making it Danilo's fastest-selling in 25 years. But that's sport, which is boring. Bring on the pop stars . . .

LOVEKYLIE

What happens? Having just announced plans to cover up, Minogue begins the year in a mirrored box sporting a pink-edged black pants and bra combo. By February she's having a lie-down, going on to wheel out the interesting 'hedge backwards with nips' shot first seen in *Pop* magazine during spring 2003. Then there's some kneeling on a chair, some sitting on a chair, some kneeling on a rug . . . there's a lot of kneeling.

Best month: May. Kylie celebrates her birthday (it's on the 28th) by ripping her bra off and sitting on a gym horse. Except the gym horse is wearing a saddle – LIKE A HORSE! Off camera, a wind machine is windy.

GARETH GATES

What happens? Gareth looks to the left (three times), and to the right (also three times), sits in a sort of white box, laughs at some French windows, inspects his feet for we don't know what, and – form an orderly queue please, ladies – wakes up naked in bed. It does seem, particularly during March and July, that Gareth is well on his way to becoming a man. Perhaps Jordan provides some useful purpose after all.

Best month: October, in which Gareth strikes his best Freeman's Catalogue Pose of Moodiness, seemingly oblivious to the fact he is waist-deep in water.

LINKIN PARK

What happens? The world's second most awful band (after Stereophonics) prove how real and gritty they are via a series of live shots and photographs in which band members grimace a lot, seeing as that is what serious musicians do, don't you know. There's real emotion in this calendar.

Best month: January. The band are standing in a line, against a wall, in tinted monochrome. Woo! That said, December is particularly nice – drummer Rob Bourdon pounds his skins in a festive Little Drummer Boy style.

EMINEM

What happens? Not much. But based on these 12 images, Em will spend four months of 2004 wearing a headscarf, three months wearing a cap, half a year wearing a white T-shirt, and one quarter of the year pointing. In real terms, that's over 91 days spent pointing at things. Perhaps if the bootleggers really do shut down his 'shit' during 2004, Eminem has a promising career working in a museum.

Best month: May, where we see Eminem with his head in a guillotine with some curious scratchy effects thrown in for good measure. This is because Eminem is not scared of taking risks – he is an edgy artist, just like famous beheaded pop stars such as, er, King Charles I.

TUPAC

What happens? An array of images take us through a life in the death of Tupac. January appears to be the month of pixelation, the filthy negatives used for February and August possibly predict strikes by Snappy Snaps operatives. The opening flap of this calendar includes plugs for a forthcoming Tupac film, a soundtrack album, a picture book, a DVD, an unreleased album, a biography, a biography of Tupac's mother, a TV movie, and a series of gospel concerts. Nice shot of his tits in March.

Best month: May, in which Tupac holds his arms aloft and smokes a cigarette. What a dude!

RACHEL STEVENS

What happens? Rachel looks pretty in some nice clothes.

Best month: March, where we find Rachel lying invitingly on a bed. 'Hello viewers,' she seems to be saying. 'You are imagining doing some unsavoury things to me. And I'm not going to argue with that.' It must be strange being in Rachel's position (as a singer, not lying down), knowing that a significant proportion of your calendar-buyers are busily inspecting your white pants for skidmarks. A time-saving fact: there are none.

ROBBIE

What happens? He's happy! He's sad! He's standing around at the end of the night with his bow tie undone in a sort of 'reportage' style! He's hanging upside down at Knebworth! He's covered in some of the most ghastly tattoos this side of the bloke outside the arcade with a spider's web across his face!

Best month: October, in which we get to see Bob's grotesque 'Elvis grant me serenity' tattoo and Bob's grotesque 'Born to be mild' tattoo. His hearing aid dangles limply around his neck, preventing Robbie from hearing the world shout, 'JUST GIVE UP AND LET WILKES ENJOY HIS ALL-NEW *YOU'VE BEEN FRAMED* GLORY!' A tragedy.

BUSTED

What happens? Busted wear some suits, look a bit quizzical, push their faces against some glass, balance dogs on their laps and take turns in front of a blue background in a variety of pictures first seen in May's excellently written official Busted book.

Best month: January. 'We've been to the year 2004,' the image seems to be saying. 'Not much has changed, but . . . In fact nothing has changed at all because this image seems to be about a year old.'

ELVIS

What happens? The King veers from the buff to the bulbous from month to month in a calendar so official that it comes with a nice hologram on the back. Looking at this now, it would appear that Elvis's early years were spent almost entirely posing for photographs taken from the left, while his rubbish period was spent on stage. Elvis wears more white tops than Eminem, making him harder.

Best month: July. Dressed in his army uniform, Elvis sits jauntily in the driving seat of a red car. He looks so happy with life, and with the prospect of going off and killing people.

BEYONCÉ

What happens? Beyoncé sports, with alarming regularity, that horrible big frizzy hair number for no discernible reason other than to make herself look better when she gets the straighteners out.

Best month: July, in which the PhotoShopping goes bonkers with a horizontal flip, some over-excited feathering, a smattering of outer glow and some dubious drop-shadow. 'Beyoncé,' says the word Beyoncé, were there any possibility that we would mistake the woman in the picture for Su-Elise from Mis-Teeq. Nice, but hardly any way to celebrate the first birthday of the record Beyoncé will spend her entire year trying to better.

50 CENT

What happens? Mr Cent folds his arms, points a bit, throws bullets at the camera like they did in the olden days before guns were invented, runs around, lays down a 'rap', wears a variety of items with G-Unit written on them, and generally wheels out a variety of press shots. He does not smile once, though he's got a bit of a cheeky look on his face in June.

Best month: December, in which Fiddy prepares to party like it's the king of kings' birthday in a fetching Gucci gun holster 'n' belt 'ensemble'. He's reaching for his gun, viewers! A traffic cone looms menacingly in the background.

CLIFF RICHARD

What happens? Everything. Absolutely everything. This is the best calendar you will ever see – and Cliff's annotated each photograph with a hilarious caption. Watch Cliff pouring some wine! Standing on a building site! Wielding gladioli! Pretending to play guitar with a tennis racket! Rocking the worst shirt 'n' slacks pattern you'll have ever seen! And a whole lot more.

Best month: September. Cliff is pictured reclining, white shorts hitched above the knee, holding a cocktail. 'Dreamin' of me and you,' reads Cliff's caption. It's difficult to know whether this image is more seductive than Rachel Stevens' March pose, though Cliff gains points for his inventive use of a hammock.

29 April 2005

WHAT GOES UP . . .

Dorian Lynskey

However eventful your year has been so far, it is unlikely to have moved with quite the same hair-raising pace as it has for the Bravery. On 7 January, a panel of music industry pundits anointed the one-year-old New York band, with only a few UK dates and one limited-edition EP under their skinny belts, 2005's most likely success story.

At the end of February their heavily playlisted debut single, 'An Honest Mistake', entered the top 10, swiftly followed by their eponymous first album. They announced a May tour, including one date at the London Astoria, which sold out in an hour. Two more Astoria shows sold out in the same time. On 29 March, Brandon Flowers of the Killers kicked off the backlash by branding the Bravery opportunistic phonies. Their success resembles less a real career than the implausibly accelerated timeframe of a biopic.

There's an old Hollywood joke about the stages of a showbusiness career: 'Who's Joe Blow? – Get me Joe Blow – Get me the next Joe Blow – Who's Joe Blow?' It was ever thus but now a young band can experience the whole cycle – from screams of excitement to shrugs of apathy – in as little as two years. 'They call it in the trade a firework career,' says DJ Steve Lamacq. 'They go straight up and it's very pretty, and then they come straight down again.'

The climate around new bands has never been as overheated as it is right now. Mild hysteria surrounds any group with at least one good song who can get through a live set without falling over. Genuine enthusiasm snowballs into frothing hype in the blink of an eye. Backlashes arrive before there's been enough time for a proper lash. Nobody has time to wait around: not the press, not the record labels, not the record-buyers and, whether they like it or not, certainly not the band.

The first bidding war Lamacq can remember from his time on

the *NME* was the Sundays in 1989. Once Britpop showed how much money could be made from so-called indie music, the floodgates opened. The joke went that if you could enter a pub in Camden walking like a band and talking like a band, then a record deal was yours for the asking; Menswear, probably the 1990s' archetypal firework band, did exactly that.

The hunger for new music in the past two or three years, however, has become insatiable. Festivals and gigs sell out within hours: harmonising siblings the Magic Numbers have just sold out two nights at London's 2,000-capacity Forum after just one limited edition, seven-inch single. Broadsheets that a decade ago regarded most pop music with a quizzical 'Who is Gazza?' fogeyishness now fight to cover bands before their first albums are on the shelves. Texas's South by Southwest festival has become an essential date on the calendar: this year British attendance tripled to 900. Competition among A&Rs and publicists to snap up new acts is at fever pitch. 'I think it's partly down to the internet and messageboards,' says Lamacq. 'Originally it made everyone a critic – now it's made everyone an A&R man.'

For a young band, being hailed as God's gift to recorded sound must be both exhilarating and disturbing because the pitfalls are many. There are groups like the 22-20s, who wait too long to release their first album and find their moment has passed while they were still trying to get the perfect snare sound. There are those, such as Hope of the States, whose albums, though promising, don't live up to expectations and are promptly deemed failures. 'It takes one bad week and it's like, they're all over,' Lamacq complains. 'Give them a chance! A lot of people will only come good on their second album.'

Then there are those (the Rapture, Fischerspooner) who find themselves signed for telephone-number sums that their minority-interest music can't hope to recover. In the frenzy of a bidding war, some A&R men demonstrate all the cool-headed common sense of an inebriated eBayer. 'There's only going to be three or four bands who break through in any given year,' cautions Frank Tope, an A&R manager for Universal Music Publishing who has signed the likes of Franz Ferdinand and Röyksopp.

Sometimes, says music industry journalist James Roberts, there's method in the apparent madness: 'Some major labels sign artists that are unlikely to recoup as trophy signings, purely to attract other cool artists. It's all part of the process of rebranding.' More often, though, the rule is: the bigger the deal, the bigger the pressure to succeed. A band such as the Thrills or the Killers, signed at an early stage for a reasonable sum, will recoup their advance very quickly. One that emerges from a bidding war can sell 100,000 albums and still be in the red.

Anyone who does manage to become genuinely successful faces stratospheric expectations for their next record. Consider the Music, the Vines or the Polyphonic Spree, all of whom delivered more-of-the-same follow-ups to a withering lack of interest. Music-making has become a kind of gladiatorial combat, in which bands battle for attention while record-buyers casually tilt their thumbs up or down, forever craning their necks to examine the next contestant hovering at the arena entrance.

It takes a certain toughness or, even better, experience to emerge unbloodied. 'It can really help a band if at least one member has been through the mill already and they know what to expect,' says Tope. Franz Ferdinand's Alex Kapranos had a recently unearthed past in a 1990s jazz-rock outfit called the Karelia; the Kaiser Chiefs rose from the ashes of garage-rockers Parva; and Snow Patrol, who struck most new fans as an overnight success, released their first record in 1997.

However well things are going, it is always best to prepare for the worst. A band can now play three nights at Brixton Academy without earning much in the way of loyalty. The Hives caught the mood with their knowingly titled 2002 breakthrough album, *Your New Favourite Band*, then found for themselves how easy it is to become an old favourite band. Music fans increasingly want one-night stands rather than lasting love affairs.

'As a consumer we've got a brilliant record, we've had some great singles, we've seen some great gigs and it's over,' says Lamacq. 'The only people who suffer from a firework career are the band themselves, who are just charred remains in somebody's back garden after two years.'

Of course, you don't know for sure you're watching a firework band until they begin their sudden descent, but the Bravery, and the rest of this year's bright young things, would be wise not to read too much into the oohs and aahs. They live their lives like a roman candle in the wind.

The Thrillers: the firework career of a fictional band

November – A few friends form a band, think of a name and play their first show in a local pub. The band's parents and friends are sighted at the gig.

January – The Thrillers record their first demos in the drummer's bedroom. (That was where the Kaiser Chiefs made their first single, the original version of 'Oh My God'.)

March – A manager and lawyer approach them after seeing them play in Camden's Dublin Castle. The band launch their website and post a handful of MP3s. (Before the Killers had played their first UK show, interested labels could hear music on their website. Steve Lamacq says: 'There's so much competition between record labels to find someone before everyone else. If a band has got good songs, they will be found – wherever they are – within six months.')

April – The A&R buzz builds. Record labels, publishers and press officers descend. Nobody dances, but there is much thoughtful nodding. Steve Lamacq is sighted at the gig. (He says: 'I saw Franz Ferdinand playing in front of 40 people [in February 2003], at least 26 of whom were people from the record industry. I said to Alex [Kapranos] later on that they were rubbish that night and he said, "Yeah, but you were a rubbish audience." And we were!')

May – Their first seven-inch is released on Fierce Panda, the independent label that has been a launching pad for Coldplay, Keane, the Music and the Polyphonic Spree. They land their first *NME* live review, full of ecstatic praise for their music and their singer's hair. An intrigued A&R scout from a US record label is sighted at a gig (American labels flew over by Concorde to court the 22-20s in summer 2003). Zane Lowe, Radio 1's excitable indie music champion, gives the single its first airing. They play a guerrilla gig, popularised by the Others and Kasabian, in a pub car park.

July – They sign a major record deal (the Departure signed to Parlophone only six months after getting together) and tour the UK supporting British Sea Power (like the Killers and the Duke Spirit). A live review uses the phrase 'the best new band in Britain' – the music press's favourite endorsement ever since *Melody Maker* put it over a cover picture of Suede in 1992. It describes approximately 74 bands every year. Their first festival appearance, at T in the Park, is warmly received. (Paddy Davis, publicist for Kaiser Chiefs and Ash, says: 'The press is wary of backing something that isn't necessarily going to follow through. If the Kaiser Chiefs had signed to Shit & Shovel Records, I'm not sure the press would have got behind them.')

September – First major label single released; it scrapes into the top 30. Showcase gig at In the City (where the Darkness were first discovered). Featured in *The Fly*, the free music magazine distributed in teetering piles at rock venues. Win a coveted slot in the *NME*'s influential Radar section, which has featured virtually every successful band of recent years. Garrulous singer says the band are into 'a bit of everything', that they want to 'make music exciting again' and that, despite the name, they owe nothing to either the Killers or the Thrills. Radio 1 and XFM start paying attention.

October – First US appearance at CMJ in New York (a spot here was pivotal for the Killers). Their singer guests on a hip dance record (the last Chemical Brothers album helped boost the profile of Bloc Party and the Magic Numbers). A publishing deal is confirmed.

November – Small headlining tour sells out. Kate Moss and Noel Gallagher sighted at gig. Small mention in the *Star*'s Hot column. The tipping point is reached. First feature in a national broadsheet, now considered a crucial part of a press campaign. (Paddy Davis: 'Five or six years ago I used to sit in marketing meetings and say a broadsheet would like to do something, and people would pooh-pooh it.')

January – With the tour fresh in their minds, critics, DJs and other industry figures vote the Thrillers as one of the 10 names in the BBC's annual Sound of . . . survey. (Now in its third year, the poll has predicted success for Keane, Razorlight, Franz Ferdinand, the Scissor Sisters, Bloc Party, Kaiser Chiefs, the Magic Numbers, the Yeah Yeah Yeahs, Interpol and Dizzee Rascal. Although Gemma Fox, Wiley and the Ordinary Boys will tell you that a poll placing is no guarantee. Lamacq: 'I've virtually stopped making predictions because everything moves so quickly – a band on the starting grid in December could be out of fashion in March. Meanwhile, the best new band of the year is probably still in the garage.')

February – The new single, a scrubbed-up reissue of their indie debut, is inescapable on Radio 1 and crashes into the top 10 (just like the Killers' 'Mr Brightside' and the Kaiser Chiefs' 'Oh My God'). *NME* puts them on the cover. Internet messageboards grumble about hype.

March – They are one of the most talked about bands at South by Southwest. (Past discoveries there have included the Yeah Yeah Yeahs and the Polyphonic Spree. Lamacq: 'Even four years ago, it was some enigmatic event miles away from home that bore no relevance. But then people discovered one or two American bands.') First album is released to positive reviews, although at least half use the word 'hype', and debuts at No 5. Festival dates are announced and the forthcoming tour sells out.

April – Back to the US for a short tour, culminating at Coachella, the country's only European-style music festival. The album is given a cautious welcome by American critics, all of whom make narky remarks about the excitability of the British press.

May – Sell-out tour coincides with the second single. Adverts for album run on E4, and the 3AM Girls are sighted at a gig. As surely as night follows day, Elton John bestows his seal of approval (previous beneficiaries include the Killers and Mylo) and buys copies of the album for all his showbiz pals.

June – A triumphant performance on the Other Stage at Glastonbury. (The Darkness, the Killers and Keane have all boosted their reputations in this way. Rachel Hendry, publicist for the Killers, the Bravery, the Duke Spirit and Nine Black Alps, says: 'A great festival gig is something record companies dream about.')

August – The Thrillers are nominated for the Mercury prize. Bookmakers make them joint third favourites at 6–1. They do not win. They appear at V festival, playing two new songs that sound much like the old ones. Have a backstage run-in with Mancunian newcomers, the Astounded, following disparaging remarks in the press about the singer's hair. *NME* runs a photograph of the two warring frontmen wearing Photoshopped boxing gloves.

October – Fourth single is released, accompanied by a 'controversial' video. Yet another sell-out tour, this time closing with three nights at Brixton Academy. Support comes from promising young turks the Siegfried Line. Nominated for three *Q* Awards. Win one, for best video. Singer becoming unbearable.

January – Win best new band award at the Brits. The *Sun*'s Bizarre column celebrates by running a year-old anecdote. The band fly off for another US tour the next day, where they are photographed for a magazine feature wearing sunglasses in front of a familiar American landmark.

February – They write more new songs on the road, some of which are about being on the road. The A&R man urges speedy delivery of a second album, reciting the words 'Stone Roses' and 'Elastica' in dread tones. The annual BBC poll features the Siegfried Line, who are described as 'the next Thrillers'. (Lamacq: 'If you've been out on the road for 18 months touring the first album, how bereft of new ideas are you going to be when you finally get back into the studio? My law of A&R is: what does the second album sound like? Do you even want to hear a second album? There's some bands where I don't even want to listen to their first album.'

June – Second album is greeted by blanket press coverage but lukewarm reviews. It sounds rather like the first one, only not as good. Enters the charts at No 5, then swiftly tumbles down. Cue disappointing festival shows, 'musical differences', talk of releasing next album independently . . .

RO
& R

ENCOUNTERS

28 June 1972

OUR NAME IS CALLED DISTURBANCE

Leroy Aarons

'Ladies and Gentlemen', comes the microphone voice of Bill Graham, 'The world's greatest rock 'n' roll band!' A tidal wave shout and Mick Jagger is suddenly there, jumping up and down like a Jack Flash-in-the-box. Is that gold dust dancing around his head? Without delay the band strikes up: And there's no denying, it is the raunchiest, flashiest, most exciting rock 'n' roll band in existence.

Gravel scratching sandpaper. Jagger, a vision in purple-sequinned, one-piece, membrane-thin silk jumpsuit, spangled and jangled with red glitter eye make-up, with sashes and scarves and a white satin cutaway. All of it undulating to Jagger's incredible witch dance.

The music gives way to an even louder roar of approval. Kids who waited in line for 20 hours for tickets and began arriving for the concert six hours ago are on their feet. Near the stage, instead of applauding, they raise a hand, palm stretched outwards towards Jagger as if to conquer the space between them, to touch. Or receive benediction?

Jagger struts, reels, camps, swishes, bumps, grinds, runs in place – he's a bantam, he's a peacock teaser, he's a drag queen, he's a witch doctor. Who is he? Who cares, man? Just keep on truckin'.

San Diego, California

This is the Stones' fifth American tour, the first since 1969 and Altamont. It will cover thirty cities in less than two months. Everybody is concerned, almost obsessed, with keeping things cool. And so far, except for a few skirmishes (with injuries and arrests) outside the arenas, usually involving counterfeit tickets, it has been that way. Tickets are being scalped for up to $45 apiece. In fact, in the four cities I covered, it looked like the most professional, disciplined rock tour ever.

‘On this tour they hand cast all the people,’ Bob Gibson is saying backstage at the San Diego Sports Arena (almost site of the Republican national convention), just before the Stones are to go on. Gibson is half of Gibson and Stromberg, the Hollywood press agents hired for the tour. ‘No amateurs. Last time it was run by people who were not professionals. We’re working with the best promoters in every city. We have our own make-up man on this tour, our own doctor, our own accountant, our own security guards and even our own guitar tuner.’

Out front Stevie Wonder, the opening act on the tour, is warming up the crowd. Someone has written a poem about Mick that found its way backstage: ‘Beautiful hermaphrodite butterfly/ Sex without sex/Hatched under grey English skies . . . Mick Jagger flew into himself one day! Miraculous dizzy flight . . .’

Jagger appears from the dressing room. He is wearing the same purple silk jumpsuit, only this time he has a blue denim jacket over it. Around his neck is a blue scarf, around his waist a red sash. He has rhinestone bracelets on either wrist. And white shoes. And the red sparkly eye paint. With all the make-up, he looks, oddly, like Nureyev.

Jagger starts limbering up, like a boxer before a fight. He moves restlessly from place to place, dropping a few words, but essentially into himself, all nervous energy. The others seem to respect that, leaving him alone. The rest of the band emerges now. Keith Richards, Mick Taylor, Bill Wyman, Charlie Watts, and the sidemen, sax players Bobby Keys, pianist Nicky Hopkins, trumpet-trombonist Jim Price.

It’s time. The band moves to a curtain that separates the back-stage runway from the crowd. Jagger is jumping now, a taut spring about to move. ‘Ladies and gentlemen, the world’s greatest . . .’

Just then, the make-up man who had been hovering around rushes up to Jagger and puts something in his hair. Gold dust sparkles!

Albuquerque

Barry Fey is nervous, all 287lbs of him. It’s 8 p.m. Stevie Wonder is halfway through his set, and no Stones. ‘That ain’t right,’ says Fey, anxiously surveying the parking lot outside the University of New Mexico sports arena. Fey, thirty-two, is a rock promoter who is handling the Stones from Albuquerque to Houston. He was an assistant manager of a Robert Hall clothing store until he heard about a group called Baby Huey and the Babysitters. 'I brought them into Rockford, Illinois, made $90, and that was the start of a great career.'

Fey will make many more times that amount promoting the Stones, but it can be a hassle. While worrying about their whereabouts, he has to be certain that three buckets of Kentucky fried chicken get delivered to their dressing room, keep an eye on the crowd, watch for counterfeit tickets (of which thousands have been printed).

'It's different, sure it's different. The business is much bigger than when The Beatles were Number 1. You have much more demand. In 1967 you had to get on the radio and say, "Please come." This year our security arrangements were so elaborate you had to have a ticket to get tickets. I was the Perle Meste of Houston during ticket sales. The concert is almost an anticlimax.'

The Stones arrive, finally, in an anonymous-type vehicle, and tumble quickly into the dressing room, a cornucopia of food, soda and liquor. Jagger, between sips of Jose Cuervo tequila, agrees to talk briefly.

What is your sense of American audiences so far this year?

'They don't seem to be quite as stoned as they were . . . I think they're more straight. Possibly younger.'

I'm talking about crowd psychology.

'Every crowd is different . . . they are different every year, every crowd, every town, every audience, every one, not the same as it was three years ago. These aren't the same kids that came three years ago.'

You once said your lyrics were crap. Do you still feel this way?

'Yeah, I'm not a very good lyric writer . . . If you can't get into 'em singing and then you can make it, even if it's just mediocre. The way you do it, you know, you can make it sound better than it really is . . .'

But it is time to go on. The crowd is hot, but so is the un-airconditioned arena. The acoustics are poor, and there was no way to mount the huge reflecting mirror, a Chip Monck innovation that bounces light on to the stage. It's going to be a bummer. You can't always get what you want.

Airborne to Denver

Jagger is in a post-concert funk. He moves restlessly up and down the aisle of the Electra turbopop charter the Stones rented from the McCulloch Oil people.

'It wasn't so good tonight,' he mumbles to anyone who'll hear it. 'It wasn't awful, but it wasn't so good.'

It's a rainy night and the pilot – who is used to ferrying middle-class retirees to Lake Havasu City, Arizona – announces there might be air turbulence. Jagger blanches.

He's very nervous about planes, Jo Bergman says. Jo is combination logistics-secretary-lady. She carries around a 500-page colour coded book which contains a day-by-day scenario of the Stones' movement, the movements of 20 others in the travelling party, and those of the eleven crew members. The show travels by air but the logistical support – two 40ft (12m) equipment trucks – are on the road all night long from city to city.

'These trucks better get there,' murmurs Pete Rudge, the 25-year-old tour manager who also conducts tours for The Who. He is worried about the bad weather.

Jagger is now bouncing down the aisle in an embroidered shirt and a pair of briefs. Fried chicken is passed around and there are cold cuts, beer, and lots of whisky.

I wanted to get the insiders' view of Jagger, the man and the myth.

Psychologists in London say he turns up amazingly often in people's dreams, claims Jo Bergman, who has known him for eight years. 'What is it, that Jagger can represent so many things to so many different people. I'm amazed he's so sane. And he is very sane, intelligent, creative, and when he wants to be, a brilliant businessman. So what are these people seeing? The eternal child-god. A reflection of themselves. Or it could it be a power thing, a shadow side. He's like Shaman.'

Steve Goekel, the make-up man: 'He seems to like to put forth an exotic and sensual appearance – the mystique sort of thing he's built up around himself. There's an emphasis on the showmanship of glitter. He likes to darken the eyes and have plastic glitter around the sides. He has a special love for gold sparkle dust in his hair.'

Lawrence Badgley, the hip-looking 29-year-old travelling doctor: 'He's always active, always shifting. He's an asthenic personality. The guy is always putting out this energy, muscular, vocal. And he takes care of himself pretty well. This reputation of devil-may-care – it's not the situation at all. Look at his body. It's well-nourished. He doesn't have any stretch marks, just very lithe. We give him vitamins every day. Uppers? No, he's just up.'

Peter Rudge, tour manager: 'He's the symbol of everything parents fear in rock 'n' roll. The devil's advocate. At the same time, Mick is very intelligent and very cultured. It's the arrogance of rock 'n' roll with the civility of a social figure. He's seen in the best restaurants, he's always on the list of ten best-dressed. He's a very professional person.

I asked Keith Richards, composer, lead guitarist and life-long chum, about the electricity the Stones generate on stage, about the mystique: 'It's energy, it's electricity, it's whisky and a few other things . . . they're just words. If there's a good band on a good night, they swing, things happen. Mystique is not going to be mystique, if you define. If it's definable, it's not mystique . . .'

5 December 1975

THE IMPORTANCE OF SPRINGSTEEN

Robin Denselow

It can hardly have escaped anyone's notice that Bruce Springsteen, the scruffy 26-year-old from New Jersey who has been hailed as 'the future of rock 'n' roll', has just completed a one-week tour in which he was to 'take Europe'. It was handled in such a bizarre fashion, and started so disappointingly, that it probably has escaped most people's notice that in the end he actually succeeded.

So after giving a lukewarm review to Springsteen's opening night at Hammersmith (to which all the usual press and trendy personalities had been invited), I'm pleased to report that once he got away from the ultra-cool audiences his show was completely transformed. The last two concerts – in Amsterdam and back at Hammersmith – actually matched up to all the torrent of publicity.

Springsteen is important because he has managed to combine the spontaneity and energy of early rock 'n' roll (which he has clearly studied hard and loves passionately), with a lyrical ability that's worthy of Dylan, writing in vivid poetic outbursts about his roots in the poorer quarters of the tacky coastal town of Asbury Park, creating a part-real, part-surreal, part-exhilarating, part-frightening world from the juke joints, the abandoned beach houses, and the back-street gangs. He's as compelling a singer and writer as Bob Marley, and as closely identified with his tough background.

Not that his music is simple as a result: there's a slow, pounding beat to most of his songs, but also a subtlety that's reminiscent of Van Morrison. He can mix quiet solo piano ballads with rock revival numbers – and the best of those, like 'Pretty Flamingo' and 'Won't You Wear My Ring' (by his hero, Presley), he mysteriously saved for the second Hammersmith show. That show also saw the best of his colourful New Jersey story-telling, his Chaplinesque sense of humour, and his ability to take an audience, within one song, from the hush of an alternative concert to a near-riot.

If he survives all the publicity, he deserves to become as influential and powerful a figure for the decade as Dylan was for the Sixties, or Presley for the Fifties. And like those two, he has surrounded himself with a manager who should become a legend for his ability to shout at people and a retinue who are there to interpret his muddy off-stage behaviour.

Springsteen's unpredictability, and the heaviness (to use the fashionable rock phrase) of his leather-jacketed manager, Mike Appel, had given that retinue the paranoid edge that so often characterises proximity to showbiz greatness. Press coverage of the tour was coordinated by the New York press officer for CBS (Springsteen's record company), an old friend of his, who for some reason begged me not to quote him by name. It was he who had the unenviable task of talking Springsteen into going to his own party, and later telling a group of Germans whom CBS had flown to London that they wouldn't be able to meet Springsteen after all because he wasn't likely to get up.

It was he who had to pacify the group of photographers with agreed press passes when Appel suddenly threw them out of Hammersmith – and the explanation, 'Well that's his prerogative', somehow didn't go down too well, especially when it was discovered that a freelance hustler in Holland, with no passes at all, had set up a battery of lights backstage, grabbed Springsteen, and got him to pose for dozens of pictures. Watching that incident, it was clear that he had no idea of the meaning or importance of any resulting publicity; he didn't know who the man was, but simply acted on instinct. His minions, set to throw the man out, faded away once Bruce had agreed. 'If the Boss says yes, that's cool,' they muttered.

Springsteen acts as if it's easy to go from a lifetime of poverty and obscurity, playing in seedy bars 'for a $30 a week maximum', to international stardom and the covers of both *Time* and *Newsweek*. But the pressures are clearly building up, and he's hit back by deciding things he won't do – like play in large halls (3,000 seats is the maximum, larger than that he'll walk out), eat anything else but hamburgers and 'junk food', give prearranged interviews, or have his time planned.

After the Amsterdam concert, for instance, he retired to his room and made rude noises and screamed 'No' to every phone caller, without bothering to find out who they were. Even Appel gave up trying to get through. It was easy to sympathise with that. It's obviously difficult to act normally, even when your road crew have searched out the most American hotel in town, when your manager is down at the bar shouting about you. His act 'transcends rock and transcends theatre – it's an experience', Appel was gesticulating, 'and he doesn't feel the pain or the exhaustion until after he's left the stage'. He went on modestly to describe his own role by saying 'art is universal, and we're just its purveyors.'

Appel does Springsteen's publicity for him, because, as he admitted in an unguarded moment, 'Bruce talks slow and drawls. If we put him on a talk-show they'd probably think he was dumb. And we can't have them thinking that about a new superstar.' Bruce obviously isn't dumb, as he showed by his wit on and off stage (quite apart from his meticulously worked lyrics), but in conversation he doesn't use one word if three sentences will do.

He has a touching naivety, coupled with flashes of insight. Asked whether he thought Dutch kids could understand the subtleties of his lyrics about growing up in New Jersey, he replied, 'Well . . . (long pause) . . . I assumed that everyone knows about New Jersey. Well it's clear what I'm on about, isn't it? When I talked about it, they understood, didn't they?' But when asked about his substandard first concert in London, he made the point that the fault can never be with the audience, but must always be with the artist.

That first concert – which greatly upset him – showed the dangers of the overkill publicity. Even Appel now admits that it wasn't up to standard, though he – to start with – did blame the audience. 'I died. I fell asleep after three numbers. I thought that England was the home of rock and kids had gone wild when Jerry Lee Lewis played here. But this time no one moved.' The explanation, as finally given by both Appel and the unmentionable press officer, is that Springsteen was put off by all the publicity provided by CBS – particularly a sign outside the theatre saying 'at last' London was ready for him. 'I didn't say anything to him when I saw that,' says Appel, 'I thought that maybe he didn't mind it. He didn't say anything either – but then we don't communicate that much. But he did mind.'

So Appel told CBS to take the signs down, and while they were about it to stop selling albums in the foyer (a reasonable move by CBS, as Springsteen has so far sold very few here). 'I just said pull them down 'cos that's what Bruce wants,' shouted Appel. 'I told them they needed me more than I needed them, and if they told me to go to hell we'd all push off home over the Atlantic.' An interesting line, considering that CBS were paying for the cost of the tour (the four concerts made £8,000, and the expenses would be around £35,000, according to Appel's lawyer). But CBS obliged. The signs came down, and by the second Hammersmith concert all the offending posters had the 'at last' slogan scratched out.

Appel didn't have quite that success with everyone he crossed. 'European radio is government radio – it stops people hearing what they want,' maybe because they didn't play enough Springsteen songs.

Whether Springsteen is a star because of the backstage rows or despite them is debatable, but Appel is living up to his ambition to be 'like Albert Grossman' (Dylan's famous former manager), though the retinue and the band already compare him to Presley's Colonel Parker. Everyone was happy when they left London – Bruce, because he'd finally succeeded, with one of his best concerts ever (according to his band) and the band because England had proved itself to be the cultural haven they'd been promised – not just because of the reaction on Monday, but because 'we found some amazing deleted Fifties' albums in Oxford Street.' As for CBS here, one (different) unmentionable official was 'just pleased to see them go'. They'll be back next year.

22 April 1995

ROCK AND A HARD PLACE

Jim Shelley

One-two, one-two. One. Two. One-two. Cleveland, Ohio. The Mid-West. The heartland of mid-America, where so many English bands touted as The Next Big Thing have fallen on their pretty, over-rated faces.

Oasis's vocalist, Liam Gallagher, is standing in the centre of a dusty wooden stage, like so many Great British Hopefuls before him, singing his heart out to an empty dancehall. 'I live my life for the stars that shine/People say it's just a waste of time . . . Tonight, I'm a rock 'n' roll star.' In the gloom of the small hall – the sort of venue Oasis haven't played back home for ages – the song, 'Rock 'n' Roll Star', couldn't be more apposite. When the band first emerged in Manchester, the song stood out as a hedonistic, escapist anthem for a disaffected, dreaming youth living in towns like Burnage, where Liam and his brother Noel (the band's guitarist and songwriter) grew up.

Then, as Oasis took the British music scene by storm, and even their most outlandish rock 'n' roll fantasies became reality, the song began to take on a different significance – one of the celebratory self-fulfilling prophecy. Here in Cleveland, though, with the band's American campaign still in its early stages, the song once again seems to be about bedroom-bound boredom, defiant dreaming.

The song ends to the sound of slow, sarcastic clapping and isolated jeering. Luckily though, we are not at the gig, but the soundcheck – the sarcasm comes from the band's soundman. Cleveland, like most of the venues on the tour, sold out long ago. Radio stations across the country are playing Oasis on 'heavy rotation' and their debut album, *Definitely Maybe*, has moved steadily up the US chart into the top 50. The *David Letterman Show* awaits. America beckons and, rather than New York or LA, it's places like Cleveland that will determine just how big Oasis can become. The soundcheck drags on.

Outside in the sunshine, a group of six or seven teenage fans wearing REM T-shirts and Nirvana badges wait for autographs. One of them, a gawky 15-year-old with braces on her teeth, is waiting to give Tony McCarroll, the band's drummer, a box of biscuits.

'Hi!?' she beams at Noel Gallagher as he walks out to the band's silver tour bus.

'Not yet,' he quips with a smirk. 'But I soon will be.' To the band's evident dismay, Cleveland, has, thus far, proved to be a drug-free zone in the debauched and drug-happy world that is Life on the Road – Oasis-style.

As Noel and I have yet to be introduced, when he reappears, I decide to break the ice by asking him if he knows where Tony is. 'I couldn't give a fuck,' he says simply, and keeps walking.

Then he sees the box.

'Hey, is that for me?' he demands, expectantly. 'Is that my cocaine?' 'No,' the girl smiles coyly. 'They're homemade chocolate chip cookies.' Noel looks at her for a moment, suspicious that this is some sort of wind-up.

'Have they got cocaine in them?' he asks, hopeful to the end. He will have to keep looking.

Later, back in the dressing-room, the band's present predicament sets Oasis off on a bout of dewy-eyed memories of The Good Old Days, The Wild Times, The Halcyon Days, before success gave them everything they had ever dreamed of, and took all the fun out of things.

With a nostalgia and fondness reminiscent of the Stones remembering the Sixties, guitarist Paul 'Bonehead' Arthurs, excitedly recalls the early days when, with five band members, two roadies and all the equipment wedged into one Transit van driven by himself, they moved from gig to gig 'like a bunch of fuckin' Vikings, invading England for the first time'.

The memories come flooding back: the fleapits they played and the TV sets they tipped out of hotel windows, the times they drove out of petrol stations without paying or did a runner from the local B&B . . . all because they'd spent the money for the whole tour weeks ago on drugs and drink.

'Ahh,' one of them sighs, contentedly, 'happy days.' 'Yeah,' someone agrees, 'great memories.'

Only a killjoy would point out that it was only a few months ago. In fact, it's just over a year to the day since Oasis put out their first single. It's been a year. Their year. Ask Oasis to put into words what the last year has been like and they'll shake their heads and, without hesitation, say 'mad'. 'It's just been absolutely mad.'

Given that Noel Gallagher writes all the music and lyrics and makes most of the major decisions concerning the band on his own, or with manager Marcus Russell, it's paradoxical that Oasis started life without him.

In August 1991, Noel was on tour in America, working as a guitar roadie with the Manchester mediocrities the Inspiral Carpets, when his mother told him his brother Liam was singing vocals with a group he'd formed with three mates: Paul 'Bonehead' Arthurs (rhythm guitar), Tony McCarroll (drums and bass) and bass player Paul 'Guigsy' McGuigan.

Noel, who taught himself guitar when he was 13 and has been writing songs ever since, saw them play and, recognising his brother's obvious star potential, offered to take over and do all the songs – but only if he had total control and 'they did it right'. 'If you're not in it to be bigger than the Beatles,' he would say, 'it's just a hobby.'

From this point on, the story of Oasis's success would become the stuff of legend, ridiculous schoolboy stuff. After months of rehearsals in Manchester, they heard that Alan McGee, whose label, Creation, gave the world Primal Scream and the Jesus and Mary Chain – was going to be at a gig in Edinburgh. They drove up and demanded a support slot. When they were refused, they threatened to burn the place down. By the end of that night, they had a deal with Creation and McGee was driving back to London phoning people at the label every 15 minutes telling them he'd done it: he had signed the future of rock 'n' roll.

On 11 April 1994, Oasis released their debut single, 'Supersonic' ('I'm feelin' supersonic/Gimme gin and tonic'), followed by a trio of classic singles – 'Shakermaker', 'Live Forever' and 'Cigarettes & Alcohol'.

From the beginning, Oasis's arrogant confidence set them apart. With a loud wall of raucous guitars, a string of smooth Beatles-like melodies, and a singer who sung in a thick Northern drawl that managed to recall both John Lennon and the Sex Pistols' John Lydon, Oasis had the temerity to sound as if they actually knew they were the first great English group of the Nineties.

Draw a line through the pivotal influences in English rock music from the Beatles – the Small Faces, the Who, the Kinks, T Rex, through to the Sex Pistols, the Jam, the Smiths, Happy Mondays and the Stone Roses – and they would all lead to Oasis.

The music press, predictably, went bananas, not only over the music but also the band's headline-hungry extra-curricular activities, which included stealing a load of golf-carts from Gleneagles, Noel's predilection for sprinkling cocaine on his cornflakes and press interviews during which the two Gallagher brothers would invariably lay into one another, both verbally and physically. 'Guigsy used to be completely and utterly stoned 24 hours a day,' Noel recalls. 'I don't think he spoke to me for four months. Tony was just totally befuddled by it all and me and Our Kid were like fuckin' Punch and Judy.'

Helped by a live reputation that put the likes of Blur and Suede in the shade, *Definitely Maybe* sold 100,000 copies in four days, and by the end of the year had sold more then 700,000. A Christmas No 2, the Beatles-y 'Whatever', completed a triumphant nine months. 'I'm quite proud of the fact that everything I ever said about the band was justified and came true,' reflects Noel later, in rather more approachable humour. 'Other than that, it's just been mind-blowing, and a total and utter fuckin' laugh.' This Monday sees the release of yet another all-new four-track EP, 'Some Might Say', a gloriously catchy, full-blooded racket as mindless and brilliant as the Pistols or Stooges in their heyday, with a flip side, 'Acquiesce', that reminds you the best punk rock was built on great pop songs.

Oasis obviously have no intention of relenting and Gallagher's talent is beginning to look almost insolently easy. 'Acquiesce', he says, was knocked off in the Severn tunnel when his train got stuck for a couple of hours.

Even more appropriately, 'Some Might Say' was also written 'out of boredom' when the rest of the band failed to show up in the studio because they were in the process of being thrown out of the notorious rock 'n' roll London hotel the Columbia, for throwing a table through the windscreen of the manager's Mercedes. The No 1 spot is taken as read.

Touring the US, though, is another story, as endless British bands regarded by the Americans as over-hyped could tell you (not least Suede and Blur, who both died a death there). Even English pop phenomena like the Smiths, the Jam or, more relevantly, the Stone Roses and Happy Mondays have all struggled there.

Trying to crack America is something of a tightrope; it could be the making or breaking of them. It can take months and months of constant touring and promotion. And the boredom and pressures (pleasures) of being on the road have driven many a band to self-destruct. Bands can return home to find the fan base that made them has, in their absence, moved on. Setting out to capitalise on the first wave of success, a band like Oasis can find that lack of time to recharge the creative batteries might ensure there is never any second wave.

In recent years, only the visually-lavish, stadium-friendly home-grown acts such as Depeche Mode or U2 have sustained their success there. If nothing else though, their gig in Cleveland demonstrates why Oasis could be destined to join them.

Whereas most American guitar bands or indie bands play up their nihilistic image or the social messages of their songs, Oasis are a good-time band. (Noel has summed up their songs as being 'about shagging, taking drugs and being in a band'.) At the same time, their lyrics strike a perfect balance between rebellious teenage disdain and romantic adolescent escapism: 'I dream of you and all the things you say', 'Let me be the one that shines with you', 'I think you're the same as me/We see thing they'll never see/ You and I are gonna live forever.' Better yet for the States, on top of a formidably meaty rhythm section, Noel's guitar solos offer a veritable nirvana for the massed ranks of America's air guitar solo exponents, with 'Live Forever', in particular, a song that is destined to be the 'Freebird' of its generation.

The Cleveland front row consists of an impressive array of teenage devotees: baby *Baywatch* blondes screaming at Liam, pogo-ing punk wannabes and all-American college kids. Oasis's only handicap States-wise is the total lack of stage show. Oasis live equals optimum cool, maximum noise, minimum effort and not pandering to anyone. As always, they blaze through the set standing virtually motionless, only occasionally breaking out into toe-tapping. Stage banter consist of cursory 'ta very much' and they make no bones about showing their irritation with the American ritual of stage-diving, as a more or less constant bombardment of kids clamber or cartwheel over the audience's heads to the front of the stage. 'Any of you touch me,' Liam warns them, 'an' you'll get a smack, knowworrimean?' To the audience's bewilderment, despite the applause, Oasis do not do encores. The show ends with the soaring groove that Oasis have honed out of 'I Am the Walrus', a finale impeded only by a barrage of ice-cubes, peanuts and bananas being thrown at the drummer, Tony. These come, not from the crowd, who go home happy anyway, but from the side of the stage, where Liam is unloading the contents of the buffet from the dressing room.

After the gig, amid the usual throng of would-be groupies, grunge fans and fanzine geeks, are a number of people whose job descriptions appear to be 'something in the music business'.

Radio playlist promoters, local record store managers and regional marketing men connected to the band's record label are here for that essential part of Playing the Game known as Meet-and-Greets. The suits are here to tell the band how much they 'love you boys', and hang out with them trying to be cool – ignoring the fact they've all got Santana moustaches and are asking the boys in Oasis if they get much time on tour to play golf or if they've ever seen a better stage show than the last Floyd tour.

Most of the band behave amiably enough (as long as the drinks keep coming) but Noel is not having any of it. He resolved to stop doing Meet-and-Greets after the record company put on a dinner for the band and the MD made a speech thanking Liam and Noel for coming by calling them 'Leland and Norton'.

'I don't give a fuck about meeting some guy from Tower

Records, the Territory of Bogarse, Ohio, who says he'll display our record better if we meet his wife and talk to him,' he complains. 'They all say, "I really want you guys to know what a great job I'm doing for your band." I just say, "You're PAID to do a great job, you fucking idiot." Bands come over here and, because the band before did meet-and-greets, it's expected they'll do them too. Well, someone will say to the next lot of bands, "Oasis never did them, so you don't have to".' By now, the alcohol is flowing freely and members of Oasis are walking up to the meet-and-greet brigade almost at random, and asking them, 'So have yer got any drugs, or what?' Noel is now really getting into his stride.

'Here's a fuckin' story, right? And you can quote me on this cos I love fuckin' stickin' it to the American record company . . .' he says, embarking on a fantastically libellous story about one of the bigwigs from Epic Records.

He has, at least, procured some ecstasy. 'Yeah, I got it from this girl who says she gets it prescribed cos she gets depressed. So I said, "That's a shame . . . Can I have six? I'm a bit depressed myself".' As the evening ends, one of the suits makes the mistake of schmoozing Noel and saying that after tomorrow's show, maybe he could come backstage so Noel could meet his wife. Noel looks at him for a moment then says, 'What the fuck do I wanna meet yer wife for?' and walks off to get another drink.

The following day, Oasis are down in the lobby by 11 a.m., in good time to sort out breakfast (a McDonald's and some Benson & Hedges washed down with a Jack Daniel's) before piling on to the tour bus to drive to Detroit. The main point of the exercise seems to be to get the food for the day out of the way nice and early.

On the Oasis tour bus, pride of place is taken by a special cactus, given to the band by U2's Adam Clayton, which appears to have produced a beautifully exotic orange flower, but which on closer inspection turns out to be a Cheesy Wotsit.

We check into our hotel. The five members of Oasis race each other down the four-star stairs, pile into the hotel's revolving door (all in the same compartment), and head off to the venue, spread out across the road like a slightly scruffier bunch of Reservoir

Dogs, ready to ruck and have a laugh, banging on shop windows, pushing people's doorbells, dodging the homeboys driving by, and threatening to pull each other's sideburns off. After years of dosing around in Manchester on the dole or doing a string of dead-end jobs, they are going to enjoy themselves. Being on the road, as Noel puts it, 'is a total laugh; it's insanity'.

By Noel's estimation, for three or four months in the middle of last year, Oasis were 'totally and utterly out of control'. They were thrown out of Sweden for causing £30,000 of damage to their hotel, thrown off a ferry to Amsterdam for starting a drunken punch-up, and banned from four chains of hotels in the UK.

'Me and Bonehead would just walk into a hotel room and empty it out the window,' Noel laughs, almost in disbelief. 'I would be doing interviews in my room or in the bar and halfway through, one of the band would come in for a fag or something. I didn't suss out that they were seeing where I was sitting. So I'd be playing it all down, saying, "It's all been blown out of proportion. It's all about the music," and the journalist would be thinking, "I'm sure I've just seen a TV set going flying past that window." ' As for the band's drug intake, Noel says he's had to tell them to cool it all down now because they don't know when to stop. 'Or rather, they do – when they run out.' Both Liam and Noel have stopped smoking dope, which Noel says he smoked 'since I was 14 non-fuckin' stop. I hope they never legalise it neither – it just mongs people out.'

Cocaine, though, is, as far as Oasis are concerned, totally recreational. As he says in 'Cigarettes & Alcohol': 'You could wait for a lifetime/To spend your days in the sunshine/Might as well do the white line.' The last time he was in Detroit, Noel remembers (rather vaguely), he ended up passing out with chest pains and spent the night in hospital. 'The doctor said, "It's a good job you're 27, cos if you were 47, you'd be dead." ' This time, he reasons, before he came out to the States, he saw the band's Harley Street doctor.

'Fuckin' Jason Donovan was in the waiting room!' he laughs, decidedly embarrassed. 'Now, he needs to see a doctor. Smoking draw was my only problem cos I've got low blood pressure so I used to faint every time I 'ad a spliff. The doctor said, "Basically, you're alright with anything that gets you going, cos you need that!"' He laughs. 'I love my doctor, man.'

Ask Liam Gallagher how he thinks he's changed in the last year and he looks away into the distance, doe-eyed and rather glum-looking and says, 'I'm just gettin' more an' more into me own little world, which is right. Feel at one in me own little world and that's what I always wanted.' Ask Noel how his kid brother has changed in the last year and he struggles to explain before saying, 'He's just got more stupid. When he was at school, he was quite normal. Now he's definitely mad. He's mental. He's not mad like some people in bands are mad. That fucker's mad. Mad. He's madder than mad . . . He's just mad.' Later when we're talking about the pressures of stardom, I ask Noel what he thinks it's doing to Liam. Without hesitation, he says, 'It's just making him madder.'

Having spent most of the last 18 months touring, life on the road is what now passes for normal life to Liam Gallagher. 'I had a month off in January,' he remembers in disbelief, 'and it done me head in.' Who knows what's going on in Liam's head? He's a 22-year-old dreamer, still trying to work himself out. He contradicts himself all the time depending on his mood, which is volatile, impulsive, extreme. He is either boisterously loud or worryingly sullen, either loves his brother to death or hates his guts; looks like a young George Best; supports Man City.

As Noel writes all the songs and makes all the decisions, he admits it's 'all a bit Frankenstein's Monster, isn't it? But to be honest, I couldn't give a fuck what happens to him. I only keep the band goin' cos if I didn't, me mam would kill me.' Even the way Liam walks – a massive, rolling swagger, palms dropped at his sides, opened out, feet splayed almost sideways, looks as if he is ready for a ruck at any moment. Totally. If nothing is happening, it probably will soon with Liam around.

The previous night, in Cleveland, the band, the road crew and assorted hangers-on made it back to the hotel just in time for last orders. 'In that case,' Liam shouted to the barman, 'I'll 'ave three double Jack Daniel's and Cokes and three beers, mate.' An hour or so later, Liam announced he was leaving the band. He was going to get some lessons, see if he can 'get as good as Our Kid', and do his own thing. All because Noel had had the temerity to go to bed early.

Next day in Detroit, and Liam is not even interested in writing anything himself. 'It wouldn't be as good as Our Kid's so why bother? I'm just into being a singer. Totally. I don't want to be a fuckin' lyricist or a fuckin' frontman, working the crowd and all that bollocks. Elvis never wrote a song in his life, did he? I don't reckon Elvis was the King though,' he says sweetly, sulking slightly. 'I reckon John Lennon was. "Imagine" is one of the best songs ever. Totally. One of the scariest songs ever. It's just . . . Imagine, innit? Imagine, like, nish, or whatever.' In New York, another of Liam's heroes, John McEnroe, came backstage to meet him. 'Mad bastard!' Liam beams, 'a fuckin' proper mad-'ead. Had a spliff and that. He's got a band, right? So he was singing us these songs: "You cannot be-ser-i-ous/Double faults hurt-my-head." Mad. Totally fuckin' mad.' Just before the soundcheck, I see him sitting on the steps of the venue, in his huge baggy trousers and striped Burberry shirt, singing to himself. He is singing: 'Merrily, merrily, merrily, merrily/Life is but a dream.'

Just before the gig in Detroit, Bonehead and Guigsy (who more and more resembles a kind of bedraggled Dudley Moore) attend a press conference for local college radio stations, answering a series of questions like, 'How do feel about the quote that Oasis is just Suede spelt backwards?' Luckily, Bonehead is in good humour, and he just stares at them manically and says, 'Yeah, but it's not is it? That's Edeus.' Asked whether they get bored on tour, Bonehead's answer is so passionate, it borders on outright aggression, as he shouts, 'You just can't, though, can ya? Don't ya see? You just CAN'T!' Someone asks if many of their dreams have come true, and the lads talk excitedly about getting to No 1 and so on before, to the journalists' total bemusement, they describe the time they went out on to the pitch at Man City for a presentation and then embark on a detailed discussion of what's wrong with City's back four.

The gig in Detroit is excellent and euphoric, the momentum

interrupted only once when, halfway through, Noel puts down his guitar and walks off. 'S'alright,' Liam tells the crowd, 'Our Kid's just gone for a piss.' The band sit down on stage and wait.

As this might suggest, Noel is less than obsessed about cracking America at present. 'If someone said, you can go home now, I'd go,' he says, sitting behind the desk in his hotel room. 'I don't think it's possible for a British band to be big in America anymore. We will be to a certain extent, yeah, but if we get to a certain level, the record company are gonna want us to fuckin' camp out 'ere, an' if it comes down to England and America, I'd rather just stay big in England.' Even Noel is beginning to wonder if Oasis can last five albums. 'I wouldn't say I envy bands who haven't had the success we have but . . . I liked it better when we had to go and prove ourselves. I've only got to fuckin' fart and it gets in the top 10 now. I might start a label, start a band that I write songs for but I'm not in. Write some songs that Oasis couldn't do – you know, for people like Rod Stewart. Also,' he grins, 'I think the time is right for the first post-Seventies supergroup: me, Remi from the Stone Roses, Paul Weller on vocals, Johnny Marr [former Smiths guitarist] on lead guitar . . .'

In the last year, Oasis have conquered all the logical steps before them and have arrived at the stage where it's all up to them. Or Noel, and manager Marcus Russell. 'We don't even have a contract,' he smiles. 'Just a handshake.' I ask him what would happen if Russell ripped them off. 'Well I'd sue him, wouldn't I?' he says, simply. Yeah, but you haven't got a contract, I point out. He thinks about it for a second, then hits upon the answer. 'Then I'd burn his house down,' he beams. 'And he knows I would.' Some things, it seems, never change.

For now, at least, the shows (and the tours and the partying) must go on. Upstairs after the Detroit show, in what passes for the hospitality room, rumours are rife of a special delivery by a dodgy-looking Mexican known as 'Mario from the Barrio'. Mario's arrival has in fact become as eagerly awaited as that of Santa Claus and the Man from Del Monte put together. The band, therefore, are in excitable mood, especially when a group of inebriated college kids – seemingly in the belief that it's a word the English find hilariously anachronistic – make the potentially fatal mistake of chanting the word 'wanker' at Bonehead.

The atmosphere is warming up nicely, and, over in one corner of the room, another bunch of louts are pushing each other around, obviously looking for a fight. One of them picks up a chair, feigns throwing it, feigns throwing it again and then launches it across the room at someone's head. 'My God,' cries one of the suits from the record company, in dismay, 'who are *those* guys?' They are, of course, Oasis.

The party over, the last few fans, loaded with the band's hospitality, finally drift away, many of them clutching signed albums as prizes.

One the cover of *Definitely Maybe*, you can see Liam lying on the floor of Bonehead's flat, staring dreamily up at a big blue globe. On the inside cover, his brother, Noel, stands centre-stage, insolently holding the globe in his outstretched palm – the world in his hands. Perfect.

Outside the venue, a couple of girls are sitting in a grey Cherokee Jeep with a bootleg of the night's gig blaring out of the stereo. From the badly recorded cacophony of guitars and electric noise, Liam's voice, emerging with increasing clarity and conviction, drifts into the night and, as the Jeep speeds away, is left hanging there. The drawl is unmistakable, as is the sentiment. 'It's just rock 'n' roll,' he sings at the end of 'Rock 'n' Roll Star'. 'It's just rock 'n' rollll/It's just rock 'n' rolllll/It's just rock 'n' rollllllll . . .'

13 July 1996

NICE DREAM?

Jim Shelley

Waking up from a bad dream is nothing new for Thom Yorke but, hours later, this morning's dream is still lingering, still bothering him. Radiohead's notoriously maudlin frontman describes it to me with all the twitchy trepidation of someone obviously reluctant to seem as if he's taking such a thing too seriously, but who can't help talking about it.

'In the dream, everybody I'd ever met in my whole life came to a party at my house and I had to be nice to everyone,' he says. 'Some people I'd been really horrible to turned up and I had to be nice to them, too. Every person I know was there, watching.' You must have had a very big house, I point out, by way of consolation. 'Yeah, I did,' he admits. 'I'm rich – in the dream, I mean. I'm rich.' As dreams go, it's not exactly difficult to interpret. Fear of fame and being submerged by it; fear of the falseness that invariably follows it; fear of changing, becoming alienated, because of it.

He knows where the dream came from – from a party the previous night following Radiohead's triumphant showcase gig in New York. Yorke stood at the back in the corner clutching a carrier bag, looking like some sort of gamin, scruffy urchin bunking off school, a gatecrasher at his own party, drinking faster and faster as the groupies and stargazers moved in. Yorke shudders.

'The thing about what happened in the dream was that I liked it. Even though it was awful, I liked it 'cause everyone was being nice to me.' This last revelation, anxiously blurted out almost despite himself, hangs in the air between us, leaving us both feeling rather despondent. We sit there for a minute in silence, pondering his hypocrisy, struggling to come up with a more positive interpretation of the dream. His blatant insecurity is not the problem. It's actually quite endearing. What's more unsettling is the possibility that this was not a dream at all. What if it's The Future? Certainly, it's not difficult to foresee Yorke's private nightmare turning into reality.

In retrospect, missing out on last year's Britpop bandwagon turned out to be the best thing that ever happened to Radiohead. Passed over by the press, as the likes of Elastica, the Bluetones and Pulp cashed in their chips to claim their 15 minutes, Radiohead became the ugly ducklings of Britpop, the Band that Missed the Boat. Gradually, though, helped by a series of stunning videos for singles like 'High and Dry' and 'Street Spirit', the months went by, the momentum grew and Radiohead's album *The Bends*, released last year, is now widely regarded as the most accomplished and enduring of the lot.

These days it's almost impossible to see the name Radiohead without the words 'the next REM', 'Britain's answer to Nirvana' or 'the U2 it's okay to like' written alongside it. Their first release since *The Bends*, the single 'Lucky', was so obviously the standout track on the Bosnia *Help* compilation that *Melody Maker* wrote, 'Radiohead are no longer capable of anything other than brilliance.' America obviously agrees, responding to Yorke's almost adolescent sense of social anxiety and unease, his dark sentimentality, embracing the band as a kind of 'Oasis with intellect'. Sometimes it seems the only choice ahead of Yorke is whether he should take on the band's new-found stadium status with his integrity intact – like Michael Stipe – or with the shameless complacency of a band like Simple Minds – and turn into Jim Kerr.

Sleepy-eyed and pale, quizzical as a cartoon with his tatty Woody Woodpecker haircut and his thin bones lost inside crumpled clothes, Thom Yorke just doesn't look cut out for a superstar's job. He's 27, five-foot-five, clean and English and indulgent, his punched-in face scrunched up into a permanent scowl.

Born with one eye closed and paralysed, Yorke grew up used to being the victim. He had five major operations before the age of six, and spent a year wearing an eye-patch and being laughed at by the other kids, who called him Salamander. Each time his family moved, he encountered a new ordeal and had to work through the same trauma. Maybe he's been getting up on stage all this time simply to shove his defects, his disability, in the audience's faces, challenging people to reject him on an even bigger scale. Except now they're worshipping him. No wonder he finds it confusing.

For years, the fuel to Radiohead's fire – their whole raison d'être – has been their sense of inadequacy and anxiety, that they would never amount to anything. They have virtually fetishised the threat of failure, cultivating their sense of imminent collapse into a permanent state. Formed in Oxford, around the time of 1991's Summer of Love, and bonded by a love of bands like Magazine and Joy Division, Radiohead were instantly unfashionable, immediately out of step. Out of time. Yorke squirms.

'It was a period of acute embarrassment. I was pretty into it at college, but there wasn't enough emotion to it. I kept trying to go to raves.' Their first EP in May 1992, 'Drill' (first chorus: 'I'm better off dead'), was refreshingly dark and insistent, invigorating enough immediately to win them a fiercely loyal following. But disaster struck when their second, 'Creep' (with the chorus 'I wish I was special/So fucking special/But I'm a creep'), became a one-song phenomenon, an American anthem of alienation and self-loathing, propelling their first album, *Pablo Honey*, into the American top 40. In a self-fulfilling prophecy, Yorke became 'the Creep guy'.

Far from providing some sort of palliative for their neuroses, Radiohead turned success into something that only made matters worse. Encouraged by their American record company to capitalise, they toured the States for months, realising too late that they were still playing material that was more than two years old – just another band that turns into the thing they hate.

'We sucked Satan's cock,' Yorke spits, with typical scorn. 'It took a year and a half to get back to the people we were . . . to cope with it emotionally.' By then, says guitarist Jonny Greenwood, they were 'operating in a kind of stasis. Thom was trying to shut off from everything. The rest of us just weren't communicating.' Sick of touring, by the time they went into the studio, they had become phobic about recording anything. Their confidence was shot.

'We were playing like paranoid little mice in cages,' says Greenwood. 'We were scared of our instruments, scared of every note not being right.' Perhaps the secret of their success is that they learnt to turn their paranoia into a virtue. Contrary to popular wisdom, it's often a band's second album that proves to be their most natural and direct expression, where they shake off their influences (in Yorke's case, early Elvis Costello) and get the confidence to be themselves.

After resting up and scrapping their early demos ('Guns N' Roses pomp rock'), they returned to record *The Bends* in majestic form. The title perfectly summed up the band's state of flux and Yorke's personal alienation that bordered on repulsion, brought on by the rigours and unreality of touring: 'Baby's got the bends/ We don't have any real friends.' The sense of malaise and self-disgust becomes more and more palpable the more you listen to *The Bends*. Greenwood has said it shocked him, 'how much it's about illness, doctors . . . it's a real medical album'. But despite its success, they still perceive themselves as having never belonged, never been made welcome – by the press or the industry. Radio play has always been denied them (too gloomy). Radio 1 refused even to put 'Lucky' on its playlist, even though it was for Bosnia.

The music press, too, has always treated Radiohead with suspicion. For a start, they can play their instruments (which is always a worry) with suspiciously mature, muso sensibilities. They have far too many ideas, layering their records with strangeness and innovation, obviously aiming for something bordering on beauty. Too MOR and too middle class, five students who first met at Abingdon boarding school, Radiohead are the sort of band who spend their time on the tour bus playing bridge. When I'm introduced to bass player Colin Greenwood (Jonny's brother), he's lending someone a book, the socio-economic history *The Collapse of Power*. Radiohead Do Not Party is practically a by-law among music journalists. When support act David Gray trashed their dressing room, the story goes, Radiohead tidied it up.

The single 'Lucky' encapsulates the sceptics' worst fears: a hauntingly uneasy ballad about Yorke's preoccupation with mortality, it includes a Pink Floyd-sized guitar solo, offering Americans unbridled air guitar and lighter-waving opportunities. The common perception was that Radiohead, like Bush or the Cranberries before them, were heading for the American mainstream, a sort of alternative version of Tears for Fears, set to follow in the footsteps of bands like James and Simple Minds and sell out as soon as possible. Watching them soundcheck in New York, I can't say you'd notice.

True, the unnaturally affable Colin Greenwood and the drummer Phil Selway fulfil the Wyman and Watts roles with foot-tapping aplomb. The others, though, can make for unorthodox, even uncomfortable viewing. Stage left, the tall, bug-eyed figure of guitarist Ed O'Brien charges around performing a series of the most overly-energetic leaps and glory poses since the Clash or the Who in their heyday. Stage right (wearing what can only be described as a pair of mid-Seventies-style 'cans'), Radiohead's second guitarist, the impossibly beautiful, charmingly bashful Jonny Greenwood appears to spend most of his time plucking agitatedly at the wrong end of his guitar. He crouches on the floor, coaxing the sort of noises more closely associated with Van Der Graaf Generator – the sort of thing that has elder critics reaching for the word 'extemporisation'.

In the middle, Yorke strums away furiously on his guitar, like an unnaturally absorbed, slightly deranged busker, blessed with the voice of an anxious angel. 'They love me like I was a brother/ They protect me/Listen to me/They dug me my very own garden/ Gave me sunshine/Made me happy,' he sings, before tearing into the chaotic chorus, 'Nice dream/nice dreeeeam'.

The others shuffle off, leaving Yorke's tiny frame performing a pretty-sounding acoustic number he's working on, a kind of emotional-protest music. With his eyes closed tight, his head hanging to one side, convulsing with spastic energy, he stands there singing his heart out, a bitter, twisted mannequin. The punchline, sung in beautiful soprano, rings round the empty hall: 'I will see you in the next life.' And then he's gone. It's like watching a nervous breakdown gone solo.

Earlier, I had been reading an interview where he summed up *The Bends* as 'cynical and nervous and not making sense. You get the feeling at the end of it that there's something wrong, but you can't work out what it is.' Sitting watching him here, it's obvious that the something wrong with it is . . . him.

His baggy maroon cords falling over his shoes, and wearing a red Gameboy T-shirt and thin grey jumper, Yorke wanders around the empty auditorium with the sort of jaunty cockiness that reminds me of a Belfast schoolboy throwing stones at the soldiers. He is, predictably, a mass of contradictions: a strange blend of snide cynicism, bitter self-pity and earnest decency. There is still something studenty about him – his juvenile sense of humour, his naff sense of outsiderness, his naively radical idealism.

He wants to change the charts, change the government, change the *NME*, and sits at home grumbling, shouting at the telly. He thinks the media should be 'creative and informing, empowering', but says it's just a distraction instead, making a spectator sport out of fame. 'The press could destroy us,' he mutters darkly. 'They have a million weapons.' He thinks things like following football or liking the Clash are 'not feminine enough' for him.

Most of all, he worries. He worries about swearing too much, about being too nice or too nasty, about not writing back to the fan mail he carries about in a duffle bag ('not exactly fountains of joy'), about what the next album's going to sound like, whether all his darkest secret fears are just being repackaged into music for people to play on their car stereos as they travel to work. He worries about whether his life is becoming too glamorous and removed or too banal, too corporate. He sits there hugging his knees and scowling into space, worrying whether he's turning into Jim Kerr.

I can't help but point out that there was a time when Kerr used to spend his interviews talking about existentialism and the Speed of Life, the alienation and anxiety of travel and global communication, just like Yorke does now. And look what a travesty he turned into. He worries about how to behave with all the screaming girls and groupies. 'I tend to run away if it's anything beyond them saying they like the music. We were at a single-sex school, so, you know . . . Anyway, I have someone that I love,' he blushes. 'So it's . . . nice.' He worries about the words to new songs, works on them dutifully, and is obviously happy that they matter. But he squirms at the idea of them being treated like poetry, that his lyrics are a distillation of pure misery.

America, in particular, fails to see the irony, the way he's prepared to send himself up. The *New York Times* started its review: 'The world is caving in on Thom Yorke. He has no real friends. He loses faith in everything every day and he thinks he'd be better off dead.' At the same time, he can't help worrying about the idea that some 12-year-old girl in Seattle is sitting in her room at this minute, listening to 'Street Spirit', trying to decide which way to kill herself.

In New York, where the 'culture of despair' is something akin to a teen craze, you can see the kids before the gig: 12, 13 years old, drinking beer, smoking dope and popping Prozac, wearing their Nine Inch Nails T-shirts and clutching their Dennis Cooper novels. During the gig, just before 'High and Dry', someone shouts something and Yorke repeats it: 'This one's dedicated to the girl who just shouted, "Help me, Thom, I'm dying."' It's the Radiohead equivalent of a heckle.

'Some famous pop star told me to lighten up. And I felt really proud of myself. I felt really good because I haven't lightened up. I have absolutely no intention of lightening up, because when I do I really will turn into Jim Kerr.' Of course, despite everything, Thom Yorke is a jolly little chap. He's tough, with the sort of cocksureness that likes to get into fights. He's prone to protecting his tetchy temper as a point of principle. He is getting fed up being treated like some sort of casualty, propped up on Prozac and poetic despair. He's started making jokes about being on heroin and attempting suicide, telling people if they want music to slash their wrists by, they should listen to the Smiths instead, even though that's what he did himself.

Still, for all his brave denials, as Jonny Greenwood says, 'all Thom's songs eventually come down to how he's feeling'. Talk to the others about him, and apart from an almost awestruck adherence to the belief that he is the most articulate, interesting lyricist of his generation, what you find is a sense of protection.

They all say that the success of *The Bends*, combined with the support slot on REM's tour last year and their largest headlining gig to date – 5,000 people in Toronto – have done him the world of good, 'given him more confidence'. Only an incident in Germany, described by the *NME* as 'Thom's tantrum', clouded the idea that everything was going swimmingly.

'I freaked out. I couldn't sing. Threw stuff around. The amp, the drum kit . . . I had blood all over my face. I cried for two hours afterwards.' His explanation – that he was ill and couldn't cope with his strange medication, that he cracked up when his voice started giving out – did nothing to allay the idea that he was undergoing some sort of burn-out, like Bowie or Kurt Cobain. He jokes about his imminent demise doing wonders for his back-catalogue, but stops when he realises it probably would.

Radiohead's dilemma is What to Do Next. What sort of band do they want to be? How big do they really want to get? 'It's a very weird position to be in,' Yorke shrugs. 'To be the stadium rock band it's OK to like. I thought it might double my paranoia level, but it's exciting. It's actually more liberating, the idea that people might wanna hear it.'

Still, he can't help but sneer about 'sit-down audiences', and admits there is something truly disheartening about hearing thousands of American kids singing 'I wanna perfect body' with none of the line's original pathos or irony.

What Yorke probably wants, of course, is the best of both worlds, something similar to the artists he most admires – people like Elvis Costello, Neil Young or Tom Waits. 'You know, just come back every three or four years, then go off and record an album down the bottom of the garden.' But he has the grace to allow himself a smirk, adding: 'Simple Minds probably said that, too.' Just thinking about it gives him an attack of anxiety, a ridiculous sense of responsibility. 'Paying the crew retainers suggests that the next record is going to do well automatically. The idea that what I do pays someone else's wages at all is just so weird. Disturbing. I'm not sure how long I'd be able to handle that – creatively. At the moment, the idea that we could be as big as REM or U2, we just couldn't handle it.'

Right now, Yorke is trying to get a life, make a life, before it's too late, so at least he has one to be taken away from him. 'It's almost like frantic desperation at the moment,' he grins, desperately. He has bought a house in Oxford (he calls it the House that Creep Built) and has been trying his hand at normal life – 'spending as much money on household appliances as possible. Taking them home to my girlfriend and saying, "Here you go." The house is still full of them, still in their boxes. It's just stuff that I bought to try and claim my life back.'

The prospect of repeating the commercial and creative success of *The Bends* must seem pretty daunting. The new songs are coming thick and fast, and the ones I heard (as yet unrecorded) sound simpler, more mainstream, more REM, with some Roxy Music synthesizers thrown in. (Those of us who are worried about the Simple Minds factor will be alarmed to hear them talking about the excitement at 'just hearing each other play'.) One called 'Electioneering' is pretty upbeat – an almost Clash-style skiffle – while 'Airbag' is another scrape with Yorke's mortal self. Another new one, 'I Promise', is, Yorke murmurs, 'about faith, in, er, a relationship. It's supposed to be quite positive.'

It's possible that Radiohead's ultimate fate will depend not on Yorke but on Jonny Greenwood, who provides the avant-garde edge to offset Yorke's perfect pop. 'The next challenge,' Jonny muses, 'is to find the great, extremely catchy atonal riff.' He's been exploring his growing prog-rock collection (luckily, so far he's found most of it 'unlistenable. The lyrics are unforgivable') and learning the viola and the flute. 'It's a bit pastoral, isn't it?' he sighs. 'A bit "One Leg up on a Log".' Besides synthesizers, he's also been getting into dub, 'which I suppose means the new stuff will be a heady mixture of Augustus Pablo meets Rick Wakeman'.

The predominant atmosphere in the band, they all make a point of saying, is 'very positive'. (Radiohead fans will, understandably, immediately start worrying.) 'I think we've got back to how we were when we started. Same kind of excitement. We're so uptight generally, I wouldn't contemplate the idea of getting complacent. We're not used to people liking us, so I don't think it'll ever happen.' Yorke, for his part, is beaming. 'All of us have been given great belief in ourselves. It's like a flash of release more than inspiration. I know we can do it now. The next album will be about that release. The way we're writing and the way we feel when we play together is about release now. And the new stuff is grateful and will hopefully be good because of that. I have every intention that the next record will be a very grateful record.' It's a nice dream.

11 October 2002

THE LOUDEST THING WE'D EVER HEARD

Richard Williams

Nowadays they wear earpieces and black satin jackets and look as though they could be packing heat. In my day – and there was only one of them – we wore medium-grey suits and school ties, and carried just enough money for the bus fare home. Funny to think that, almost 40 years ago, we were responsible for protecting the Rolling Stones from fan and foe.

As members of the school music society, we were allowed to act as ushers at all the local concert halls. Normally we would turn up in our school uniforms and politely show people to their seats for an evening of Purcell or Hindemith. But when Monday 2 March 1964 came around, we found ourselves entitled to participate in a very different kind of experience.

This was not the Rolling Stones' first visit to Nottingham. Five months earlier, soon after the release of their first single, they had played two shows at the Odeon cinema, below the Everly Brothers, Bo Diddley and Little Richard (who had been added by the promoter after the tour's early dates had failed to attract enough interest). Although the single had not been a hit, the buzz was already about. For some forgotten reason, almost certainly to do with a lack of cash, I missed them at the Odeon, which made the chance to see them for nothing at the Albert Hall – a miniature version of the better-known one in Kensington Gore – even more attractive.

The music society probably had no more than 20 or 30 members, who met for occasional record recitals and debates: Viennese dodecaphony versus English pastoralism, that kind of thing. In the days after the Stones' concert was announced, the secretary was deluged with applications, most of them from boys who would have had trouble distinguishing a C major scale from a hole in the ground. They were out of luck. Only existing members, it was said, would be allowed to act as ushers for the Rolling Stones.

So it was that, after a day spent studying Chaucer and the

principles of local government, a couple of friends and I were to be found shuffling our feet nervously in the backstage dressing room (the very one we had used a fortnight earlier for the school's spring concert) as Mick Jagger, Brian Jones, Keith Richards, Bill Wyman and Charlie Watts draped themselves over the furniture and acted nonchalant.

We were 16; with the exception of Wyman, who was already 27 but not admitting it, the Stones were all 21 or 22. In their elephant-cord hipsters, tab-collared shirts and Carnaby Street suede laceups, they exuded an ineffable and hopelessly unattainable cool. At that stage, the burden of debauchery sat lightly upon them. When invited, they signed their names on a paper napkin without demur. They showed no surprise at the presence in their dressing room of a group of boys in school uniform, although even at that stage they would probably have chosen to die rather than show surprise at anything at all.

Half an hour later I was stationed in the middle of the first of several rows of seats immediately behind Charlie Watts's drum-kit. Being a drummer myself, I could hardly have been granted a finer vantage point. Not, as it turned out, that I would get very much time to study the subtleties of Charlie's hi-hat technique.

The hall was packed, which meant that there were about 900 people present, probably none over 20, and evenly divided between the genders. At the cutting edge of teenage tastes, rhythm and blues had taken over from the Mersey beat. Chuck Berry's 'Memphis, Tennessee' had recently made the top 10. The Stones themselves could be heard playing their cover versions of obscure R&B songs on *Saturday Club*, the BBC's radio pop show. Their unspectacular first single had been a brittle, twitchy cover of Berry's 'Come On'. That was what the boys were interested in.

But with 'I Wanna Be Your Man', a much poppier song given to them by John Lennon and Paul McCartney, the Stones had reached No 13 in the charts a few weeks earlier. Much to their surprise, this bunch of hardcore blues enthusiasts started to find themselves being mobbed by pubescent girls. They had been seen on *Thank Your Lucky Stars* and *Ready Steady Go*, where it was noted that their hair was longer and shaggier than the Beatles'. Even more important, they did nothing to ingratiate themselves. Lips were curled and smiles were sardonic. Where winsome Paul McCartney grinned, shook his head and went 'Wooooo!', Mick Jagger did a sinuous little Nureyev-goes-to-Harlem dance and shook his quadruple maraccas like voodoo implements, a portrait of self-absorption. When he sang Muddy Waters' 'I Just Want to Make Love to You', the word 'love' was elongated and lubricated in a way that made it mean something quite different from the 'love' in Cliff Richard's songs. The girls were there because the Stones were sexy in a new and disturbingly exotic way.

So there I sat in the front row of the choir seats, with a few feet of stage between me and Charlie's Gretsch drums, flanked by girls who were already flushed with anticipatory arousal, conscious of my duty and wondering what came next.

As soon as the Stones emerged from the stairwell that led from the dressing room up to the stage, that question was answered. When they walked into the light there were screams, and tears, and within moments the first attempt was made to get close to a Stone. Doing something about that, it turned out, was supposed to be my responsibility.

Luckily these were the early days of Sixties pop hysteria. Certain rules of decorum still applied. A minimal degree of physical restraint – even when applied by a 16-year-old in a school tie – seemed to work. The attempt to make contact, it appeared, was more important than the success. But those attempts continued throughout the set, which meant that I have little memory of what the Stones played that night, or how they played it. What I do remember is that they performed their new single, a version of the Crickets' 'Not Fade Away' set to a storming Bo Diddley beat, and that they were the loudest thing I'd ever heard – even though each guitarist had only one small amplifier on stage, while the vocal amplification was consigned to a pair of primitive column PA speakers.

What must have been an hour, or getting on for it, passed like five minutes. It was new and strange and totally exhilarating, whether you were invading the stage or defending it.

I left the hall carrying the unexpected prize of Charlie's

drumsticks, which he handed to me as he left the stage. Halfway along the shaft of each one was a huge jagged notch, as if the stick had been gnawed by a large rodent. Etched by the repeated impact of the wood against the steel rim of his snare drum, this was tangible evidence of the force with which he drove the band's backbeat. Late that evening at the Don Juan coffee bar I gave one of the sticks and the autographed napkin – the signatures of all five original Rolling Stones on one piece of paper! – to a dark-haired girl who liked poetry and R&B and, I hoped, would look on me with favour as a result. She took the drumstick and the autographs but gave nothing at all in return.

You can see what the night was like by watching the video of *25x5*, the documentary made by the late Nigel Finch to celebrate the Stones' first quarter-century, which includes footage shot at the Albert Hall – the real one this time – during a concert two years later. In London the bouncers were not schoolboys but middle-aged men with dark suits and uncompromising expressions. They show no compunction in grabbing a pretty blonde in a Biba striped minidress – she could be the third Shrimpton, a sister to Jean and Chrissie – and hurling her back into the stalls. As a shocked Keith Richards tries to hang on to his Gibson guitar while escaping the stage, Brian Jones laughs hysterically in his face at the madness of it all.

By then they had laid aside their repertoire of songs borrowed from the R&B masters. Under the influence of Andrew Oldham, a Tin Pan Alley apprentice who was only 19 when he followed up a tip and went to see them at the Crawdaddy club in Richmond, they had begun writing their own songs. Oldham saw from the example of the Beatles that original material would be needed if his group were to outlast most of those thrown up by the beat boom. And he had spent enough time hanging around the offices of music publishers to know that copyrights were where the real money could be made.

'They were bad boys when I met them,' Oldham told a journalist recently. 'I just brought out the worst in them.' But were they really so bad, so unwilling to compromise with the establishment? For all their insolent posturing, as early as their first single they were prepared to avoid controversy by changing Chuck Berry's 'some stupid jerk' to 'some stupid guy'. In 1965 they shot a US TV promotional clip for 'Satisfaction' in which the line 'And I'm trying to make some girl' was fudged. In 1967, promoting 'Let's Spend the Night Together' on *The Ed Sullivan Show*, they amended the title line, which came out as 'Let's spend some time together'. A year later they complied with Decca's horrified rejection of the original artwork for *Beggars Banquet*, which depicted a graffiti-covered lavatory wall. And as late as 1975 they accepted the need to censor *Starfucker*, which re-emerged as *Star Star*.

But Oldham told the world they were bad boys, and the world was anxious to believe him. If the Beatles' importance was 75% musical and 25% cultural, with the Stones the proportions were reversed. The Stones connected with an audience that was emerging from the age of deference and was showing the beginnings of an interest in sociopathic and transgressive behaviour. Their appeal had less to do with the music than with their listeners' ideas of themselves. The Stones were the oil on the hinge of the doorway that led to the garden of earthly delights, and the music was just an excuse.

Yet when Jagger and Richards sat down early in 1965 and turned an old Staple Singers gospel song into 'The Last Time', they were creating the first great riff-driven rock song. They followed it with 'Satisfaction', 'Get Off of My Cloud', '19th Nervous Breakdown' and 'Paint It Black', all within barely a year – their golden age. As Shawn Levy describes in *Ready Steady Go*, his study of the forces that created Swinging London, they made a fruitful connection with the *jeunesse d'orée* of the time, the young acid-head aristos and heiresses of the King's Road, whose foppish decadence filtered into songs such as 'Play with Fire' and 'Lady Jane'. From 'It's All Over Now' to 'Brown Sugar', they made great party records. Over the long haul, however, they were hugely inconsistent. Moments of brilliance could not disguise the fact that, during an era of phenomenally rapid evolution, they were always a couple of paces behind the Beatles.

It took a while for Jagger and Richards to find a way to speak directly to their audience. Lennon and McCartney had always done it: 'Love Me Do', 'Please Please Me' and 'I Want to Hold Your Hand' were aimed straight at the shopgirls and secretaries in the front row at their gigs. But the Stones, having borrowed their early repertoire, started off as if they were addressing the women who populated the cotton fields and juke joints of the Delta. It was not until Oldham forced them into songwriting that they found their voice and – in 'Stupid Girl', 'Under My Thumb' and 'The Spider and the Fly' – their targets.

Over the years there has been no shortage of reasons to be sceptical of the Rolling Stones. A random selection might include their involvement in Godard's dreadful *One Plus One*, the girl's blouse Jagger wore in Hyde Park, the pathetic flirtations with evil, the phrase 'child-bearing lips', Jagger's acceptance of a knighthood, and the mere existence of 'It's Only Rock 'n' Roll', rivalled only by 'We Are the Champions' as the most banal and unnecessary song produced in the name of 'rock'. The death of Brian Jones left them without a musically inquisitive intelligence, although the arrival of the gregarious Ron Wood in 1974 supplied the social glue that held them together in the 1980s, when the relationship between Jagger and Richards was at its most fissile. Hardly a single one of their albums is solid all the way through, and some have barely a redeeming feature.

There is also a pervasive sense of shoddiness clinging to their early output. Mostly this is the legacy of Oldham's decision, soon after taking them on, to sign the band to Decca Records, reasoning that the label that had missed the Beatles would want to compensate by trying harder to promote their potential rivals. Nor was the situation helped when, in 1966, he passed their management over to Allen Klein, a New York music industry veteran who successfully renegotiated their various deals on much better terms but was slow to cough up the proceeds. In 1969 – the year of drugs busts, Marianne Faithfull's suicide attempt, Brian's death and Altamont, the ultimate bad trip – the Stones finally rid themselves of Klein. 'He did very good deals for us,' Bill Wyman said, 'but I think he was really looking after himself.'

Klein's compensation (part of 'the price of an education', in Keith Richards' phrase) was the continued ownership by his company, ABKCO, of the Stones' Decca recordings. And now his son, Jody H Klein, is named as the supervisor of the long-awaited Rolling Stones Remastered project, in which the original tapes have been remastered with the aim of recreating the sound that the musicians heard in the studio.

A few weeks after I first saw them in Nottingham, the Stones arrived in California to begin their first American tour, which included 12 shows in 18 days. Tomorrow night they play Ford Field in Detroit, six weeks into a five-month tour arranged to celebrate their 40th anniversary. Last week, talking about his relationship with Jagger, which began when they were both four years old, Richards told the *New York Times*: 'You can get rid of the old lady, but I can't get rid of Mick and he can't get rid of me.' Their longevity is a marvel, but no inducement could persuade me to go and see them in a sports stadium, where they have never been anything more than a rock 'n' roll circus act.

In a more helpful environment, something very different emerges. Watching them rehearse for the *Exile on Main Street* tour in a small cinema on the shore of Lake Geneva 30 years ago, it was easy to see what Oldham glimpsed in the back room of Richmond's Station Hotel on the night he decided he could make them stars: a perfectly tuned mechanism too often obscured by the scale of tours aimed at sustaining expensive lifestyles.

You can still hear it on the earliest of the old recordings, in the wonderfully relaxed drive of 'Down the Road a Piece', a rackety roadhouse blues, or in Bo Diddley's 'Mona', a concerto for reverb-drenched rhythm guitar. At such moments the layers of powder and paint accumulated over decades dissolve to reveal once again the lithe outline of a sometimes great band.

On that night in 1964, I was too busy detaching girls from Charlie Watts's shoulders and putting them back into their seats to notice the details. Now I wish I could say for sure whether Brian was playing his teardrop-shaped Vox Phantom guitar, or if Keith accompanied the final chord of each song with the decorous little bow that can be seen on all surviving footage from their early gigs. But one thing I do remember. No matter how many girls were trying to drag him off his stool, Charlie never dropped a beat.

19 May 2003

NOT A PERFECT DAY

Simon Hattenstone

Lou Reed is a bit of a hero of mine. When I was nine, 'Walk on the Wild Side' was No 10 in the charts, and there had never been a record so languid and funky and cool and sexy. Doo de doo de doo de doo . . . So many of us wanted to be Lou with his shades and leathers, making out with the hes-that-were-shes and the shes-that-were-hes in the happening New York. A few years earlier, as the boss man in the Velvet Underground, he became the godfather of punk. Some songs, like 'Heroin', screeched with feedback, talked about the desire to nullify life and struck a chord with so many young people. Others, such as 'Sunday Morning' and 'Pale Blue Eyes', were so tender, so ethereal, they barely existed.

Thirty-plus years on, he is one of our more unlikely survivors. He has seen off heroin and alcohol, and outlived his mentor Andy Warhol, heartbreak chanteuse Nico and Velvet Underground guitarist Sterling Morrison. He restricts himself to water and Diet Coke, t'ai chi and wholesome foods, and he is still making records. Many of them are about loss and memory, growing old and evaluating life. A few months ago he released a double CD, *The Raven*, based on Edgar Allan Poe poems: although it was widely derided for its pretensions, the crystalline purity of a handful of songs touch the soul like in the old days. Now he has released a double-CD collection, *NYC Man*, which takes us from year zero to the present, and he is touring Europe to promote the albums.

Today he is in Stuttgart. It's not quite Berlin, where Reed made probably the most depressing album ever and named it after the city, but downtown Stuttgart is pretty bleak in its own right. I've heard bad things about Reed being uncooperative in interviews, but it's probably apocryphal. After all, I've been vetted by his people, and the sun is shining blissfully.

Reed is playing at the local concert hall, which looks made to measure for Reed in its concrete misery – the Barbican meets

Belmarsh prison. We wait expectantly. Eventually, a people carrier draws up. A man in hooded sweatshirt jumps out, shadow boxes and runs inside: the camouflaged Reed makes it inside unimpeded. There's only the photographer, Eamonn, and me waiting, but Reed has lost none of his star quality.

After a quick snack, he is ready for a photograph. He's a small man but well-built – big pecs, big belly, tight T-shirt. He's 61 years old. He grips my hand and eyeballs me. 'Hi,' I say. He stares. 'He's not doing the interview in here, is he?' he asks the PR. No, she says. 'So he doesn't need to be here for the pictures.'

I'm sent off upstairs to a sterile, empty room to wait for him. He's not been that friendly, but once I tell him how I grew up to 'Walk on the Wild Side', we'll bond. There is so much to talk about: the smack years, if he can remember them; flirting with death; how his parents sent him for a course of ECT when they thought he was gay; how his relationship with a transvestite inspired *Transformer*; how he went back to live with his parents after he quit the Velvets and worked as a typist for his accountant father; how he interviewed celebrity fan Vaclav Havel; how he recovered his karma thanks to t'ai chi and his love for partner and performance artist Laurie Anderson.

I hear footsteps. It's the PR, Ginny. Bad news: Lou wants to soundcheck before we talk. Good news: we can listen. On stage for more than an hour, he drives his band relentlessly towards perfection. I'd forgotten what a great guitarist he is. After the soundcheck, I'm packed off back upstairs.

He walks in silently, with swaggering B-movie menace. Of course, he'll act the hard man, but my copy of *NYC Man* is on the table and once we start talking about his greatest songs he'll relax. I know he will. Hey, I say, when I look at this record it makes me feel nostalgic for my youth, and I didn't even write the songs, so God knows what it does for you. He gives me a withering look. 'No, that's not what occurred to me. I was interested in making them sound as good as I can make them because the original mixes really hold up because they are recorded onto tape and they sounded really good.'

Ah, typical Reed – hiding his heart behind the technobabble. So didn't it take him back, remastering all these classics? 'I told you, I was interested in the sounds. There are things on some of these tracks that have bothered me for ever.' He sounds as if he means it. Good actor, this Lou Reed.

I tell him I've been listening to *The Raven* and couldn't help noticing how reflective it seems. On one song he says one thinks of what one hopes to be and then faces up to reality; on another he asks if he had a chance to converse with his former self, what would come of it. They are familiar themes. In 'Perfect Day', written in 1972, the apparent idyll is undercut by the line: 'You made me forget myself, I thought I was someone else, someone good.'

'You can't ask me to explain the lyrics because I won't do it. You understand that, right?' He gives me another look. Anyway, he says, this is just the character talking. Yes, but has he ever considered what his older self could teach his younger self, and vice versa? 'I can't answer questions like that. What is it you really wanna know, because if it's personal stuff, you won't get it. So, you know, whaddya want?'

Reed has said in the past that he may as well be Lou Reed because nobody else does it better. I ask him if he thinks of Lou Reed as a person or a persona. 'I don't answer questions like that.'

Fine, I say, you tell me what we can talk about. But I don't feel fine. I feel unnerved and upset. 'We can talk about music, is what we can talk about,' he says.

But we can't, because if I ask what he felt like when he wrote 'Heroin', or what the line 'shaved his legs and he was a she' was inspired by, that would be an encroachment. For Reed, everything is personal, except the mixing desk.

So I press ahead with the music. Back in the 1970s, he and David Bowie and Iggy Pop were regarded as an unholy triumvirate. They broke down all kinds of barriers – between pop and performance art, male and female, lyricism and cacophony. There was a fluidity in their world; nothing was strictly defined. 'I don't know what you mean,' Reed says. Again, he stares me out, his tired eyes the colour of blood and chocolate. 'I haven't a clue what you're talking about.'

But I bet he has. Reed makes me feel like an amoeba. I want to cry. Look, I was a huge fan of yours, I say. 'Was?' he sneers. I still am, I say, but I'm less sure by the second. I desperately try to stick to the music. Soon after his most commercial album, *Transformer*, Reed made his least-commercial record, *Metal Machine Music*, an album of feedback. Some critics said it was his joke on the pop business. Is there any validity in that? 'Zero.' Is it something he can enjoy? 'Well, I can.' Which of his songs does he like best? 'I don't have a favourite.' Favourite album? 'I like all of them.'

Warhol, the Velvet Underground's mentor, believed that art shouldn't be tinkered with to appease the market. Did he teach Reed to value his own work? 'It was great that Andy believed in us.' Warhol fell out with Reed before his death, complaining that he never gave him any video work. I ask Reed if he wishes they could have made up before he died. 'Oh, personal questions again.'

But isn't the music shaped by his experiences and relationships? 'Don't the people you're around shape the music, is that what you're saying? Everything does.'

So why won't you talk about them? 'You're not going to leave off that, are you? OK, let's not do it. We're not getting along. OK. You want to ask questions. I told you I can't do it so I can't do it. Thanks a lot. So I'll see you.' He's off.

I shout after him, thank you, I've come all the way from England to see you, let's talk about what you want to talk about then. He sulks back in, and walks around me, as if weighing up whether to hit me. He sits down. 'You wanna talk about music or not?' But, of course, he doesn't want to talk about anything.

I tell him that he's intimidating. (Actually, he's like the class nerd who worked out obsessively and graduated into the playground bully.)

'I'm not trying to intimidate you,' he says, mock softly. He looks pleased. 'I said don't ask me personal questions.'

OK, then, can he explain *The Raven* to me? He tries and fails, but he does manage to say it took four years to make. Did it upset him that, after all that time, so many critics slated it? 'I don't know anyone actually who does care what a critic says. Y'know, I was with Warhol, with Andy, and the things they would say about him, up to and including when he died . . . and, of course, now he's quite possibly the top American painter.'

The Raven features a singer, simply called Antony, with a wonderful, shimmering voice – almost castrato. I ask Reed where he discovered him, and say that he looks as if he could have popped out of Warhol's Factory 40-odd years ago. He says that his producer Hal Willner found him at the Meltdown music festival on London's South Bank. 'After 15 seconds we thought: "What an amazing voice". Now, typical of you as an interviewer to say something as cheap as "Oh, he looks like somebody who could have been around the Factory," as opposed to, "What a great voice".'

'I was going to come to that.'

'Well, you could have started there.'

'You never gave me a chance. Why are you so aggressive to me? What have I done to you? Why are you being so horrible?'

'I'm just pointing things out to you.'

I'm lost for words. 'I used to buy your records,' I say pathetically.

'You used to.'

'Are you really this aggressive in real life?'

'Didn't we just go through this? OK, fuck, you don't want to talk about music. Antony is someone who could have been in the Factory,' he mocks. 'You don't say what a beautiful voice, my God!'

'Have I got to sit here and fawn to you? I was going to say he could be in the Factory because he's an original and his voice is stunning and ghostly. But you didn't listen long enough before attacking me.'

'I didn't attack you. As attacks go, that is pretty mild. Come on! Come on! Stop! Who you kidding?'

I ask him if he's happy. Listening to his bile, I can't help thinking this is one unhappy man. I apologise for the personal question.

'Jesus Christ!'

'I'm not a music interviewer. I do general interviews.'

'Hahahahaaa!' And he is really laughing – even if it is the cruellest laugh I've heard. 'Well, that explains it!'

OK, who's your music hero? 'I love Ornette Coleman. I love Don Cherry. I love the way those guys play. Just my God!' For one second, he seems to be engaging. But only a second. 'If you want to know records I like, on the web pages there is a top 100 or something like that.'

I ask him whether we can discuss martial arts – strictly in the context of music. (There is a martial artist in his show.) He nods. 'I always thought martial arts was the most modern choreography we could have right now, and I always wanted to put it to music.' What does t'ai chi do to his head? 'I try to do it three hours a day. It does a lot of things. Mainly focus.' And calmness? 'I call calm "focus".'

Reed and Laurie Anderson were vocal campaigners against the war. How does he define himself politically? 'I don't. I'm a humanist.' What does he think about America at the moment? 'These are really terribly rough times, and we really should try to be as nice to each other as possible.' I think he's being ironic, but there's no hint of a smile.

31 May 2004

'PEOPLE DON'T KNOW HOW TO BE OUTRAGEOUS ANY MORE'

Emma Brockes

I'm worried I won't recognise Lemmy, since, for reasons he is not himself coy about, he is often photographed in the middle distance, in low lighting, or under a hat. But there he is, unmistakable, stalking through the pearly LA light in black jeans, black boots, black shirt, black chest hair and a black cowboy hat, moving with the arachnoid gait of a pantomime child-catcher. We are to meet at his local, the Rainbow Bar and Grill on Sunset Boulevard, where Marilyn Monroe met Joe DiMaggio and where the hoarding on the wall advertises a band called Sick Sex, featuring a big-chested woman with the word 'Slayer' written across her torso in black marker pen.

'They're shut?' says Lemmy, pulling up. 'Oh, fuck.' He thinks for a moment, takes down two chairs from a table on the terrace and, giving the photographer a $100 bill, sends him to buy Jack Daniel's and ice from an off-licence round the corner.

Lemmy, whose real name is Ian Kilmister, has lived in Los Angeles for 14 years, but still sounds like Les Dawson. 'People don't know how to be outrageous any more,' he growls, pointing out a corner of the terrace where, in days gone by, couples had sex in full view of the bar. He looks wistful, then cross. 'If you tried that now the feminist people would go fucking nuts.'

Lemmy has fronted the heavy metal band Motörhead for almost thirty years. He is 58 and weather-worn, his trademark moles the size of toadstools. For the first time in his life, he is thinking of getting rid of them in case they turn malignant. He has incongruously fine LA teeth, which he had installed after his natural ones were pulled out as a child. They make him look a bit like Alec Guinness. 'Really?' he says thoughtfully. 'Fine actor.'

With the rehabilitation of Ozzy Osbourne having proved to be so lucrative, Lemmy is the obvious choice for a copycat follow-up. He is much smarter than Ozzy, although he has taken just as many drugs, and pulls off that same far-out contrast of screaming about death in his art while exhibiting good citizenship skills in his life. He used to leer, 'If Motörhead moved in next door to you, your lawn would die,' but he hates bad manners and holds a wide range of socially responsible views on topics from classroom discipline to the failures of feminism to the links between Dick Cheney and Halliburton. If he didn't swear so much, he would be an excellent addition to the panel on *Question Time*.

For several reasons, however, it is unlikely that Lemmy will ever become a mainstream pin-up. He lives a few blocks from the bar in a messy two-room apartment with décor that MTV might find hard to reconstitute as 'cuddly'. 'It's full of Nazi memorabilia,' he says, grinning, 'which horrifies Americans no end. I've had people come in there and say, "Oh I can't go in, I'm half Jewish." And I say, well, my black girlfriend doesn't have any problems with it, so I don't see why you should.'

His most valuable piece is a Luftwaffe sword with a Damascus steel blade, worth $12,000. 'I bought it for $6,000. I find it fascinating and colourful, and beautiful if you want. It's beautiful for the wrong reasons, but it's still beautiful. Also, it's a very good investment. It goes up every year by about 40 per cent.'

Lemmy doesn't like credulous Americans, but he dislikes the English even more. 'I've always liked America because it's . . . eager. Whereas the British are resentful. They still haven't gotten over losing India. The British get on my tits all the time.' One of the tattoos on his arm reads 'Born to lose, live to win', and he was, he admits, a bit of a loser for the first 10 years of his life. The only English kid in a Welsh school, he was bullied and himself became a bully. 'We used to have this kid – we'd tie him up and burn him. With matches. I don't know why we did it, probably because he let us and he kept coming back.'

Lemmy's father was a vicar who left when his son was still a baby. Lemmy doesn't like religion much. He did, however, grow out of bullying, when he got a smack round the head from the friend of the boy he was picking on. 'He was just trying to save his mate. And I thought that was a much better thing to be doing than bullying. Cured me instantly.'

Lemmy is a natural aphorist. 'We can't have everything 'cause where would we put it?' he says. And 'Growing up in America is like being taught to be stupid.' And 'I think all things are alive. If they're not, how do they fuck you over so much?' When he says, 'Never give anything up,' he is referring to drugs more than the traditional pop substitute, dreams. Lemmy has taken a lot of drugs, which he says have undoubtedly made him a better person. Jimi Hendrix gave him his first fix, in 1967, and he took copious amounts of acid until he got bored with it and, in 1975, switched exclusively to alcohol. He is never hungover, he says, because he is never entirely sober. 'You ever do acid?' he asks. No, I reply. 'Mmm. Perhaps you should. It gives you a new angle on things. Several new angles. I wouldn't undo having done it.'

How did it make him a better person? 'It made me more analytical. It made me more tolerant. And it made me realise that anything is possible. Anything. It's all random, everything is random. We like to put our patterns on things, but nature never wrote a straight line. Where are the Romans now and their fabulous buildings? Wrecks overgrown by nature.' He chunters with laughter.

Has Lemmy had bad times on it too? 'I've only ever had one bad trip, which was given to me by this asshole. But you get out of it. You drink orange juice like it's going out of fashion. I saw people as animals once, I saw 'em as rats and dogs. Big rings round your eyes. Whatever you do, don't look in the mirror. All the flesh melts off your face. And you are sick forever. But I took another one the next day, you know, just to get on the horse.'

In his new album, *Inferno*, he sings songs with titles such as 'Terminal Show' and 'Killers' and 'Suicide', which includes the lyrics 'Stay clean, be true, do everything you can do'. They are perversely joyful and Lemmy has always insisted that his music is about celebration. In Motörhead's heyday, in the early 1980s, they did gigs with huge pyrotechnical displays of fire and neon and, on one occasion, 'a fucking train that came out on wheels'. I must look doubtful – my dislike of heavy metal is hard to hide – and Lemmy asks suspiciously what music I listen to.

There is a fraught pause. Mostly show tunes, I say. 'Beg your pardon?' says Lemmy. I repeat myself. Lemmy looks at me like I've confessed to killing his grandmother. 'You should be nailed to the fucking cross,' he says. There is another pause. 'What, Andrew Lloyd Webber?' I make a face. No, I say. 'Oh, she turns her nose up at Andrew Lloyd Webber.' He sips at his bourbon. 'Oklahoma?' Yes. 'Fucking hell.'

There is a heavy metal hall of fame on the wall behind him. He asks me to identify some of the people on it. Alice Cooper. Steve Tyler. Ozzy. I'm doing quite well. 'Who's that?' says Lemmy, pointing. Er. Don Johnson? 'For fuck's sake. David Lee Roth.'

Lemmy nearly got married once, to a French woman whose father was a rich doctor from Montelimar. But he had the good sense, he says, to realise he isn't the marrying kind. He thinks monogamy is an outmoded style of living. He has several girlfriends whom he says he's not that fussed about but keeps going back to. 'You know how it is.' He also has 'two and a half children'. The first he had at the age of 18, to a girl of 15; the child was adopted. His second son lives near him in Los Angeles and is a record producer; they have a good relationship. And he has what he calls 'half a kid' in France. 'Because me and my roadie went with this girl one night and the next night . . . I was young, I was a fool. Anyway she's called it Lemmy, but it has glasses like, so I'm not sure. And it speaks only French. I met him when he was about eight. He didn't look like me. But then he didn't look like Graham either. Maybe it was a third party. Under cover of darkness.' I'm surprised she hasn't come after you for maintenance, I say. He shrugs. 'If she does and it's mine, I'll pay, I don't care. At least I owe him that.'

The talk turns to politics. Lemmy hasn't wanted to vote for years, he says. Politicians are all 'assholes' (it's one of the few words he pronounces with an American accent). The last politician he would have voted for was Harold Wilson. 'But I'd have been wrong.' He despises Bush – 'a fucking peanut farmer' – and of British politics says, unexpectedly, 'I believe in the royal family. They may be blockheads, some of them, but at least they're trained blockheads. From the day they're born they're trained.' He finds Charles 'intellectually vain' and believes Diana was killed in a conspiracy to stop her marrying Dodi. 'She was unfaithful first,' he says.

No she wasn't, I say. 'Yes she was,' he says. 'With Hewitt.' No she wasn't, I say. Charles was unfaithful with Camilla first. 'No he wasn't,' says Lemmy. Yes he was. This goes on for some time. It is tiring arguing with Lemmy. He will never admit to being wrong.

'What about feminism?' he says, out of the blue. 'It's made a lot of women very unhappy.' He furthers a sophisticated argument about the women's movement failing to provide for working-class women. Then, less convincingly, he says, 'What about "person-hole cover"? And "efemincipation", 'cause they won't have the word man in it?' Those are just the extremists, I say. 'Well, the trouble is they're the ones you hear most. The idiots have the loudest voices.' No one listens to Andrea Dworkin any more, I say. 'Yes they do,' says Lemmy.

Again, the debate goes back and forth, as does the dispute following his statements 'Gay people are made and not born . . . Look at the rent boys on Sunset Boulevard' and 'Women only go into prostitution 'cause they want to'. Eventually, exhausted, we get up to do some formal pictures. Lemmy has green eyes and black hair and I tell him he looks like Scarlett O'Hara. 'Good film, *Gone with the Wind*,' he says.

If his 15-year-old self could see him now, what would he think? 'Probably, who's that cool old guy?' I am humming under my breath. 'Oklahoma?' asks Lemmy. 'I do quite like that Andrew Lloyd Webber song. From *Cats*. What's it called? "Memory"?' He smiles. 'Sends shivers up your spine.'

30 July 2004

US AGAINST THE WORLD

Betty Clarke

April 2003. Pete Doherty and Carl Barât are in their living room, at the top of a narrow flight of stairs in a Victorian terraced house. Around 40 friends and fans are pressed up against the kitchen cabinets, squashed on to the solitary couch and curled around a spiral staircase, watching the duo jolt around their microphone stands. This is the Albion Rooms, the flat in London's Bethnal Green that Doherty and Barât have shared since signing their record deal. They've lived together before – on and off for the past few years – but this is the first home they've lived in knowing they could pay the rent.

The Libertines have just released their first album, *Up the Bracket*, and been hailed as Britain's best new band. Even at this ramshackle performance, it's easy to see why. Barât and Doherty have a formidable charisma; their music is a thrillingly rowdy mix of spiky guitars and rebellious harmonies. When an irate neighbour starts screaming, it just inspires them to play louder. Later, Barât is wrestled by a friend, breaking a window and causing shards of glass to fall over a police van pulling up below. Barât and Doherty grin as they discuss who should placate the boys in blue.

The 15 months since that night have seen the Libertines break up, make up and almost fall apart. Doherty's drug problems have led him to a spell in Wandsworth prison, followed by various stays in rehab. Barât, bassist John Hassell and drummer Gary Powell have performed without him across the world. Barât and Doherty's relationship – according to their bandmates, never an easy one – has disintegrated to such a degree that they are no longer talking. How did the greatest rock 'n' roll band in Britain end up here?

In a hotel room in New York, Barât is hunched over an acoustic guitar. As night creeps into morning, he'll run through various Libertines songs, try a few Beatles numbers and play lots by the

Doors. He begins new single 'Can't Stand Me Now' – a bruised portrait of how Doherty and Barât's relationship has deteriorated – before suddenly stopping. 'Do you have any idea what it was like for me to tell Peter he couldn't be in the band?' he asks, his eyes welling up. Then he grabs a bottle of beer and loses himself in the song.

Next day, a bleary Barât is sitting on a bench in New York's Central Park, commenting on every bird, creature and jogger that passes by. What he doesn't want to think about is the Libertines. The band have a new album to promote, and he has spent the past 10 days talking to the press on his own. Now he's exhausted. 'I've sat down with people for interviews, they've started asking me questions and I've gone into deep personal stuff,' he says. 'Then they say: "OK, so what's the name of the band again?"'

It's hard to remember it was the music that made anyone care about the Libertines in the first place. That and the chemistry between all four members of the band, an unpredictability that inspires magic and mayhem in equal measure. Combining the power of the Clash and the melodic beauty of the Beatles, their songs capture the angst of the disenchanted and swoon with the poetry of the Libertines' private world, Arcadia – a vision of England in which no one is tied to societal rules, and in which everyone is free to do as they wish.

It was a shared belief in Arcadia that forged the initial bond between Barât and Doherty. 'It was something that a lot of people had laughed at,' says Doherty. 'Or maybe I'd never found quite the right person to share it with. With Carl it was glaringly obvious that we'd found each other.'

Doherty is in his new flat in east London. Wearing a suit, he is at pains to show how nice it is. He points out the roof terraces, the clean work surfaces and only slightly chaotic bedroom, trying to negate the image of a squalid drug den promoted by a Sunday tabloid. The desire for reassurance is unmistakable.

Sitting at his kitchen table, Doherty ponders his first impressions of Barât. The pair met through Doherty's older sister; Barât had been playing pub gigs since he was 16, and Doherty hoped Barât – older by two years – could teach him to play guitar.

From the start, he thought Barât was a 'genius'. For Barât, Doherty was 'a little pipsqueak'. None the less, Barât admits there was something there. 'I liked his drive and persistence. I was secretly envious of some of his character and I think he must have been of mine.' They fought often, but became the best of friends. 'I was completely devoted to him,' says Doherty. 'It was us two against the world,' Barât agrees.

After a couple of years they adopted the name the Libertines and set sail on the good ship Albion, a self-created romance drawing on English mythology, British films and literature of the 1950s and 1960s, *Hancock's Half Hour*, Chas & Dave and skiffle music. Now all they needed was a band. Hassell knew of the pair through a mutual friend; he joined as bassist after 'Pete turned up on my doorstep with a book of poetry under his arm, stroking my cat'. After several months of performing everywhere from kebab shops to an old people's home, they found a manager and a drummer, Gary Powell. At last, 'the Albion task force', as Barât calls it, was in place.

'It was a real campaign,' Barât says of their determination to get a record deal. 'Personally, I said: "We're gonna get these bastards."' What Doherty remembers was Barât being depressed, convinced it would never happen. 'Carl just reaches this point where there's no talking to him at all. It took media hyperbole and fans' adoration to drill into him that, yes, you can play guitar. Yes, what we're doing is good.'

Their potential was finally spotted by Geoff Travis, head of Rough Trade. 'They were alive, alive to a degree that you just don't see,' he says. 'They were hilarious, entertaining, jumpy, songs coming out of their ears.' The Libertines were signed to Rough Trade in 2002 – and celebrated in typically idiosyncratic style. 'We got a bunch of money,' says Barât, 'ironed it and put it in the fridge.'

But over the next few months, living and working together began to take its toll on Doherty and Barât's relationship. 'We were a little bit like Morecambe and Wise for a while,' says Barât. 'But I've always been really in my own space, and we didn't have that in the Albion Rooms. In the end, I had to get out because of Peter's new friends.'

The 'friends' were Doherty's new-found crack cocaine buddies. 'I had to throw crackheads out of Pete's room,' Barât says. 'I knew from previous experience with other people that it was pointless to ban it. But I made very clear that I didn't want it around and I didn't want Pete doing it.' That intimate show in their front room in April 2003 was Barât's leaving party.

May 2003. The Libertines arrive in New York for the first time and play a triumphant show at the tiny Lux in Brooklyn. Afterwards they go back to their hotel to celebrate. Barât and Doherty sit with their guitars, playing Chas & Dave songs to a small group of friends. Everyone is happy. It doesn't last. The next day, the band are in a recording studio and Barât is eager to do some work. But Doherty has brought some friends in with him. The tension is unbearable.

'Pete and his friends having their little crack fun,' remembers Barât. 'They're singing this song – which is my tune – adding and changing bits. Then a girl says: "Come and sing, it's fun. Shall I teach you the words?"' Barât left the studio and New York soon after.

Doherty remembers it differently. 'I knew I had a better album than *Up the Bracket* in me and I wanted to record it. But I was told we've got to keep touring, keep promoting. That was the first time I realised we were on a conveyor belt.'

A few days later, Barât flew back to America and Doherty. He wasn't prepared for what he'd find. 'He was hanging out with some English kid. I went into his room and found syringes. This guy, who was obviously preparing to introduce Peter into the world of jacking up [heroin], turned to me and said: "Pleased to meet you. I don't think there's enough for you."' Infuriated, Barât smashed the syringes against the wall. 'Peter seemed kind of pleased I'd done it.'

It didn't stop Doherty's drug problems becoming more noticeable. He seemed to be withdrawing into a world the band had little to do with. The Libertines had always performed guerrilla-style gigs – shows in tiny pubs with no stages, to hordes of fans. But people were starting to wonder if the desire for drugs wasn't Doherty's motive for staging these events. Doherty says this is ridiculous. 'If I want drugs, I don't have to do a gig to get them. I do a gig when I feel shit, because I need to be playing. There's no drug in the world that can compare with playing music.'

Still, Barât was suspicious. And when Doherty asked him to play a gig on a rooftop in east London in June 2003 – even though it was Barât's birthday – he refused. What followed was chaos. The band were about to tour Europe – only Doherty didn't turn up for the tour bus. Then he decided he wanted to join the rest of the band in Spain. 'That was a bit rude,' says Barât. 'He hadn't bothered with the rest of it. And he was absolutely off his napper.' It was decided that Doherty should not return to the band. And it was down to Barât to tell him.

'It was the hardest phone call I've ever made,' he says. 'I phoned him from Paris and said: "Don't come." He was gobsmacked. I don't think he thought I was capable of it. I think he knows why I did it. But, in a childish way, he won't forgive me.'

Worse was to come. While the tour continued to the Far East, Doherty had a brief spell in rehab. He left, then he broke into Barât's flat in Harley Street, London. When told the news, Barât says he felt himself 'descend a bit deeper into this very painful world'. Doherty had publicly betrayed him. Powell is more forthright. 'I was pissed off at Peter's lack of self-worth,' he says. 'It was Peter once again crying out for attention and the only way he could do that was burgling his best friend. There were millions of people he could have done that to. He chose Carl.'

Reflecting on the events of last summer, Doherty stares at his kitchen table. 'I can't equate it with even the slightest idea I have of reality,' he says. 'Things like being kicked out of the band, going to prison, are so horrendous, I think it's gonna take me some time to talk honestly about how I feel about it. I'm managing, so far, to shut it out pretty well. I've never been to prison. I've never been kicked out of the band, never been in a band called the Libertines. That's the way it has to be.'

Sitting in Central Park, Barât looks no less unhappy. When he heard that Doherty had been given a jail term, he says: 'I kind of broke down. It's a stupid reaction, but I thought: "I've jailed my friend." But that's bollocks.' He jumps up and walks away before mimicking the joggers who eye him suspiciously. Before long, he's smiling again. 'Sorry,' he says. 'If I get emotional, you won't get anything out of me.'

At the time, Barât held things together, leading the band as they continued touring and played Glastonbury and the Reading/Leeds festival. 'I couldn't give up,' he says. 'There's a part of Pete that says, "It's all about me." If I'd let him believe that, it would have really fucked him up.'

When Doherty was released from prison in October 2003, Barât went to collect him. 'I didn't want the bad guys to get him,' he says simply. Photographs of the meeting say more than either Barât or Doherty do. Arms wrapped around one another, they stride away from the prison, Doherty clasping his regulation HMP bag full of his belongings. The relief and joy at seeing each other is clear. In part, this is what is so frustrating for the rest of the band. 'Peter knows,' says Powell, 'that nine times out of 10 he will be forgiven for his acts.'

That night the Libertines played an impromptu celebratory gig in Chatham, Kent. This time, it seemed the good mood would last. That same month, Alan McGee became their manager (Powell had asked him to do so at the Reading festival); in November they played three sold-out dates at London's Forum. The shows were amazing: Barât's new-found confidence was a revelation, while Doherty just looked happy to be able to play.

But behind the scenes, the same problems were returning. After each gig, Doherty would disappear. Barât was looking strained again. 'The drugs were obviously back,' he says. 'And the behaviour was beginning to come back, too.' He describes Doherty on drugs as paranoid, over the top, needy. It was at this time that security guards were brought in to protect Barât and Doherty, from each other as much as anyone else.

February 2004. The Libertines' name hangs above the door at London's Brixton Academy. For the band, who had struggled so long to be heard, it felt like a victory. And though Doherty was still distant – and enjoying playing with his new band, Babyshambles – he appeared to adore every moment on stage. But on the last night of the Libertines' three-night residency, he stormed off in the middle of performing 'Can't Stand Me Now'.

'He had a little freak-out, didn't he?' Barât says, smiling. 'I thought, "His temper's got ridiculous. That's the drugs." As it turns out, he thinks I looked at him a funny way during "Can't Stand Me Now".'

Doherty stands by his reason. 'It had taken six, seven years for him to say it, to say the truth: can't stand me now. He sang it to me and I thought, "You're right. We've used each other, got here, but underneath it all, you're not my mate." So I kicked his amp over, smashed his guitar and cut myself up.'

Doherty reappeared on the stage with thin lines of blood covering his chest. Barât wasn't amused. 'I did fuck all. What upset me was that if I hadn't got back on stage, he wouldn't have come back. When he heard me on stage, he fucking legs it back to get a big round of applause. I could do that.'

Later that night, band-mates and friends waited outside the dressing room, feeling fraught. No one was sure what might transpire between Barât and Doherty. But when the door was finally opened, there was no atmosphere, no strangeness. The pain had been buried once more. 'The worst thing they did,' says Powell, 'and are doing, is to ignore the fact that things have gone wrong between them. They've never once tried to sit down and talk to each other.'

'Sometimes I get in denial with the problem,' admits Barât. 'If I just forgive Pete, then it'll be fine. And it would do me no good to have a blow-up. Pete loves a blow-up, there's almost no point in giving him that. It's a double victory of silliness.'

The following month, the band, accompanied by their security guards, started recording their second album. Working together was difficult – on the very first day, Barât and Doherty got into a fight and had to be wrenched apart – but successful. From opening track 'Can't Stand Me Now' to the unbearably poignant closer 'What Ever Happened to the Likely Lads?', the frustrations and love that still lurk in the Libertines weep from the album like an open wound.

His recording commitments with the Libertines over, Doherty

should have been basking in his accomplishments. Instead, he was battling his drug addictions. A previous stay in rehab hadn't helped, so now he tried the Priory. Not that he wanted to. He did it, he says, for the band. 'To show them I was making an effort, because I know they don't like those things [drugs]. Even though I feel I'm in control.' He had two spells at the Priory; each time he lasted a week. Was Barât surprised? 'Disappointed,' he sighs. 'Not surprised. Never surprised.'

Doherty maintains: 'I came out of the Priory clean. First time in a while.' Even so, he decided to travel to Thailand for a more radical rehab programme at the Thamkrabok monastery. Barât felt hopeful. 'I was proud that he'd taken such a big step as to go to Thailand. I thought it might help. I forgot you can go to Bangkok, just down the road, and get the best stuff [heroin] in the world.'

Doherty soon left the monastery to visit the capital. 'To get the most out of that place isn't to approach it like, "I'm going to recover from a drug,"' he says. 'It's to enter on a spiritual journey within yourself to find that precious thing you might call a soul. All I could think of, though, was songs.'

Soon after, Doherty returned home – and immediately landed in trouble. Having been stopped by the police while driving a friend's car, he was found in possession of a flick knife. A night in police custody wasn't quite the welcome home party he envisaged. The rest of the Libertines, meanwhile, had had enough. They released a statement announcing that until Doherty was well, the band would continue without him. It was the last thing Doherty wanted. 'When I think about it,' he whispers, 'I just feel like putting a bullet through my head.'

At his kitchen table, Doherty is reflecting on a spread in the *Sunday Mirror* that claims he turned his girlfriend into a crack addict. Though accepting that he opened the door to tabloid scrutiny, he says he had no choice. 'That's the only way to communicate with the Libertines. Carl doesn't answer my calls, doesn't call me. It's a way of saying, "Hello? I'm still around."'

Barât isn't convinced. 'He loves to air his dirty linen in public.

It just happens to be mine as well.' So far, he's resisted the urge to fight back in print. 'I just want Peter to clean up,' he says, earnestly. 'I want music. I don't want a chat show.'

And yet, the feeling remains that if Doherty and Barât were to talk to each other, past hurts could be plastered over. Doherty certainly thinks so. 'All he has to do is come and talk to me. If he came round and said: stop taking smack, stop taking crack, I'd do it. I'd do anything he wanted.'

'I'd love to talk to Peter,' admits Barât. 'It's so tempting sometimes and he knows that. To be honest, he knows he can manipulate me, which is why he wants to see me. Which is why I won't see him. I'm not talking to him until I know he's chosen me over the drugs. It's not about talking to me, it's about him doing it for himself.'

23 July 2004. It's the opening night of The Libertines: Boys in the Band, an exhibition of photographs by Roger Sargent. Sargent has followed the band since they were first signed by Rough Trade and the show is a rollercoaster of emotion. From the cheeky grins of the early days to the tired faces of recent shots, it's clear that in two years in the spotlight, the band have grown up fast.

Doherty walks into the gallery, staring at the pictures of himself. But his first thought is for Barât. 'He's still in America, then?' he asks, knowing that press commitments have kept Barât away. He wanders away to look at the photographs. It's the closest he can get to Barât for now.

Two days later, Barât flies back to England from New York. On the way home, he drops into the exhibition. As he stands looking at the pictures, his smile changes to a frown. 'There's more of Peter than me,' he says, only half-joking.

June 2002. Doherty logs on to the new fansite libertines.org and posts the following message: 'My brother and I are not rivals. We are shipmates and best friends and the greatest songwriting partnership in the world.' If the Albion is to sail again, those are words Doherty and Barât must remember.

26 November 2005

A SENSE OF WONDER

Simon Hattenstone

When Steveland Judkins was a little boy, he decided to jump from the roof of the shed in his back yard. He wanted to take risks, live a little, like other kids. Yes, he was blind, but what was the worst that could happen? His brother warned him that his mother was coming, and if she saw him jump she'd beat the stuffings out of him. Steveland jumped, and at that moment his mother walked past and miraculously caught him in her arms. Sure, she went on to beat the stuffings out of him, but it had been worth it. And he'd known he'd be OK. He always had faith.

Similarly, he has always been a raging optimist. But he has said that if he could see – specifically, if he could see the horrors we inflict on each other – he might be less willing to believe that love conquers all. 'I might have been made militant by what I'd seen.'

Steveland Judkins grew into Steveland Morris when his mother, who till then had brought her children up single-handedly, remarried. Steveland Morris grew into Little Stevie Wonder after being spotted by Motown boss Berry Gordy at the age of 10 and dubbed the boy wonder. And Little Stevie grew into a six-footer, lost his Little moniker, sold 100 million-plus albums, and became one of the most influential figures in the history of popular music.

A couple of weeks ago he was in London, explaining why it had taken him 10 years to make an album of new music, and why his faith is still undimmed. He became emotional when he talked about the pain of the past couple of years: the deaths of his first wife, singer Syreeta Wright (who wrote the lyrics for 'Signed, Sealed, Delivered'), and his brother Larry Hardaway. And he became equally emotional when he talked of the joy of the past few years: his second wife, fashion designer Kai Millard, gave birth to two sons (children numbers six and seven for Wonder) – Kailand, who is now four, and Mandla, who was born this year on 13 May, Wonder's own birthday. The wheel of life has kept turning, and he has continued to thank his God.

I first experienced 'Stevie Time' at a press conference at the Savoy hotel. He answered question after question, occasionally stopping to knock out a tune on the keyboard in front of him. After an hour, Paul Gambaccini, who chaired the event, announced, 'OK, one last question.' 'No,' Wonder said. 'Five more questions.' And another five. And another. And so it went, till every last question had been answered.

A couple of days later he gave one of the greatest gigs I have seen, at the historic Abbey Road studios. His voice was superb, by turns swooping and soaring, honeyed and roaring, cajoling and bullying. There was a song for everybody – the politicised funk of 'Living for the City', the soufflé-light ballad 'You Are the Sunshine of My Life', the ecstatic spiritual 'As', the belligerent reggae of 'Master Blaster', the rocking Moog of 'Superstition', and of course the unapologetic schmaltz of 'I Just Called to Say I Love You'. Has one man ever appealed to so many audiences?

Wonder's new record is called *A Time 2 Love*, and it is something of a return to form – it's neither great nor consistent, but there are a handful of blastin', funkin', lovin' grooves to remind us of Wonder's genius. Although his message may not have changed, the context has. It has always been a time to love in Wonder's world, but now even more so with the threat of global terror. He acknowledges the cynical and dangerous, rails against the forces of hate, but ultimately his hope wins out.

There is a sense of rebirth at the gig. He plays the best songs from the new album, and his daughter Aisha Morris joins him on stage for 'Positivity'. Aisha was first heard, crying, on 'Isn't She Lovely' when she was only a few hours old. Now she is closing in on thirty, beautiful and embarrassed, and singing 'Isn't He Lovely' back to him. It's a yucky-gorgeous moment.

At Abbey Road I get my second dose of Stevie Time. The gig, being recorded for Radio 2, is due to last an hour. But Wonder just plays on and on. After three hours he calls it a day. He's always been like this – once he gets going, he can't stop. Unsurprisingly perhaps, he doesn't obey the conventions of day and night. He often records through the night, and sleeps through the day.

The day after the gig, his entourage is hanging around a London hotel, waiting for him. He is an hour late, but everyone is relaxed. Sure, he will turn up, but not just yet. His brother Milton, who handles his press, is testing me. 'You wanna know something? OK, what was wrong with the title of his first album, *The 12-Year-Old Genius*? Give in? OK, he was only 11 and a half, but we had to say he was 12 because he was too young to play live.'

Milton says Wonder is due in a couple of minutes. 'What star sign are you?' he asks.

Capricorn, I say.

'You'll never be short of money, then,' he says.

He leaves the room and a few minutes later reappears with his brother on his arm. Wonder is now 55, heavily framed and paunched. He wears a grey-black outfit, with 'By God's Grace' stitched into his shirt alongside the tree of life. His receding hair is corn-rowed from the back of his head down to his shoulders. He looks so different from the cool, skinny Afro-haired Wonder of the 1970s.

He shakes my hand and sits down. He seems uneasy. There is muttering about the absence of a keyboard. I'd been told that he likes to have a keyboard with him, that it is almost an extension of his body. Instead, he taps away at a Braille machine.

I ask him where he has been all these years. He smiles. Even he appears bemused by how he could have created so much so quickly in the early days and so little recently. 'Ten years is a long time, but I think when you're in it and you're doing life, you don't really see how long that is.' He is totting up the years as he talks. 'If I really did the math, well, between 1963 and 1973, a lot of things happened, like "Blowin' in the Wind", "Uptight", "If You Really Love Me", "I Was Made to Love Her", "Once In My Life" . . .'

As he mentions every title, I hear the giddy choruses in my head and want to sing along. 'Then you think 1995–2005 and obviously there was not much that I did musically.' He sounds apologetic. 'But a lot of personal family stuff happened. A lot of changes happened – good, bad and wonderful.'

People forget that artists have lives to get on with, I say. He grins. 'That's why I don't regret the time. Perhaps if I'd done 10 years [doing nothing but music] between '95 and 2005, what I had to say by 2005 might be boring.'

His career now spans five decades and breaks down into distinct periods: three amazingly productive, one less so, the drought, and now, hopefully, a late burst of creativity. At 12, as Little Stevie Wonder, he topped the US charts with his third single, the harmonica stomper 'Fingertips Part 2'. He briefly disappeared, returning with a broken voice and a surge of hits in the late 1960s. Even as Little Stevie he crossed the black-white divide. He also wrote and produced songs for other Motown artists, notably 'Tears of a Clown' for Smokey Robinson and the Miracles, and 'Loving You Is Sweeter than Ever' for the Four Tops.

His songs were full of light and air – the best of gospel mixed with the best of soul. His singing and playing, his finger-clicking and foot-tapping, his smile and laughter all suggested the transcendent, the ecstatic.

It wasn't just his music that made him unique: he was a phenomenal businessman. In 1971 he came of age, hired a good lawyer and renegotiated his contract with Gordy. He insisted on autonomy as producer, writer and performer – unheard of at Motown. In 1975, he renegotiated again, for an astonishing $13 million. To a great extent, he was a one-man band, playing all the instruments on many tracks. Wonder was a control freak, demanding yet always loved.

From 1972 to 1976 he produced a series of albums (*Talking Book, Innervisons, Fulfillingness' First Finale, Songs in the Key of Life*) that rank with any in pop history. He was as influential as the Beatles, the Stones, Bob Dylan or Bob Marley. He didn't invent a genre but he extended its boundaries every which way. His music nodded to blues and R&B, reggae and jazz, funk and prog rock. But at the heart of everything there was soul. He continued to write for other people, but he was so attached to his music that often he couldn't bear to give it way. 'Superstition' was meant for Jeff Beck, but he kept it for himself. At the age of 26, he peaked with the magnificent double album *Songs in the Key of Life*.

During this period, everybody wanted a slice of Wonder – he toured with the Stones, played with John Lennon, hooked up with a number of leftist-liberal political activists. As Wonder matured musically, so he did politically. This synthesis was perhaps most perfectly expressed in 'Living for the City', a song about poverty, racial tension and hopes dashed. It is as much a soundtrack to the 1970s as Scorsese's *Mean Streets* and *Taxi Driver*. Songs such as 'He's Misstra Know-It-All' and 'You Haven't Done Nothin'' attacked the corrupt Nixon administration. Wonder's music defined an era, as did his Afro, his bright sweaters and his peaked caps.

Songs in the Key of Life was followed by the ambitious concept album *Journey through the Secret Life of Plants* in 1979. It was critically mauled and a commercial failure. Despite one more massive-selling album, *Hotter than July*, he seemed to lose confidence and began to withdraw. The gap between records grew longer and longer. He occasionally re-entered our lives – more often than not with sentimental schlock such as 'Ebony and Ivory' (recorded with Paul McCartney) and the ubiquitous 'I Just Called to Say I Love You'. He seemed almost wilfully determined to erase his achievements from public consciousness. But it was impossible. No amount of naffness could detract from his greatness. Then, after 1995's ghastly punning *Conversation Peace*, there was nothing.

Did the barren period reflect the fact that so much was happening in his private life? 'No,' he says. 'I think that had very little to do with it at all. I just think that unless you have something you really want to say, you can't be all over the place.' Yes, there has been another marriage and new children and tragic deaths, but he still spent most days playing and working out in his recording studio, even if the material didn't come up to scratch.

With few exceptions, popular music artists have found it harder to create as they age. Not least because 'pop' has so often been fired by youth, idealism and rebellion. Wonder talks of the need to start with a new canvas every time he goes into the studio, to start all over again. No wonder there has been such a huge gap between records.

Did he fear that he might never again record new music; that he had nothing left to say? 'I never felt that. It's when you stop living that you don't have anything to say.'

Steveland Judkins was born in Saginaw, Michigan, in May 1950. He was a month premature and overexposure to oxygen in the incubator (common at the time) caused his blindness. His mother Lula took him and his five siblings to Detroit when he was three.

Does he remember the first time he heard music? 'I remember when I was three or four listening to the radio and being curious about how the whole thing worked.' Then when his mother bought a TV he was even more awed. 'I was like, "Man, you can see people on this thing?" I held my ears to the speaker and imagined what was being shown on the screen.'

Lifelong blindness is inconceivable to a sighted person. Does he think the imagination becomes a form of sight in itself? He nods. 'I think it is because you create a sense of very vivid places you can go to, and see what's going on in your mind.' He often talks about 'seeing' things – casually and without irony. As far as Wonder is concerned, he does see, he just has a different way of doing so. A few years ago, he visited a specialist who offered him an operation to make him see. Wonder never bothered. He has said that on balance he was happy as he was.

When he was a little boy, his mother didn't like Steveland to leave the house in case he hurt himself. So he stayed at home and listened to the radio: Junior Parker, Little Willy John, Bobby Bland, Bobby Darin, Neil Sedaka and his hero, Ray Charles. If Ray Charles, black, blind and poor, could make it, anybody could. Wonder once said: 'The two advantages I had at birth were to be born wise and into poverty.'

Steveland banged out tunes on pots and pans with spoons. Lula, who worked as a seamstress and cleaner, doted on him. She shelled out for musical instruments, and by the time he was four he could play piano, organ, drums, bongo and harmonica. His first public performance was unplanned. He was at a club with his mother and stepfather, the live music was blasting out, and he was beating the table in time. 'They just said, "Come up and play the drums," so I went up, beating the drums and being crazy.' By nine he was a seasoned performer at church. In fact, he had already been expelled for playing rock 'n' roll at the piano. But he didn't yet feel confident in public arenas because he couldn't grasp the parameters of a stage. When he joined Motown, the label paid for him to attend a school for the blind.

Did he ever curse his blindness? 'No. I've never felt, "Oh my God – why did you do this to me, God?"' Once his mother's fears for him eased, he grew up much as any boy would – he went into people's back yards, climbed their trees, nicked the apples and pears, got into scraps. Was he tough? 'I was very small, but I got into trouble. I got into fights over silly things. You know, "She's my girlfriend . . ." I was a little kid – seven, eight, nine . . . "She likes me!" "No, she likes me!"' And he impersonates his hard-assed petulant little self perfectly. Were people less likely to hit him because he was blind? 'No. When we would fight, it was on. It was not about being blind.'

Was he always a ladies' man? He throws his head back and grins ecstatically. 'Well, life is good and lurrve is wonderful.' He repeats himself, rolling his tongue round 'love' even more lasciviously. 'You know life is good and lurrrrrve is wonderful.'

When did he first discover that? 'Not so soon that I shouldn't have known, but not too late to be unaware.' That's very diplomatic of you, I say. 'Yaknowhadamsayin? I can say by the time I got married I was definitely not a virgin.' In the past, he has described his love life as complex. Details are sketchy about his private life, and he seems to like it that way. Of his five oldest children, most appear to have been with Yolanda Simmons, whom he never married but has always remained close to.

What do women see in him? He thinks it through carefully. 'I think I have a nice personality. I'm intelligent, and I think I'm not hung up on myself. If you're hung up on yourself, you are hung up.' He thinks too many celebrities are self-obsessed.

In the 1980s, he recorded less, and became involved in more causes. He got himself arrested at an anti-apartheid protest outside the South African embassy, befriended Nation of Islam leader Louis Farrakhan, and fought for the recognition of Martin Luther King – a campaign that culminated in his song 'Happy Birthday' and the granting of a national holiday, Martin Luther King Day.

Today, he seems ambivalent about politics. He doesn't even particularly like the word, preferring to talk about social justice.

Maybe there has always been a tension between his faith and his desire for political change. One second he seems to say we must leave everything in God's hands, the next that we have to fight for our rights. 'I just basically say what I feel about a position or thing,' he says. The bottom line is that 'when we do the right thing by each other, then God will do the right thing by us. I truly feel that way.'

Isn't it to your credit that you haven't left it all to God, that you have agitated for change? 'Well, some say yes, some say no. I've had people say to me, if you hadn't done the King holiday stuff and all that, you would have been more accepted. Whatever! Some people say, you need to just do music, and forget about all that. But that's not me, you know.'

Others have said his politics are too saccharine. He tells me he has met George Bush, and I ask if he gave him a mouthful. 'Well, he knows my politics and I know his. There was no need to get into some kind of thing. My mother used to say this: "When you feel you've got to tell it all, just go in the closet, close the door and talk to God and be done with it."'

Wonder often plays at the Church of God in Christ near his home in Los Angeles, and plans to make a gospel album next as a celebration of faith. Has his faith ever been challenged? He shakes his head. Not by racism, not by blindness, not by terrorism, not by the car crash that nearly killed him in 1973.

Does he think Bush has made the world more dangerous? 'Look,' he says, anger against American imperialism goes way deeper. 'This whole thing was set in motion long long ago. I mean, people are still arguing and fighting about dropping the [developing world] debt, and it's a joke to me. It's a joke because look at how much has been taken from Africa. God has given every continent on this planet some natural resource we can use to survive, for trading or whatever. But the world powers go and turn over the areas and take whatever they do, work out those ridiculous contracts . . .'

And then there is the misappropriation of religion. While Bush talks about having God on his side and Islamicists talk about jihad, Wonder says both take God's name in vain. 'People can't say this is a holy war. The people suffered, while their leaders made the money from deals. We're living in a mad world where people do mad crazy things. The God that I believe in doesn't believe in bombing, and the Allah that I respect for Muslims doesn't believe in terrorising innocent people.'

He says he was distraught when John Lennon was killed 25 years ago, but not shocked. 'Imagine', with its plea for a world without religion, always seemed a dangerous song to him. 'After he died I couldn't stop crying whenever I heard "Imagine", but I wasn't surprised that he'd been shot. The guy said he shot him because he said he didn't believe in Jesus, and I remember when I heard "Imagine", I thought, "Somebody's not going to like that."' Which of the great dead pop artists does he miss most? 'My God!' He doesn't know where to begin. 'There's John Lennon, Marvin Gaye, Bob Marley, Luther Vandross . . .' He considers Gaye's despairing *What's Going On* one of the greatest albums.

I'm sitting in front of Wonder. He's wearing shades with the *A Time 2 Love* logo printed down the arms. It's a terrible thing to admit, but there's something pleasing about the fact that he can't see me: I feel he can judge me objectively rather than by appearance. There are no distractions. For a moment, I start to envy his blindness. While his head sways like a metronome as he talks, he seems endowed with an inner stillness. He has a gift for intimacy.

I tell him that there are ducks sculpted into the chair arms, and find myself guiding his hands. 'Oh yeah, I saw that,' he says. Does he think there would be less prejudice in the world if we were all blind? I rephrase the question: would we find other ways of discriminating? 'Human beings always have to have things to complain about. Blind people can be just as prejudiced, but it's not based on what they see; it's based on what they've been told.'

He tells a story about travelling home from school one day. 'There was a little boy saying, "Purple niggers, green niggers, orange niggers, blue niggers, white niggers, black niggers . . ." He was a white guy, a little kid, blind.' His point is that the boy had no real concept of race, but it didn't stop him discriminating.

We talk about Hurricane Katrina, and the fact that so many

black people were left stranded in its midst. On television, it looked like 1950s America, I say, a separatist society. He wouldn't go that far. 'I don't see it being like the Fifties. But yes, there is still a divide.' Is it more economic than racial these days? 'In certain instances it is economics and class, and in other instances it is racial. People have to begin to feel that . . .' He stops. 'No, let me put this a different way. When every single person can feel when they see a black kid being beaten up by a white kid that this could be one of their own kids, when people start to care like that, we'll be moving forward.'

Wonder asks about racism in this country and refers to the Stephen Lawrence and Anthony Walker killings. He seems happiest when asking questions: about this country, about my life.

Look, I say, I've got some important questions. What is your favourite Stevie Wonder album? 'It depends on my mood. I might have an *Innervisions* mood. But if I'm in a romantic mood, I wouldn't put on my stuff at all.' Who would he put on? 'I'm gonna do Luther, I might do Beyoncé, I might do Usher. I'm not gonna put on my stuff. I can't make love to my own stuff.' That's remarkably modest of you, I say. 'I tell you, I can't.' He thinks there would be something tawdry and narcissistic about it.

Were children six and seven conceived in the presence of Luther or Beyoncé? 'Erm, we didn't have any music. We made our own music. I don't need no music to get my groove on.' He's now relaxed, joking, chewing the fat.

'Hey, when is your birthday, by the way?' he asks. 29 December, I say. 'You're Capricorn. Hey . . .' Yes, I say, I know I'm never going to be short of money. He nods, impressed that I know.

He talks about his plans to get busy again. There's the gospel album, and a jazz album, and a children's album, and he'd like to act in a film, and do a world tour putting on a fancy show with special effects. He seems so happy to be back. Wasn't he frightened that after 10 years away nobody would be interested in Stevie Wonder?

'It's a chance you take,' he says. He pauses, and thinks it through. 'No,' he says. 'You know, I have always had more faith than fear.'

15 April 2006

MADE IN SHEFFIELD

Alexis Petridis

The Spotted Pig has a fair claim to be called the hippest restaurant in Manhattan. A kind of upmarket gastropub, it has a Michelin star and rave reviews – its low-carb alternative to gnocchi is apparently to die for – but the food is overshadowed by its celebrity connections. Beyoncé eats here. Liv Tyler pops in for lunch. One of the owners used to manage the Smiths, the head chef came recommended by Jamie Oliver, and its investors are rumoured to include everyone from Bono to Fatboy Slim. It's so hip that the *New York Times* sent a writer to review not the food but the background music. 'They played Air, a French pop group,' he noted approvingly, 'before segueing into a homage to Apple Records, then some reggae dubs.'

But all of this counts for little with the Arctic Monkeys' 19-year-old drummer, Matt Helders. He emerges from his taxi and regards the Spotted Pig's tastefully discreet fascia with a wary eye. 'We've been 'ere before,' he sighs. Like the rest of the Arctic Monkeys, Helders speaks with a broad Sheffield accent. 'I ordered chicken livers on toast for starters. I didn't really know what it were. I just ordered it. They brought it and...' His voice trails off, as if he can't find words to describe the horror. He wrinkles his nose. 'I ended up scraping it all off and just eating the toast. When the waitress came back, I said to her, "You lot should be arrested for serving this muck."'

Tonight, however, Helders will be spared the hell of an offal-based starter. The Spotted Pig is hosting a party in honour of Coldplay, who played an arena in New Jersey earlier this evening, and the Arctic Monkeys have been invited. Bassist Andy Nicholson has cried off, pleading fatigue – 'I find that sort of thing reet awkward, so I stopped in bed,' he says the following day – but Helders, guitarist Jamie Cook and frontman Alex Turner dutifully mount the stairs to the restaurant's first-floor bar. It turns out to be both tiny and comically overloaded with celebrities. Jay-Z arrives in a chauffeur-driven vintage Rolls-Royce. He is followed, in short order, by Chris Martin and Gwyneth Paltrow – who get a round of applause on entry – the rest of Coldplay and Moby. Then there is Michael Stipe, who will later request an audience with Turner, and Courtney Love, who will later attempt to engage in conversation Turner's partner Johanna, before one of the band's road crew sharply intervenes, on the harsh grounds that 'after what happened to Nirvana, you don't really want Courtney Love talking to your lead singer's girlfriend'.

However indifferent you may wish to appear, it is almost impossible to stop yourself craning at the entrance to see who's going to turn up next, although Cook seems to be having a good try. Maybe his jaded air tells of the ennui that comes when you've recorded the fastest-selling debut album in British history and have a serious distrust of showbusiness trappings (when the Arctic Monkeys were being wined and dined by a plethora of British record labels, Cook stubbornly insisted on paying his share of the bill at the end of every meal). Or perhaps it is simply the result of the events of the previous evening, which sound remarkably like the kind of thing Turner writes songs about. Abandoned by the rest of the Arctic Monkeys party in a downtown bar in the small hours, Cook managed to fall off his seat, was ejected from the premises after an altercation with a bouncer, then hailed a cab only to discover he couldn't remember either the name or address of his hotel.

Tonight, as Manhattan's A-list crowd into the Spotted Pig, he lurks behind a pillar and discusses his previous job as a tiler in a tone of voice you could easily mistake for wistfulness. He was still doing bathrooms last May, when the Arctic Monkeys' vertiginous ascent to success had begun: he finished one off for a friend after coming back from a sold-out tour, because he had promised he would. 'It were reet good. You'd get in the van at five on a Monday morning and drive to London, stay four nights, then drive back to Sheffield on Friday afternoon.' He smiles: 'You can charge 'owt for tiling in London.' Cook's attention is suddenly drawn to the table in the centre of the bar, where the biggest celebrities are seated together, although in this instance it's not the succession of multimillionaires who have caught his eye. 'Look at Helders' top,' he chuckles. Indeed, the drummer certainly stands out among the bling and casually worn designer labels, wearing a lurid orange tracksuit top. 'Whenever we get sent free clothes and that, there's always something you pull out of the box and think, "Nobody is going to wear that." And every time, Helders comes in and, straightaway, he goes, "I'll have that."' And with that, Cook departs to meet his cousin, who has been deemed insufficiently important to attend Coldplay's party.

If you want a metaphor for the astonishing speed of the Arctic Monkeys' success, then look no further. None of them is legally old enough to drink in America (a fact that led one magazine to abandon plans to put the band on the cover, after liquor companies threatened to pull $500,000 of advertising). One of them is wearing a frightful tracksuit top. Barely 18 months ago their ambition apparently extended no further than getting to play a gig somewhere other than Sheffield. And here they are, chatting to Jay-Z and Gwyneth Paltrow.

Can their astonishing success be replicated in the US? Adhering to the long-established rule that any British band who get through their set in New York without the audience throwing litter at them must automatically be reported to have stormed the US amid scenes unwitnessed since Beatlemania, one excitable journalist has already dubbed the current tour 'the next phase of Operation Arctic Monkeys: World Takeover'. The truth is a little less hysterical.

The Arctic Monkeys have received critical raves in the *New York Times* and rock magazine *Blender*, and been described in *Rolling Stone* as 'one of the most exciting bands on the planet'. They have been introduced by Matt Dillon on *Saturday Night Live* and their tour has sold out. But their debut album, *Whatever People Say I Am, That's What I'm Not*, has, thus far, sold well rather than spectacularly: certainly not enough to panic the apparently omnipresent James Blunt, whose *Back to Bedlam* took up residence at the top of the US chart some time in January and shows no signs of vacating for the foreseeable future.

Manager Geoff Barradale says there is 'no big plan to "crack" America', and the Arctic Monkeys tour bus certainly doesn't feel like the white-hot epicentre of a world takeover bid. Someone has been writing slogans with their finger in the dirt caked on its sides. Given that most of these slogans seem to involve Sheffield United and internecine rivalries with other areas of Yorkshire – '100% BLADES', 'LEEDS = SHITE' – you rather suspect that someone was one of the Arctic Monkeys themselves. Inside, the bus bears the distinctive aroma of a vehicle in which a rock band and its road crew have been sleeping for some weeks. 'Sometimes I think about other bands and I wonder if they have conversations about their ambitions and that,' muses Turner, as he sits amid the debris of the bus's rear lounge. 'Everyone else seems to know what they're doing a lot more than we do. I read about other bands and it's as if they had a big meeting when they started and worked it all out. But we started just for something to do, because all us friends had bands. We never had a manifesto or 'owt. We just wrote songs and it came out like this.'

Back home, one popular theory suggests that the Arctic Monkeys may simply be too British for US ears. In the past, Americans have welcomed culturally specific, socially observant English rock bands with the same warmth and eagerness with which Helders greeted his chicken livers. The artists usually held as the Arctic Monkeys' forebears made few ripples in the US. There were hardly any Stateside takers for the Jam, and none at all for Mancunian punk-poet John Cooper Clarke or Pulp. The Smiths remain an acquired taste and even the Kinks only really tasted success after they toned down the irony and wry observations and transformed themselves into a straightforward stadium rock band. If they proved too parochial, then what chance do the Arctic Monkeys have of making themselves understood, with their accents, their references to *Some Mothers Do 'Ave 'Em* and their song called 'Mardy Bum'?

A fair proportion of their US press to date has concerned itself with explaining the band's more arcane references. *Rolling Stone* informed readers that chavs were 'white working-class stock characters, ridiculed for their gaudy tracksuits and hard-partying lifestyle, and known for loutish behaviour and conspicuous consumption'. *Blender* magazine dispatched a reporter to Sheffield's High Green district to get a flavour of the Arctic Monkeys' exotic background, while Turner says he feels 'a bit silly playing "Mardy Bum" over here, a bit like I don't know where to look'.

For their part, all the Americans I speak to get a bit huffy when I suggest they might not get some of the more recherché nuances in Turner's lyrics. 'Sure, I understand them,' says one female fan, who has travelled across the country, 'but I'm kind of an Anglophile. Mardy means pissed, right? I'd never heard of Frank Spencer, but I Googled his name, so now I know.'

'I don't think it's a big problem,' agrees Craig Marks, editor of *Blender*. 'It may be equivalent to a southern hip-hop record being understood in Sheffield. It would be a little bit of a challenge, but lyrics like "I think she looks good on the dancefloor" [sic] are not vague, they're not in cockney slang or anything. Alex's ability to tell relatable stories to teenagers is one of the strong points and unique qualities of the group.'

The crowd at the New York show, however, tells a slightly different story. It includes Liv Tyler and Amanda de Cadenet (''oose that?' asks a bewildered Cook when her name is mentioned), as well as a sizeable number of British ex-pats. But towards the back of Webster Hall, I find an intriguing split in comprehension. To my right are two men in their mid-20s so overwhelmed by the Arctic Monkeys experience that they seem to have gone native: they are not only word perfect in every song, but have cultivated both a Dick van Dyke-ish English accent for the purposes of singing along, and a slightly inscrutable chant that they deploy between songs: 'ENGLISH BOYS!' they yell. 'ENGLISH BOYS!' But to my left are a group of locals who spend the entire gig in a state of advanced befuddlement. 'WHAT DID HE SAY?' bellows one, as Turner thanks the audience for coming and informs them he's fond of New York. 'I NEED A TRANSLATOR!' I tell him what Turner just said. 'Awesome!' bellows the gig-goer, relaying the information to his friends, before turning back to me with his palm outstretched. 'High five!'

Quite aside from the possible need for subtitles, there may be another barrier to US success: the band's reputation for surly, difficult behaviour. The vast fanbase they gained through steady touring and fans sharing their songs on the Internet means they attained British success without compromising: they refused to appear on *Top of the Pops* and rarely give interviews. 'There's no commandments, no manifesto to what we turn down,' insists Nicholson. 'People ask us to do things and you think, "I'm going to feel reet stupid doing that," so you just say no.' He shakes his head. 'I'm amazed at what people will do to get their photo in a fucking magazine.'

One result of their reluctance to do press and appear on TV is that, 360,000 album sales on, a slightly intimidating air of mystery still surrounds the Arctic Monkeys. In lieu of hard facts, a variety of lurid rumours has gained currency. The most diverting suggests that, far from being the work of a keen-eared and preternaturally gifted 20-year-old, the Arctic Monkeys' lyrics about prostitution, recalcitrant girlfriends and taxi rank rucks are written by manager Barradale, formerly the frontman of dimly remembered indie rockers Seafruit. 'That's a good 'un,' says Nicholson, in a tone that suggests he doesn't think it's a particularly good 'un at all. 'Have you heard any of Geoff's songs?'

In fact, the band's members are noticeably less truculent in the flesh than advance publicity suggests. Turner is quiet and clearly deeply uncomfortable with being singled out for attention, but he is never less than scrupulously polite. Nicholson's face seems naturally to arrange itself into a look of profound disappointment – something about him makes you think of Bobby, the perennially disenchanted son in *King of the Hill* – but in person he is charm itself, possessed of a bone-dry wit. Helders and Cook, meanwhile, are an absolute hoot, which seems at odds with their relentlessly pessimistic interviews in which they are much given to predicting imminent disaster for their careers. 'Every silver lining has a cloud,' says Helders when the dictaphone is pointed in his direction. 'Our history teacher, Mr Staunton, always used to say that. There's a downside to everything.'

If the kind of intransigence that has become their trademark seems odd back home, it is unheard of in America, where bands are expected as a matter of course willingly to press the corporate flesh and smile their way through interviews with gormless DJs. 'There's no way around it,' says Craig Marks, of *Blender* magazine. 'Over here, if you want to sell a lot of records, you have to go to local radio stations in Dayton, Ohio, and shake the hands of men with satin jackets.' There seems little chance of the Arctic Monkeys doing that in the foreseeable future.

Today, they are due to appear on MTV, where they will be filmed performing live and then interviewed. They don't seem exactly overjoyed by the prospect – 'Check this shit out,' mutters a rigidly unimpressed Turner as they arrive at the studio. The interview passes with all the zip and good humour of an agonising death after the Arctic Monkeys refuse to introduce themselves to camera. 'It's our company policy that we don't introduce ourselves,' says Nicholson, flatly. Initially, at least, the only one who seems willing to answer any questions is Helders, whose idiosyncratic approach to designer freebies is once more much in evidence – the top part of his head is almost entirely obscured by a vast pair of sunglasses – and whose answers invariably involve bands no one in America has ever heard of, and who lies: 'I like East 17, me. They were a reet underground dance act in Britain.' The interviewer's smile never slips, but when she attempts to direct an inquiry about the band's influences to Turner, he stares at the floor and his answer tails off first into monosyllables, then into indistinct noises, then into silence: 'I dunno, really. Songs are more influenced . . . by different events . . . than . . . artists . . . I . . . don't . . . huh . . . hmm . . .' Things pick up marginally when Nicholson, apropros of nothing, tells her that he used to be a champion tapdancer, 'then I pulled me 'amstring and it were all over'. It's difficult to tell if she pursues this line of inquiry because she believes him, or simply because she's relieved that someone is talking about something other than East 17, but she asks about his dancing partner. 'Me partner's dancing with someone else now,' says Nicholson, his expression even more mournful than usual. 'I don't like to talk about it.'

While MTV's interviewer heads off to have her smile removed by a crack team of surgeons, the Arctic Monkeys tour bus drives to

Philadelphia and a seedy ballroom in what is self-evidently the least salubrious area of town. Backstage, Turner wearily ruminates on his night with Manhattan's glitterati at the Spotted Pig. 'It were weird. They seem strange people, like. A bit glazed. All sat on a table with everybody staring at them. If they just stood around with everyone else, nobody would be looking at them, would they? I feel in them situations almost like. . .' He sighs. 'Not an imposter, but do you know what I mean? I like to be in normal situations, me. I just want to be in the same atmosphere as everyone else.'

Outside, the venue is heaving. As in New York, there are British ex-pats waving St George flags, word-perfect wannabe Yorkshire-men and a healthy sprinkling of bewildered frowns. The Arctic Monkeys sound fantastic – taut, explosive and exciting. Turner tries to talk to the crowd, but he's drowned out by cheering and chanting. 'You're not even listening to me, are you?' he complains. ''Ow rude.' They play a new song called 'No Buses', and he ends the gig jumping into the audience, still playing his guitar.

Afterwards, his mood seems to have lifted. 'There's worse things you can do in life,' he says. 'I keep forgetting that. You only think about things within what you're doing, so there's always bad things about it. But if you put it on the grand scale of things, you think, "Oh, shurrup you dickhead, there's worse things to moan about than that. You've got the opportunity to write songs for a living."' His eyes shine, and for a moment Alex Turner seems neither weary nor jaded nor rigidly unimpressed. 'You're proper fucking blessed.'

3 November 2007

BETTER THE DENIM YOU KNOW

Simon Hattenstone

Francis Rossi and Rick Parfitt walk into the green room, looking ashen. The eternal rockers have just won £50,000 for charity on *Who Wants to Be a Millionaire?* but you wouldn't know it.

Rossi: 'I lost weight there, I tell you. I can't believe it. Chess as the opening question.'

Parfitt: 'I had no idea – I've never played chess in my life.'

Rossi is embarrassed. How many knights on a chessboard was the first question. He answered two. Wrong, they faced the ignominy of leaving with nothing. And that's when fate, or some kindly producer, intervened. Apparently this question had been asked before, so they had to scrap it and start again. Second time round, the boys did rather well.

'It was the most nervous I've ever been,' Parfitt says. He's in his 59th year, his hair still golden-blond, lush and long. He is dressed in black, wears shades in the studio, a diamond earring, a watch that P Diddy would die for, bangles galore, every inch the rock star. He and his new wife (his third) are off to Spain, where they now live. Rossi isn't as stylish – thin, grey rat-tail trailing down his collar, leather jacket, white socks. He still lives in Purley. He says he's never been fashionable.

The same could be said of the band. But their history is remarkable – more than 100 million records sold, 65 hit singles, and one of the most recognisable sounds of the 20th century. Only the Rolling Stones and the Who can match them for longevity. But whereas those two have always been cool, Status Quo came to be regarded, somewhat unfairly, as kitsch and a little bit rubbish.

They have been blamed for most of rock's ills – the rise of the denim waistcoat, air guitars, 'Rockin' All Over the World' as a sporting anthem. And they've been ridiculed regularly – for suing Radio 1 when the station refused to play their singles, for writing the same song again and again, for starting the tradition of men dancing with their thumbs in their pockets while swaying like willows. Yet they rocked as hard as the best of them, and lived harder than most. After the drinking years, and the cocaine years, and Parfitt's quadruple heart bypass, it's incredible they're still here, let alone preparing for another European tour.

I was 10 when I got into the Quo. I was ill and confined to my bed, and thought they were about as cool as cool got, until Roy Wood and Wizzard came along. I bought three of their albums in quick succession – *Piledriver*, *Hello!* and *Quo*. I loved the fact that their one-word titles had as much conviction as their heads-down, no-nonsense, mindless boogie. Most of the songs had only a handful of words ('Get down deeper and down/Down down deeper and down/Down down deeper and down/Get down deeper and down') and I loved that, too, because it made them easy to sing.

The Quo have always prided themselves on being a band best experienced live and thunderously loud. Rather than touring to promote their albums, they release an album to promote their tour. The new record is called *In Search of the Fourth Chord* – a wink to the notion that they know only three chords. When I tell Rossi about my old Quo collection, he nods and says, yes, they are regarded as the classics. 'If you actually sit down and listen to them, there are some great moments, but there's a lot of shite, too.' He has never had pretensions.

I've not been an active Quo fan since the 1970s, but I have admired them from afar and with metaphorical earplugs in. How does a band keep going for 40-plus years? Where do they find the energy and will to perform night after night in different cities all around the globe? Doesn't constant touring screw up their lives and drive them mad? Or maybe it's the other way round – the constant touring is a manifestation of their madness. I'm going on the road with them to try to find out.

A week later we meet at 7 a.m. at the GMTV studios. The whole band is here to perform their single, 'Beginning of the End'. Aside from Rossi and Parfitt, the other three members are relative newcomers. Keyboard player/guitarist Andy Bown says, 'For the first 20 years I used to say I was the new boy.' He has been in the band 31 years now. Bassist John 'Rhino' Edwards replaced original member Alan Lancaster 20 years ago, and has settled in nicely. The band have been through a few drummers – Matt Letley is still feeling his way after only seven years.

Everybody is looking for Rossi and Parfitt. Lyane Ngan, the band's PA and wardrobe dresser, reckons they've sneaked off for a fag. The boys are always sneaking off for fags. They return just in time, slightly giddy, hammily blowing smoke away from their mouths. Their manager, Simon Porter, is handing out copies of the new album.

I can't stop singing 'Rockin' All Over the World'. Lyane hears me. 'You're a closet fan!' she says. I think it's an accusation.

Was she a fan when she joined them? 'Oh, no!' The band regard Lyane as their sixth member. She's always with them on tour. While waiting to perform on TV, they are discussing crosswords. Rossi and Rhino are disappointed with the *Guardian*'s Saturday crossword – not big enough. Parfitt and Rossi spend most of the interview talking about how much they stank in the old days – they'd come off stage soaking, screw their clothes into a ball and wear them the next day.

We head off for breakfast at a greasy café in London's West End. Two eggs on toast, sunny side up, for the boys. Occasionally people stop them for autographs. It's hard to miss Rossi and Parfitt with their hairdos.

They met when they were 16 at holiday camp where they were performing – Rossi with the Spectres, who later became Status Quo, and Parfitt with the Highlights. 'People thought Rick was a bit flash, which he is. And a lot of people thought he was gay – a lot of that is that cabaret part of showbusiness when you've got to camp it up. He's definitely not gay. I like camp people, I like gay people, they don't seem to have the hang-ups of the rest of us.'

They became friends, but Parfitt didn't join the band until they recorded 'Pictures of Matchstick Men'. It hit the charts in the UK and US, and it's still their only American hit. He started playing guitar at 10. His parents would take him to the working men's club in Woking every weekend. His mum played the piano well, his dad played the comb badly. 'Dad would always say, "Are you going to put your guitar in the boot?" and I'd say, "Noooooah, I don't want to," and he'd say, "You don't have to play it, just put it in the boot anyway." Of course, in those days everybody got up and did a turn. So I'd end up on stage.' He won a number of talent competitions at Butlins, usually singing 'Baby Face'. Was he really good? 'No, not really good. I was a bit of a novelty – this 11-year-old kid playing a guitar that was bigger than him. I've still got the certificate – Butlins junior talent competition winner, 1960.' Both Rossi and Parfitt left school without qualifications. Rossi was expelled on his last day, to his bemusement.

Rossi idolised Little Richard. 'I think that's where we got the energy. To me it's synonymous with doing rock 'n' roll. If you don't commit physically, rock 'n' roll doesn't really work.' Rossi's father, who was second generation Italian, owned an ice-cream company, but they weren't as rich as his friends imagined. He often heard his dad arguing with his mum about the need to budget better. At school, he was a smartarse. 'I was sat in a class, probably 11 to 12 years old, and they'd already moved me to the front because I had my feet on the desk, and my French teacher said, "You're going to be a pop star?" And I said, "Yeah", and she said, "Well, if you're going to tour, and you go to France, you'll have to speak French", and I said, "No, because I'll have somebody to do it for me." I was dead right about that, but wrong about not learning the language. I've now realised I have quite a thirst for knowledge and particularly language.' He's teaching himself Italian.

Both his parents are dead now. He misses his dad hugely, especially his food. 'Some of the food he made. God! Italian. My favourite is *pasta e fagioli*, pasta with beans, soupie thing, gorgeous. The older I get, the more I'm into food.' Has it taken over from drugs and alcohol? 'When you grow up with Italians, food is important. I've always been like that with food. Apart from when I was doing cocaine – there was no food whatsoever then.'

Radio 1 is celebrating its 40th birthday and Quo have been asked to record a message. 'Happy birthday, Radio 1,' Rossi says. 'You're almost as old as us.'

'You can sing happy birthday if you want,' the producer says.

'You'd rather we didn't . . . You are awful . . . but I like you,' he answers in his best Dick Emery voice.

'Thanks for your support, you've been great,' Parfitt says.

But things haven't always been great with Radio 1. When Quo sued the station after it ruled that the band were too old hat for airplay, they lost and it cost them an estimated £500,000. Was it a good move? 'In hindsight, probably not,' Parfitt says, 'because we were accused of attention-seeking. But it wasn't like that at all. We had to get it off our chests because it was really annoying us.'

At the Beeb today, Rossi and Parfitt record slot after slot. They play a pop quiz with Ken Bruce, discuss Parfitt's blue, red, brown and gold pixie boots with Mark Radcliffe, and for another show are asked about their heroes over the past 40 years. Parfitt names sportsmen Michael Johnson, Colin Jackson, Jonathan Edwards and Carl Lewis. 'Johnson is possibly the greatest 400m runner of all time. The beautiful thing is that he always wore gold running shoes. He never expected to come second, did he?' Rossi names Jeff Lynne, legendary producer and founder of ELO.

They skive off to the loo for a sneaky fag, and return grinning. As we leave the BBC, an elderly man with a distinguished voice calls out, 'Can you stop for one old fan?' It's the DJ David Jacobs, now in his 80s, the first man to play Quo on the radio in 1968.

'Still here, you? It's lovely – great that you're still doing it,' Parfitt says.

'I've done my ankle in. I'm limping along like the old man I try not to be,' Jacobs says.

'It doesn't show on radio,' Parfitt says.

'No.'

'Lovely to see you.'

'Lovely to see you, too.'

'Incredible,' Parfitt says. 'What a legend, David Jacobs. Fantastic! He is the David Jacobs! That's made my day, that has.'

Parfitt's got a lovely, sunny disposition. He's a firm believer in karma, and says that after plenty of rough times he's never been happier. His daughter drowned in a swimming pool at home when she was two, and he has said he considered killing himself at the time. In 1997 he had tests for chest pains. As he was leaving hospital, he was hauled back in. 'They told me that if I didn't have a quadruple bypass I could be dead in 24 hours.' A few years ago, he had a throat cancer scare – the nodules were removed and turned out to be benign. Since then he has been trying to stop smoking (he is down to 10 a day from 50–60), and living more sensibly.

He got married for the third time last year – just two months after meeting Lindsay, a businesswoman in her late forties. Was she a fan? 'No. She had no idea who I was. She thought Status Quo had ceased many years ago.' He shows off the diamond earring and two-euro bangle she bought for him. 'Apart from being beautiful, she's very nice. It's nice to have a woman on your arm that you know you can take anywhere – no matter what the company is. She's brilliant.'

Rossi and Parfitt are almost as well known for their sexual exploits as for the drugs. I ask Parfitt if he's been in love many times. 'No, never. Not like this, anyway.' Did his other wives know? 'No, I don't think so. I always felt there was something missing, but I was never sure what it was. Now I know. When it does hit you, it's an unbelievable feeling.' When he goes on the road, he's going to take Lindsay with him, he says. 'We didn't get married not to be together. Life on the road takes its toll – it's a crime, really, to a marriage. It's asking a lot of any wife or partner to endure half their life alone.'

Rossi roughly divides up the decades. In the 1960s, their management convinced them that psychedelia was the way ahead, so they wore their gaudy colours and had a hit with the haunting 'Pictures of Matchstick Men'. They looked trendy and individual, but Rossi says it was a manufactured individuality. All the time, they just wanted to get down and rock. In the 1970s they did just that – they turned faded denim into a uniform, grew their hair even longer and found heavy-guitar heaven. They had a series of huge hits, many of which sounded the same as the last one. Rossi loved the early Seventies, but after that it was drink and drugs. In the Eighties, they split up for a year. Rossi argued with co-founder Alan Lancaster ('He wanted to be really macho and it's not ma thang'), regrouped and opened Band Aid with 'Rockin' All Over the World'.

'Rockin' All Over the World', a cover of a John Fogerty song, somehow defined them. Perhaps it was too ubiquitous for their own good. It became shorthand for naff, stadium rock – fans of every football team that reached a cup final would rock all over the world. That's when it became really unfashionable to like the Quo. In the 1990s, the Quo discovered a new sensitivity and attempted to reinvent themselves. It didn't work. Now, as they approach their pension, they have gone back to their roots. Some of the songs on the new album are co-written by their former roadie, Bob Young, who with Rossi wrote many of the classics, such as 'Caroline' and 'Paper Plane'.

We're in Lille, France, at a venue holding 1,600 on the third floor of a shopping centre. Road manager Dave Salt has transformed the place into Quo HQ – Quo catering down the corridor, Quo Internet café, Quo relaxing room, Quo sleeping room. They travel heavy with three huge coaches: one for the band, two for the crew. There are Quo signposts on all the walls, so nobody gets lost. Salt is ferociously organised, despite having to hobble from room to room – he's twisted his knee, which is in a brace.

In the room next door, Parfitt is dressed in a white towel and rock 'n' roll medallions, and blow-drying his hair, which seems to stretch halfway across the room. He waves the hairdryer at me. 'Hello, love.' That would make a great photo, I say. 'No, I'm too fat.' He's also crocked, and feeling sorry for himself. He stumbled last night and has a nasty bruise along his instep. Everything is beginning to hurt. Lindsay isn't here, and he's missing her. The days are long and boring, and he occupies himself with talking to his family on Skype, talking to himself in his made-up language and telling jokes. He'll be halfway through a story before you realise he's simply building up to a punchline.

We're talking about the days of excess. 'God, yeah,' he says. 'They were wild. I once went to one of those, you know, dressing-up parties and I went with a naked girl on me back. And the host said, "What have you come as, Rick?" And I said, "A tortoise." "A tortoise," he said, "but you've got a naked girl on your back?" 'Yeah, that's Mi-chelle."'

Actually, he says, he was horrible back then. He spent £3,000 a week on cocaine. 'Through the late seventies and all through the eighties I was a bit of an ogre. I fell into the sex, drugs, rock 'n' roll big time, and Richard, my eldest son, saw me at my worst. It was a big shock for him and he deserted me. I don't blame him 'cos I was just not with it, I wasn't here.'

What was he like? 'I was a maniac, just mad and wacky.' Violent? 'No, I don't think so much violent as just out of it most of the time. Coke makes you talk complete bollocks, you link up with people who want you for who you are rather than what you are, and because you've got the coke. Richard drinks socially, but he's never touched any drugs in his life because he saw what it did to me, so in one way it was positive.

'Richard has described me as turning into a Mr Hyde. He said, you just became a different person, and it was almost like being out of a movie where you'd wake up and all the facial hair had gone and the claws had been drawn back, and you wake up and you're this normal person for a very short space of time until you decide to drink the potion again. For three or four years he didn't talk to me, and he came back to me at about 14. Wisely his mother kept him away from me. In fact, it made Richard quite ill.' He had bad nerves? 'Yeah. He was frightened of me.'

Richard is 32, in his own band, and the two are close. 'We have a lovely relationship now.'

Rossi is in the relaxing room, boiling over with frustration. There's one clue left on the *Times* crossword and he can't get it. 'Forceful, intense. Blank e blank e blank e blank t. Forceful? Fuck it.'

Give me the clue again, I say.

'Same fucking clue, it won't help, will it?'

He spends the days listening to music, reading, doing crosswords, exercising and sleeping. He practises two hours a day on his guitar, often just going up and down the scales, playing jazz, keeping his fingers nimble. Despite the image, he is an accomplished musician. Does the three-chord taunting bother him? 'Anybody who knows anything about music knows that we know five chords. It's not three, it's five. And what you can't do with five chords ain't worth doing, really. It's always been based round the old 12-bar boogie shuffle rhythm that Chuck Berry started off. I guess in the Eighties it annoyed me a bit.'

There are two high points to his day – eating and playing. Quo travel with their own catering team and twice a day they turn the latest crappy kitchen space in the latest crappy venue into an upmarket restaurant. Three courses, four options for the main. 'Ravioli this evening, ah!' He sticks his fist in his mouth and chews on it. 'Forceful, intense. Blank e blank e blank e blank t. I do crosswords all the time, that's how I learned English. I had no education.'

Can we cheat?

'No.'

At home, he can happily go months without seeing people or leaving the house. When he's in the mood, he talks 60 to the dozen – there is nothing he doesn't have an opinion on.

I'm on the phone to my partner, and she gets the clue. 'Vehement,' I shout at Rossi. He doesn't look pleased. 'Vehe. . . you cow. I hate you,' he shouts into the phone.

Late afternoon, and Parfitt's off on one of his surreal riffs. 'I've got to get a haircut. What does that mean? It should be I've got to get my hairs cut. Hello, can I have my hairs cut? That's what it should be.' He's bored.

Early evening, and the boys are even more bored. 'It's the worst, waiting to go on, the last hour. If it was cancelled now I'd be elated,' Parfitt says. 'As soon as the lights go down and the drone starts, that's when it gets good. That's when we start cavorting. We talk about food constantly on stage. . . it's always about food.'

Have the fans got older? 'Yeah, they've got older. And younger. It's anything from eight to 80. Some nights it's like a crèche down the front. It gets to 10.30 and we're halfway through "Down Down", about 860 decibels, and there are seven to eight kids asleep in the pit. Just asleep. Gone.'

Actually, one beautiful little boy on the front row looks younger. He's wearing mufflers and leaning against his dad. A couple of rows back are an English couple who have been given the tickets as a 40th anniversary present from their children.

8.50 p.m., and Toot the road manager gives the 10-minute warning. 'Still bored,' Parfitt says. Then the five-minute warning. 'That's your last piss, like your mum tells you before you go out.'

Two minutes. And they're on. The lights go down, the dry ice swirls, Rossi stands with his back to the stage, Parfitt is coiled, his guitar slung low at groin level. I'm to the side of the stage. He give me a thumbs up. And they're straight into 'Caroline'.

It is unbelievably loud and tight, with elements of pantomime thrown in. 'This is one from years ago,' Rossi says. 'Well, they're all from years ago.' On the song 'Gerdundula', they play four guitars in two sets of pairs – each pair does the fretwork of the other guitar while strumming his own. It's quite a feat, and surprisingly tuneful.

I've become proprietorial about the Quo and want the crowd to love every song. I hear the insistent chug of an old hit, get excited because I recognise it, and invariably find it's actually a different song. Come on the Quo! Come on you medallion-clad, white-trainered, axe-wielding heroes.

At the end, they come off exhilarated. There are Marlboro Lights and wine waiting for them. 'Feel this,' Parfitt says. His shirt is soaked. The crew are waiting with dressing gowns and head towels, the shirts are whipped off and within seconds they look like post-fight boxers heading off into the night for the next city.

Rosenheim, in Bavaria, Germany. The hotel next to the venue is inundated with Quo fans. Bettina Mueller, 42, has come from Austria, and has been a fan for 27 years. 'The madness started when I was 15 and I was on an exchange in Bournemouth. There I bought a single of "Caroline", and that was it.'

'Status Quo is a life philosophy for me,' Bernd Reinhardt says, 'a positive way of looking at life.' The fans look different now – smarter, the denim less distressed, the hair shorter. Some even wear cords.

The boys have just done eight gigs in nine nights and they're knackered. Parfitt is picking up more injuries by the day and is feeling sorry for himself. 'I'm a bit of a wounded soldier. My bad leg has put my back out which has put my neck out. And I've got toothache and my left arm's numb.' Then there's the tinnitus – a ringing in his ear alleviated only when he can hear the crickets back home in Spain. 'I'm not getting any younger, and to put in this massive effort every night, it does get to you. We used to say,

"When we get to 40 we'll have to slow down." Here we are 20 years on and we still haven't slowed down, but I do feel it much, much, much more these days. We've had 90 shows this year, which is well over 100 nights away. So next year I'd like to spend some time at home and relax – maybe do around 60 shows.'

He cheers himself up by telling me a new joke. It's an unusual Parfitt joke – it's funny. 'The other day I discovered my dog was a locksmith,' he says. How come? 'I stuck a poker up his arse and he made a bolt for the door.' He's still obsessing with language, and its correct usage. 'You know how we say we'd like a cup of tea? Well, it's not a cup of tea, is it? It's a cup with tea in it.' This thesis has evolved into a whole Quo language which involves breaking down words by their syllables and adding 'with it' or 'with them' in between. 'It's immature, I know, but it amuses us. It's a load of boll with ox in them.'

He plays me the Christmas single he's just written. It sounds a bit like Wizzard's 'I Wish It Could Be Christmas Every Day'. 'Sweet, isn't it? I always thought we should do a Christmas record. I wrote it in Spain with my mate Wayne.' He thinks about it and he's off. 'And lucky enough it didn't rain so it wasn't a pain, 'cos that would have driven us insane.'

Everyone's raving about the supper tonight. I choose the halibut fillet with scallops, dauphinoise potatoes, veg melange and pesto tapenade. Lovely. Afterwards I sit down with 'the other three'. Drummer Matt Letley says he joined the band because Rhino the bassist told him to. What was he doing beforehand? 'A bit of ironing.' Rhino – who tells me within seconds of our meeting that his son is studying philosophy at Cambridge – won a scholarship to the Royal College of Music to play violin at 11. What does he like about being in the Quo? 'They don't sound like anybody else. There's never been a band more aptly named than Status Quo. Changes are few and far between. I'm still pretty close with Rick, I'd say. Francis is quite an enigma. He's a nice man, but he's an enigma. You don't ever really know what he thinks about you. Francis doesn't go out. He's a very private man. He's got his own circle of friends and he chooses not to involve me with them, but that's all right with me.'

Does it bother him that, after 20 years, he's just one of the other three? 'Well, it's the brand. The brand is Francis and Rick.' Is that annoying? 'I don't give a flying fuck. When we're on stage, and that's the only time you're in the now in the whole day, there's five of us. Francis might do all the talking and the guitar solos, I don't give a toss because it wouldn't work otherwise.'

Rhino is a man of strong opinions. He thinks the Quo have cheapened themselves recently with stunts. To coincide with the new album, a competition was run in the *Daily Mirror* to win gold pendants. 'It's born out of necessity, I suppose. If people aren't playing your records, you've got to get it out there one way or another.'

Andy Bown joined in 1976. That must have been when they were off their heads? He smiles. 'Oh yeah.' Was he as bad as the others? 'I didn't go to their extremes. I'm a great believer in everything in moderation but, yes, I did introduce the band to a selection of controlled substances, yeah.' So he's responsible for Rossi's damaged nostrils? 'No, he's responsible for that. Never use a crappy dealer.' Can he see the band retiring? 'I just don't know any more. When I joined, Francis said, I reckon we've got three or four more years left.'

Rossi has already completed today's crosswords. He offers me some of his beetroot, ginger and celery juice. He likes to keep fit these days. Is it true he can thread a cotton bud through his nose? 'You wanna see it, do ya?' He winces, as he inserts the bud. It looks horrible. 'I've got to show it to some kid that we know has started doing coke. I said, "Bring him over because if we don't put him off, he's fucked."'

Parfitt and Rossi are chatting, and I'm looking at the back of their heads. Even from behind, you'd know it's them. What's amazing about their relationship is not simply that they have stayed together so long, but that they have such a deep love for each other. Parfitt talks about his three marriages and 'one long-term partnership with him', which has outlasted them all. Do they ever argue? 'Not really fall out,' Parfitt says. 'We just go quiet on each other. Something happens and we don't talk to each other for a few days, then it's gone.'

'Once we fell out,' Rossi says. 'He threw a towel at me and I threw it back at him. Seriously, if either of us got to the point where we hit each other, neither of us would come back from that. If we hit each other, it's finished. Simple.'

Rossi has eight children from three different partners, and is now a grandad. Is it the need to support the kids that keeps him going? 'Partly. I need the money, I've got a lot of kids in education. We were ripped off a lot of years ago, so we're nowhere near as rich as people think. Plus there's something in me that needs to do it; that insecurity to show off in all of us. I think of those people who have integrity in terms of music, or like to think they have, but they still have to go and do it. Two people who come to mind are the grumpy old Irish fella, Van Morrison, the grumpiest fucker in the business, and Sting – he was a teacher, an intellectual. Now what does he go on stage for, love of music? I don't think so. It's just 'cos we want to show off. If you just love music, you'd stay at home, study music, make it for yourself. There's something in us that wants to go and stand in front of people so they can tell us we're good.'

Even now, he says, he's trying to prove himself in some way he doesn't quite understand. 'It's like this carrot's been hanging there for fucking years and I just can't reach it, whatever I do, and I keep thinking I'll get there, and it will all be all right . . . Maybe it's that my parents aren't here to say, "Good boy, you've done well." I have this thing that I'm gonna get there, then I can rest when I'm older. But I'm 58 now . . . 58, fuckin' hell. Come on, isn't that too much? Then Uncle Keith and Uncle Mick are still doing it, so I feel a bit better.'

Has he ever cut off his ponytail? 'Nah. I'm thinking about it because I think it looks stupid now. Whether I will or not is another matter because I suppose that vanity thing . . .'

8.50 p.m., and 10 minutes to go. Five minutes. Two minutes. The hall is packed. The lights go down, the dry ice swirls, 5,000 hands are raised, and those chugging guitars build towards a familiar intensity. Parfitt and Rossi grin at each other, contented.

ROC
& R

B-SIDES AND RARITIES

23 October 1969

REVERSE CHARGE DIALOGUES WITH A BEATLE BY PROXY

Victor Keegan

Rumours that Paul McCartney is dead, which have pushed the Beatles back to the top of the charts in America, are only part of a new surge of Beatlemania which is sweeping across the United States. I know because, unfortunately, my telephone has proved an all too accurate barometer of the Beatles' popularity in the United States.

Hundreds of people have rung my number day and night from America, where it has a magical significance, asking to speak to characters associated with Beatles songs. This has built up to a crescendo in recent days.

'Hallo, can I speak to Sergeant J. Pepper?' says a typical voice, courteous, charming – and with the charges reversed. For months I bravely lost nervous energy in an attempt to discover the secret of why all America wanted to ring me. Late at night I would awake as if in the midst of a nightmare and reach shakingly for the telephone to hear: 'I have a collect call for Mr Billy Shears from Chicago, Illinois. Will you accept?'

No calls were accepted, but as they grew more numerous and the American operators more intrigued (I am almost on Christian name terms with some of them), it turned out that I was being rung because of rumours that if you rang a magic number concealed on the sleeve of the *Magical Mystery Tour* album you would be able to hear the Beatles, be translated to mysterious romantic lands, and various other refinements. The resurgence of Beatlemania in the States is now taking teenagers on a magical mystery tour, courtesy of Bell Telephone, which ends iconoclastically at my telephone number.

A girl from California, who did not transfer the charges (she will have to learn the hard way), said she discovered me through gazing at the word Beatles, written in stars on the album sleeve, reversing the image in the mirror, and then reading backwards. If you screw your eyes up a bit, and let your imagination roam after a few scotches, you can just about squeeze my number, 834 7132, out of it. And if you do not believe this, hundreds of teenagers and others have done just that.

Most of the callers ask for Billy (or Mr William) Shears, who appears on the Beatles' Sgt Pepper LP, though why they ask for him especially I have never discovered. Others ask for Mr Kite, Mr Henderson ('the Hendersons will all be there'), Ivor Cutler, George Martin, Derek Taylor and other less familiar names.

John Lennon, Paul McCartney and George Harrison are frequently asked for, but never Ringo . . . Now that's the stuff real rumours are made of.

The nightly dialogue is conducted with callers in Chicago, New York, California, Florida and a host of other States. Over the past few days, as rumours of Paul's death (denied categorically by Apple in London) have mounted, the telephone would have been ringing almost continuously if it were not off the hook.

Most people want to hear that Paul is alive (asking through the operator) and once I confirm that, they refuse to believe that they have come through to the wrong number. One caller asked if Paul was alive and then added: 'Can you give me any information about the R and D mortuary?'

Yesterday, before leaving for work, I put the telephone back on the hook and it rang almost immediately. A voice with a Southern drawl said: 'Hallo, sir, this is John K. Roberts, Radio Corporation of Florida. Can you tell me and my listeners if Paul McCartney is alive?' And so on and so on.

My favourite was Jane from Milwaukee, whom I shall miss dearly. She had tried the combination 834 7132 on all American exchanges. She told me: 'I was sitting by the fire puzzling the quiz out, when I suddenly realised that the number must be in England.' She cooled noticeably towards me when I confessed I was not a Beatle, but for a moment or two I knew what idolatry was.

In spite of months of questioning I have been unable to trace the origin of the mythology of my telephone number. Most people seem to think it was started by some local radio station and then spread like a forest fire. The only common link of the calls is the consistent use of Beatles song language ('Is it true Paul died Wednesday morning at five o'clock?')

Most callers sound perfectly self-confident, not to say a little 'high', and quite unapologetic about ringing up on a transferred charges basis in the middle of the night. On the rare occasions I have been able to question them about how they came to look for a telephone number on the album, they merely say: 'Oh, I got it from a friend of mine.'

Yesterday my magical mystery tour ended. With a feeling of relief, tinged only slightly with regret, I finally decided to get my number changed, severing in one blow a transatlantic link that has been with me on and off for many months. I rang the operators' supervisor expecting some sympathy for my disturbed nights. Instead she appeared to be thrilled to the bone. 'That's marvellous,' she said. 'You should be able to sell that story to the newspapers for a fortune.'

Alas, the unknown penalties of being a newspaper reporter.

25 November 1994

SUCKED IN AND SOLD OUT

Bob Stanley

My parents ritually humiliate me with the story of how, as a toddler, I'd twist two shoe-polish tins round and round, make musical noises, and pretend I had my own reel-to-reel tape recorder. Pop has been an obsession of mine for as long as I can remember; yes, music was my first love and it will be my last.

To appear on *Top of the Pops* was a dream on a par with playing for England at Wembley. In the same way that *Van Der Valk* seemed an 'important' programme because my parents watched it, it was on late and there were no jokes in it, appearing on *Top of the Pops* always seemed very important.

As I turned teenage, and was drawn into British post-punk by Joy Division and Postcard records, what became 'important' was to stay independent, keep your style and dignity, and not to sell out to the major labels. Yes, I fought the war against rockism with John Peel and Pete Wylie. And yes, I embraced the 'new pop' of the early Eighties, totally thrilled by the sights of pop subversives like Dexys Midnight Runners, the Human League and the Teardrop Explodes on *Top of the Pops*. The Clash never meant a thing to me because their refusal ever to appear on the show revealed an immense lack of style.

So the stage was set, and when, more by luck than judgement, I ended up making a record at the start of 1990, my dreams and dogmatic principles were firmly intact. Saint Etienne would stay fiercely independent – never would we walk that rockist road of major labels, encores and hippy festivals. Little did I know.

Illusion number one was smashed to smithereens on our first tour of Japan. At this point we played 40-minute sets, the length of an LP – anything longer was self-indulgence. The set in Osaka seemed to have gone down very well. After we'd been backstage, slapping our backs constantly for 10 minutes, I thought I'd venture out into the crowd and meet the dozens of autograph hunters who would doubtless be waiting for us. For some reason, the crowd was still facing the stage. A confused fan asked me when the second set was going to start. Errrm, that was it, I explained helpfully.

It turned out that the Brand New Heavies had played for three hours (gulp) the week before, and that was what the crowd expected from us. Worse yet, the tickets had been the equivalent of £30, which we'd put down to the Japanese cost of living. We later discovered that tickets for Michael Jackson's show cost £35. Quite inadvertently, we had become capitalist scum.

We had sneeringly met a major label representative when our first single was out as a white label and picking up a lot of club plays. A lardy chap from Polydor took us to a West End bar where the Walker Brothers' 'The Sun Ain't Gonna Shine Any More' was playing on the jukebox. 'They were fucking great, the Righteous Brothers,' said Lardboy. 'Look, I'm putting my cards on the table,' he semi-whispered. 'I'll give you a £5,000 advance if you sign to Polydor.'

Our jaws dropped. The cheek of the man. 'I can tell you're shocked. I know it's a lot of money, but I think you boys are worth it.' After a year living on principles and salt and pepper sandwiches, we signed to a major label for everywhere excluding Britain, where we stayed equally principled and poor independent, Heavenly.

The main reason for the deal was an A&R man (no names, no law suits) who had an endless supply of yarns about when he worked for the Stones in '64, how he'd been chased around his kitchen in '66 by a knife-wielding Marianne Faithfull, that sort of thing. The fact that he had photos of beefeaters and royalty on his office wall didn't bother me at the time. I trusted this man's judgement implicitly, and signed my life away. Within seconds he was trying to coax our singer, Sarah Cracknell, away for a solo deal. My last shred of respect for the man disappeared when, for his birthday treat, he made his (vegetarian) assistant dress up in a pair of ill-fitting, ultra-skimpy hot pants, before sitting her at the dinner table and forcing her to eat a sausage in a suggestive manner.

Saint Etienne never said no to charity work until we were asked to play for handicapped children at Chessington World of Adventures. We turned up, poked our heads into the tent where we were going to play, and the place was mobbed with 1,500 berserk kids watching a clown show. When the clowns had done their bit, Judith Chalmers went on and said, 'Now we have Saint Etienne, here's their singer, Sarah . . .' In the three minutes or so that Jude and Sarah were chatting, the tent emptied at an incredible rate. We played to the 50 poor souls who were wheelchair-bound and unable to escape.

I often wonder how I'd think of Saint Etienne if I was still just a pop fan. I like to think that I wouldn't be too hard on us. Even though we do put records out on a major label, play encores, do Glastonbury, and everything else I used to despise. I guess I've sold my soul for rock 'n' roll.

21 September 2001

A TALE OF TWO DISC JOCKEYS

Dave Haslam

Dave Cotrill is a DJ. Every few months he goes to a function room upstairs in a pub on the edge of Manchester city centre, down the wide streets behind Piccadilly station, under one of the iron bridges, well away from the bustle of the city's club and bar hot spots on Canal Street, Oldham Street and Oxford Road. He goes where there are few cars, no taxi ranks, no gangs of drinkers swaying down the pavement, to a pub on the corner of Fairfield Street called the Star & Garter. The main door is always locked, so he goes in the side entrance. When he walks in, there are four or five customers congregated around the bar downstairs, sipping pints. This is unregenerated Manchester, untouched by the digital, global, corporate world; there's no stripped pine, no chrome, no theme, no menu, no cloakroom, no Chardonnay, no champagne.

He goes upstairs to a room that's available for hire. It's 9.30 p.m. The decks have been set up on a trestle table on the stage. He clambers up on to the stage with his records. It's a one-man operation: he hires the room, does all the publicity and plays all the records. He has with him three boxes of records – not the swish metallic record boxes festooned with logos and airline stickers that the top-notch DJs would have someone carry for them, just plastic crates, which he carries himself. His crates are full of records by the Smiths, and the records the Smiths singer Morrissey has made during his subsequent solo career. Tonight, as usual, Dave will be hosting a Smiths/Morrissey night, a one-man disco dedicated to the man who infamously called on his listeners to Hang the DJ.

Dave also carries with him a slide projector and a bedsheet which he hangs at the back of the stage. He dusts down the in-house DJ equipment, turns on the power and checks the leads are plugged in. The Star & Garter's DJ equipment consists of two old-fashioned Citronic decks built into a crumbling black console with a mixer. The mixer has no crossfader, and the decks, needless to say, have no pitch control and no slipmats. There's a 20p piece glued on top of each stylus, weighing the needle down to prevent the records jumping. The set-up is state of the art 1978.

Dave has been running the Smiths/Morrissey disco since 1994. It takes place every few months. It's the only DJ job he's ever had; nobody has come down to one of his nights and headhunted him, snapped him up to do a festival or a gig somewhere else, although occasionally he has branched out and run a Smiths/Morrissey disco in London. The last one at the Liquid Lounge in King's Cross was OK, but not as good as the Manchester nights.

The Star & Garter doesn't have queues. When I get there I worry, not just because there's no queue, but because there are also no doormen, and at first, I'm not sure I've come on the right evening. At the bottom of the stairs there's a middle-aged lady in a purple anorak collecting the entrance money. It's £2 before 10.30 p.m. I pay and go upstairs. I can hear 'I Started Something I Couldn't Finish' as I walk through the door into the room, which is already half full. The hall holds maybe 200 people, with Dave, his records, and his slides on the stage to the left, chairs and tables to the right, and a bar in a room off to one side. There's no VIP bar (naturally; there are no VIPs). Somebody gives me a leaflet advertising the sale of a West Ham Boys Club T-shirt; apparently Morrissey wore a similar shirt on his last tour in Britain. I ask the T-shirt salesman if it's the same design as Morrissey's. 'No, but as near as I could get it,' he replies. There's a fruit machine, but it's been turned off.

Tonight, pints of Stella in plastic pint pots are £1.30. I could probably buy a round for everyone in the room for the same price as drinks for four in Ten, or China, or some other London bar. I don't, although half an hour later I get Jane a pint of cider. She's celebrating her 26th birthday.

Jane has been coming to the Smiths/Morrissey disco for five years. She's on Dave's mailing list, so she gets advance warning of when the events are going to take place (every couple of months, always on a Friday, and a special every year on the Friday that falls nearest to Morrissey's birthday). Dave has more than 100 people on his mailing list, and most of them are in the room already.

I look for somewhere to sit. There's no room around any of the tables, but there's a bench running along the side wall next to the dancefloor with a couple of spaces available. It turns out that this is where the true devotees sit. I'm next to Bill from Wigan. He's in his late 20s and he, too, is on Dave's mailing list. Something has gone wrong recently, though, and he hasn't been sent any information about tonight, but he ended up here anyway.

He was on a night out in Wigan with his mates, but they went looking for some decent music. They ended up in Warrington (why Warrington? 'Don't ask,' he says). Eventually Bill and his friends found themselves in Manchester, at the Thirsty Scholar. I didn't even know it was still open, I tell him. While they were there he picked up a flyer advertising tonight's Morrissey disco, so they came straight over.

Talking to Bill is difficult, and not just because the bench is near the speakers. Morrissey fans know all the words to all the songs and throughout the evening, they sing them raucously. As we sit chatting on the bench, Bill will suddenly start singing, so about one out of every four things he says are lines from Smiths songs. I choose what to respond to as it's clear he doesn't expect a reply every time. Dave plays 'Girl Afraid'. Bill gets up to dance, and I go and talk to Dave.

At home, Dave listens to Scott Walker, David Bowie, Prince, some old soul and French pop from the 1960s like Françoise Hardy. He's very disciplined about what he plays at the discos, though. Probably a good 95 per cent of the records he plays are songs sung by Morrissey, 3 per cent are by other groups, and the remaining 2 per cent are Smiths instrumentals. He has a clipboard on the table next to the decks on which he writes down the names of the songs. 'I sometimes forget what I've played,' he says, 'and I never like to play anything twice in a night.'

At the beginning he knew most of the audience, and they became friends and regulars, but he's been doing this for seven years and a lot of the original audience has drifted away. Now he doesn't know many of the crowd, although just as he tells me this a couple of lads come into the room and wave to him.

So how does he know what to play?

'There are certain things that I know are going to be popular.'

Like anything with Morrissey singing on it?

'Yes.'

There are a surprising number of younger people there. No toddlers, of course, but 18- and 19-year-olds, which strikes me as a bit odd considering that it was 1986 or 1987 when the Smiths were at their height. Somehow the Morrissey cult is still strong enough to renew itself with fresh-faced new disciples. According to Dave, it is the more recent converts who are the most devoted and eager. They're the ones totally consumed by Morrissey: 'The younger ones are definitely the ones most likely to want to hear just Morrissey and the Smiths – and the ones who have quiffs. The ones into them originally wouldn't have quiffs.'

I ask Dave if these older Smiths fans are broadminded enough to want to hear some house or garage or something. 'I don't know,' he says, 'I mean, I don't know what all those different dance things are called, but some of the older ones I speak to used to go to the Haçienda.'

The Haçienda nightclub seems like a long time ago and a long way away. Here, at the Star & Garter, there are photocopied A4 posters stuck up with Sellotape on the blackwashed walls advertising punk nights. Also on the wall is an advert for next week's Manic Street Mania, a night of records by the Manic Street Preachers, also £2 before 10.30 p.m., but not organised by Dave. He tells me that other people have hired the Star & Garter for tribute nights. There was one night that featured records by James. There was also a Belle & Sebastian night and, predictably, some of Belle & Sebastian actually came to it.

Many of the gathering crowd at the Star & Garter are wearing genuine antique Smiths T-shirts, while others have come dressed in plain T-shirts, with scribbled tributes to Moz daubed in indelible black pen on them. The prevailing colours of the clothes are black and dark denim. Many of the girls are wearing skirts with flower prints, and some of them are dressed like Miss Havisham: gothic, I suppose, wearing long black dresses, clumpy shoes, widow's weeds. They dance in groups, rather than couples, or singly. There's one couple dressed in Gap light khaki combat trousers and canvas trainers sitting at a table about ten yards from me. They are clearly in the wrong club.

Dave plays 'Golden Lights' by Twinkle – a song that the Smiths once covered – but the dancefloor clears. Jane comes over to sit next to me. She arrived here on her own. After about four or five Smiths songs, Dave plays something by James. 'He never plays much else besides Morrissey and the Smiths, does he?' I say to Jane.

'No, not really, but he'll throw in the odd weird one.'

Like James?

'Yeah, or the Fall.'

What about Motown?

'No.'

A bit of disco or some funk, say by the Fatback Band?

'No,' she says, 'you won't get any disco music here.'

We change the subject. She admits to me that her job is about as inappropriate as you can get for a Morrissey fan: she works in a McDonald's. Tomorrow she has a day off. When she asked her boss, the man had said, 'Why, is it another Smiths night?'

'Come back in two months,' she says to me, 'and it'll all be the same.'

Dave then plays the acoustic Sandie Shaw version of 'Jeane' and five people get back on to the dancefloor – a group of four girls and a boy, tall, with black floppy hair and adidas trainers; he look like Alex James before he met Keith Allen. The girls are smiling and doing a skippy dance but he's just standing there on his own, gently rocking and touching and hugging himself. It's a bit creepy. I go to the bar to get Jane a drink.

I have to bring the drink back across the dancefloor, which has filled now, to the strains of 'How Soon Is Now?' (sample lyric: 'I go home and I cry and I want to die'). Everybody is singing along. Even the Gap couple are dancing, singing the words to each other; it turns out they're Smiths fans after all. Then Dave plays 'Still Ill', and suddenly Bill weaves his way across the dancefloor to me. 'Does the body rule the mind or does the mind rule the body?' he asks me. 'I don't know,' I reply.

For the throng, dancing is a sideways swivel of the hips; their feet are everywhere and nowhere. Many of them twirl invisible gladioli above their heads. They dance with their hand on their hips, but primarily with their voices. When Dave plays 'Everyday Is Like Sunday' the dancefloor fills and the crowd roars the chorus. I nearly spill my pint on to Jane's lap.

Jane says that when the night started it used to be full of Morrissey lookalikes. Back then, she remembers, 'All the boys looked like him and everyone brought flowers.'

Did they?

'Yeah, I brought daffodils.'

And then what happened?

'I grew up.' She laughs.

I'm still amazed at how young the crowd is. I must be one of the few people in the room old enough to have seen the Smiths play. Jane never saw them, although she has seen Morrissey during his solo career. The last time she was a bit disappointed, not by him but by the crowd: 'There were all these students there, who must have been into Morrissey for like a year or something.'

I ask her what she thinks would happen if Morrissey walked in now.

'Well, we'd all jump on him.'

A few minutes later I'm back bothering Dave as he tries to cue the next record up through his headphones. I ask him if Morrissey or any of the other members of the Smiths knows that the night exists?

'I don't know.'

What would happen if Johnny Marr came in?

'I don't think people would leave him alone. I think they'd ask him questions.'

What, like 'Why did you split the Smiths up?'

'Er, no. I don't think they'd ask that.'

Would you ask him to sign your records?

'I don't really bother with things like that.'

As we talk, a few dancers come over to the stage and ask Dave to play certain tracks. It's all very polite. There's no one asking, 'Have you got anything good?'; nobody is giving Dave any sort of a hard time. He's giving them what they want. Do any of the audience get aggressive when they ask for records?

'You can get one or two but that's usually because they're drunk, really.'

Does he ever get any shady characters down here?

'Um, once or twice we have had some shady people in, but I don't think they were here selling drugs.'

So, what happened; did these shady people start fighting?

'No, they just stood there and then they left. We never have fights. Sometimes it gets a bit rowdy and if somebody has had too much to drink, they might start acting daft and pushing people on the dancefloor, but nobody would start fighting.'

Does anyone ask to hear something a bit different?

'No, they never want anything else, although somebody asked me once for Dinosaur Jr. But they didn't get aggressive.'

He waits for the record to finish so he can put another one on, and then he tells me about his proper job. He works for a company that helps find work for people in places like Salford and Bootle. His employers know that he moonlights as a DJ: 'I have told them, yes, but I don't know what they think.'

Does he think their image of a DJ is somebody living a very glamorous lifestyle?

'No, I don't think they think what I do is very glamorous.'

I take a quick look round the Star & Garter dancefloor. They would kind of be right, wouldn't they, Dave?

Dave has played a few floor fillers but now he's playing one of the more miserable dirges from Morrissey's back catalogue, and the dancefloor has thinned out again. Dave is DJing in a totally different way to the way Seb Fontaine does it at Cream, or Steve Lawler does on the Space terrace on a sunny Sunday in Ibiza. If I were behind the decks, I'd be looking to build the atmosphere, peak it, hold it there, take it down again, bring it up, climax, encore. But Dave's set isn't like that at all; it seems like he's just throwing the records on one after another. There's no underlying thread, no sense of programming or progression. But this is a different world.

I ask him if he ever hangs out with other DJs. 'I don't know any other DJs,' he tells me. So if Paul van Dyk walked in now Dave wouldn't recognise him? 'No. Paul van Dyk? No, I've never heard of him.'

Dave isn't on that loop – clubs, promo records. He's not interested in going to Cream, Fabric or Gatecrasher. He's happy doing his own night: 'I used to go to indie clubs, but not any more. The last club I went to was the Venue because it was all bottles 50 pence but it smelled of sick and everybody was about 14.'

The gaps between records are getting longer. He's like a jukebox, full of the audience's favourite tunes, with somebody pressing random buttons. But then why should he follow the disco rules? He's entirely matching the audience's expectation, after all. If he started some nifty cross-fading, he'd probably be booed off. He's not even standing up; he's sitting behind the decks, only getting to his feet to change the slides. Next up; a picture of Viv Nicholson.

Morrissey doesn't like dance music, does he?

'I don't really know. I don't believe anything he says in interviews because he always seems to contradict himself.'

He's never said he likes dance music though, has he? He's still up for burning down the disco and hanging the DJ as far as we know.

'Yes, but I don't know if he means it literally.'

Do you think he would burn down this disco?

'I've no idea.' Dave is getting wise to me. 'I don't know if his limousine would find the Star & Garter,' he says.

Dave has been a fan of Morrissey since 1988, just after the Smiths split up. The first record he heard by Morrissey was 'Suedehead'. Of course, 1988 was the year of acid house, an episode stubbornly resisted by Morrissey. 'I could never begin to explain the utter loathing I feel for dance music,' he said.

It's gone midnight now, and there won't be many more people coming to the Smiths/Morrissey disco. Those that are here will stay until 2 a.m. I ask Dave if he pays his mother wages for taking entrance money: 'Yeah, I do, but, I mean, she'd probably do it for free. I've never made much money, but then I'm never out of pocket.'

Have you ever had a big night, loads of people in and it's been bonanza time?

'No.'

I ask him to put me on the mailing list. I tell him I'll be back, and I do go back. The next time was Morrissey's birthday. Somewhere in Los Angeles, where he now lives, Morrissey was probably out with friends, but 200 of his most dedicated followers were in an upstairs room at the Star & Garter. Unfortunately there was no screen on the birthday night because some faulty wiring on Dave's slide projector blew the fuse when he plugged it in. The Star & Garter was full, but there were no birthday balloons. No cake. No candles. No disco biscuits. Just the way they like it.

29 March 2003

ROCK BREAKS

Bill Borrows

Whatever you do, don't mention the F-word. Or the K-word for that matter. Fish and Kayleigh are, of course, synonymous with the band in the minds of the general public, but to mention either to any of the devoted fans attending the Marillion Weekend at Butlins in Minehead (yes, you read that correctly) will instantly 'out' you as a fully functioning member of society.

'Look, that is just such a cliché,' explains Steve from Leatherhead. 'All you people ever go on about is Fish and Kayleigh, there is so much more to Marillion than that. Fish left Marillion in September 1988. That's almost 15 years ago.'

'What do you mean by "all you people"?' I ask. 'The press?' 'No, all of you. All the rest of you.' 'The great mass of humanity?' 'Yes, basically. Everybody who isn't here.'

Steve was, it has to be said, inebriated. Less than a minute after delivering his impassioned speech and bringing our conversation to an abrupt end, he missed the automatic door and walked straight into a pane of strengthened glass, spun round to see if I was still looking and threw his hands in the air in a gesture of frustration and despair before stumbling straight into a family of five who were attempting to enter the Butlins Skyline Hall, the focal point of the whole camp. 'Wanker,' shouted the father as Steve ploughed on in a speed walk that was neither a mince nor a jog.

It was an extremely rare example of interaction between two groups of people who had been voluntarily shoehorned into the confines of a holiday camp in Somerset and recognised each other as members of the same species, but only in a visceral sense.

One group sauntered around the complex in the regulation working class uniform of jeans, baseball caps, hooded tops, leggings and trainers. The other ambled about in Marillion-branded fleeces, peculiar trousers with more than a hint of the harlequin, walking boots and a variety of T-shirts that embraced every tour the band had undertaken since Ronald Reagan was last in the White House but also suggested a certain loyalty to Ozric Tentacles, Rainbow, Megadeth and several IT companies. Think of the Royle Family on holiday at a Bill Bailey convention.

Steve Rothery, guitarist with the band since 1979, agreed that it was one of the more surreal locations the band had performed. 'When two worlds collide,' he ventured, backstage on the morning of the third day. 'It is surreal,' he added. '[The inspiration for the event] came from the Stranglers who did a similar thing at Pontins,' explains Mark Kelly, who joined the band as keyboard player in 1981. 'We did Pontins last year but this time it has been incredible.'

There is no denying that. The weekend at Minehead (with a 2,200 capacity and 600 more than the previous year) was sold out weeks ago at prices between £130 and £160 per person, and fans from 26 countries including Brazil, Canada, Indonesia, Mexico, Norway and Poland were in attendance.

A group of five German die-hards, all wearing black and orange tour jackets, had never been to England before. 'Why are you here?' 'Marillion, they are the best.' 'And what do you make of it all?' 'The weekend is brilliant.' 'Do you like England? Or what you've seen of it . . .' 'Yes, of course, but we can't believe people stay in these . . . camps.' Hmmm.

For the fanatic, the weekend has everything: the band play three times ('From 9.30 p.m. – whenever they stop!'); there are signing sessions which snake out of Jumpin' Jaks nightclub, past the bouncy slide and almost up to the Harry Ramsden's concession and take about three hours to navigate (nobody gets their bosoms signed but a woman asks if she can slap Mark Kelly's bald head and, having received an answer in the affirmative, does so); there's a pub quiz (sample question: 'Which Fish-era songs reference Chaucer?'); a question and answer session with the band and, of course, a chance for certain members of the audience to get up on stage and perform a favourite song with their favourite band.

Darren Newitt, an architect, dares to play Kayleigh and gets a fantastic reception from the crowd but perhaps it's different if you are on the inside. It's a middle-class, Manson family type thing. Even the PR woman is a fan – a very rare thing, let me assure you.

The Friday night concert was filmed and ready to buy on DVD on the Sunday afternoon (a world record, apparently). They sold 1,700 copies at the site and the merchandising alone took almost £70,000.

A young Butlins employee from Birmingham, manning a stall at the venue which was trying to get rid of the kind of flashing neon necklaces and bracelets you might expect to find for sale on a rug in the streets of Paris, confessed, 'It's mental. We normally get tribute bands but it's rammed tonight. Who are all these people?' 'They are Marillion fans.' Blank look. 'Tell me you've heard of the band at least.' 'Never heard of them, mate. Who are they?' 'How old are you?' 'Twenty.' 'I'm sorry, forget we ever met.'

On the second night the venue is even more packed and rocks to the extent that the floor actually starts to move up and down. This is not a journalistic device, it is an architectural point of order.

The hall is on the second floor and, as Mark Kelly avers, 'I was actually becoming quite concerned. From the stage it looked like the audience was disappearing two feet and then coming back up. You could see these heads and then you couldn't and then they reappeared.'

'I thought we were all going to fall into the disco downstairs,' laughs Rothery the next day. It was an alarming experience in so many ways, not the least of it being that I actually enjoyed it. There you go, I've put it in print. Let's just draw a discreet veil over that and move on.

There were people who looked like the owner of the comic store in *The Simpsons* everywhere, singing to themselves and dancing like someone trying to locate small change in a snowdrift.

Meanwhile, as the least physically prepossessing band in the world communed with their constituency, there was a hen party from Wales downstairs which amounted to 36 women from the valleys impersonating WPCs, but for the addition of fishnet stockings and the number 69 on their epaulettes. There was also a stag party from the south-east of England, with men dressed as Batman and the gorilla from *Trading Places*. Obviously.

In the Swinging Shillelagh Irish theme pub a young man from Mansfield asked, 'What are all the smellies doing here?' before his girlfriend interjected, 'And when did you last have a shower?'

The Marillion audience could not be drawn on their fellow campers beyond the occasional, 'What do you think they think of us?' 'Really weird' would be the standard response.

On marillion.com Mark Kelly lists his favourite things as 'magic tricks, fossil hunting, brass rubbing, Snickers, unicycling, juggling'. Rothery prefers 'nuclear fusion, gadgets, car numbers, *Star Trek*, chocolate chip cheesecake and plectrum tiddlywinks'.

While self-consciously ironic, not one of these pastimes seems to be available for any of the people who are sleeping on the mandatory plastic incontinence sheets at Butlins. But then I don't think the Marillion fans are really there for the crazy golf, five-a-side football pitches or the smash-a-plate stall.

'There's a guy who came from Australia last year,' says Kelly, 'and he sold his drum kit to get here. He's come again [this year] and he reckons he sold his house this time. Another bloke told me that if it wasn't for the band he would have nothing in his life.' 'And what did you say?' 'What *do* you say?' Is it too late to say I'm sorry? Perhaps.

23 March 2007

HAIL, HAIL, ROCK 'N' ROLL

Laura Barton

I watched one of my friends fall for the Hold Steady recently. It was as if his heart just gave way and he tumbled, without grace or finesse, but with delight. I knew he'd got it bad because he'd email me their lyrics and sing their riffs as we walked to lunch. 'I guess you're old enough to know,' he wrote one afternoon, quoting his new love apropos of very little, 'certain songs they get scratched into our souls.'

It can be difficult, sometimes, to discern whether you simply have a crush on a band or if you really love them; whether their songs have merely got whipped up in the spring weather and the scent of fresh earth and sent you giddy. Some bands you inherit, of course – Van Morrison and Leonard Cohen, Dion and the Belmonts, Duke Ellington, music that soaked into me from my parents' stereo, as syrup into a sponge. I love their records the same way I love my parents: unquestioningly and unerringly, as if they shaped my musical features, the way my parents made my mouth, my nose, my eyes.

Then there have been the bands I found myself, bands that have changed my life: Pixies, the Velvet Underground, the White Stripes, the Mountain Goats. I remember the first time I heard the Pixies: in my best friend's lilac-painted bedroom, on her black twin tape deck, her long freckled fingers pressed rewind and play. There they sat, in the three and a half minutes between Bauhaus and the Dead Kennedys, on a compilation made by her older brother. My heart just stopped. The way traffic does, with a screeching of brakes, and a pause.

You love a band like this forever. Years later, you will still have pangs for all the things you did together. All those Friday nights on the back seat of the bus to town, with a bottle of Buckfast, my best friend and I, trying to howl like Frank Black. The hours the Velvet Underground and I laboured over my art homework together, me with my hands shiny with 4B pencil, Lou Reed weary from singing 'Heroin' for the 16th time that day. The days the White Stripes walked me through the streets of London, serenading me with 'Hello Operator', 'Astro', 'Suzy Lee'. Their new blues and the city spread out before me, succulent and ripe.

Musical crushes only placate you, they merely tell you what you want to hear, in a voice you've heard before. Bands you love seem to answer a question you didn't even know you were asking. They seem necessary in your life. And you feel like Black Francis did when he sang: 'But hey/Where/Have you/Been if you go I will surely die/We're chained.'

I'm half in love with Elvis Perkins just now; I've been playing his album on rotation, working my way through song by song, slowly testing their strength. Because liking a new band is like climbing a tree: you place your weight on each branch with trepidation, in case it cannot carry you; you try to discern if it is a sapling love or a true, oakish thing.

My mother always told me that she knew she loved my father when she just didn't want to be without him, and that's pretty much how I feel about the bands I love, they have taken hold in me. It's as if all the time you have been up in the lofty branches, their roots have been spreading down in the very ground of you.

The last time I truly fell for a band it was for the Mountain Goats. Two summers ago, I played *The Sunset Tree*, and found songs that seemed both familiar and surprising, as if I had turned over a stone in my own garden and discovered all kinds of wiggly creatures living under there.

There's one song in particular, 'Pale Green Things', that got scratched into the soul of me, a song of seaweed and Indiana sawgrass, death, wet leaves and horses in the paddock. It's a song, too, that makes me think of how it is to feel that love for a band rising up new inside of you: 'Coming up through the cracks' it goes, 'Pale green things/Pale green things.'

15 June 2007

SGT PEPPER MUST DIE!

Paul Lester

Ever get the feeling you've been cheated? It's meant to be a classic album, but all you can hear is a load of boring tripe . . . we've all felt that way. And so have the musicians we asked to nominate the supposedly great records they'd gladly never hear again.

Tupac Shakur, *All Eyez On Me*
Nominated by Mark Ronson, producer
This was Tupac's biggest record, and is seen by rap fans as the greatest latterday hip-hop album. But I've never got the cult of Tupac. Sure, he was in a lot of pain but he never said anything particularly clever – Notorious BIG. was far superior. People really related to the emotion in his voice, but it didn't resonate with me. No one would doubt Tupac's 'realness' – he was shot nine times, for God's sake, and he began recording this album hours after being released from prison – but it doesn't compare to Biggie. Dr Dre produced it, and I didn't rate his production, either.

Problem was, Tupac was so prolific. He would write fifty songs in a weekend. Maybe he knew he was going to die, so he recorded relentlessly. I bought it at the time because it had one song on it that I'd play in clubs, but one out of 20 isn't great. In fact, there are 27 tracks on it – it started the trend of putting loads of songs on rap albums. Tupac wasn't up there with Dylan – Dylan was a brilliant poet. Eminem is probably the Dylan of rap, whereas Tupac just sounded like he was whining.

Nirvana, *Nevermind*
Nominated by Wayne Coyne of the Flaming Lips
It's better to be overrated than underrated. Besides, it's not the musicians' fault *Nevermind* is overrated – it's the public's, or the critics'. But you don't find yourself ever longing to listen to it, because there were – still are, in fact – so many mediocre bands that sound like it, that you're constantly experiencing it. I never

get out *Nevermind* and think: what great production, what great songs. *Nevermind* had a poisonous, pernicious influence. It legitimised suffering. The sainthood of Kurt Cobain overshadows the album: Kurt's lyrics, his attitudinising and navel-gazing, were hard to separate from the band's image. You can never just hear the record. For me, *Bleach* and *In Utero* are superior. Even the album cover seems cheap: that stupid dollar bill just seems to have been airbrushed in there. If Alice in Chains had done it, we'd have thought it was a joke, but because it was Nirvana we thought it was oh-so-clever. If you think you're going to hear an utterly original, powerful and freaky record when you put on *Nevermind*, as a young kid might, Christ you're going to be disappointed. You're going to think, 'Who is this band that sounds just like Nickelback? What are these drug addicts going on about?'

The Beach Boys, *Pet Sounds*
Nominated by Luke Pritchard of the Kooks
Of all the albums that get written about as 'classics', this one least deserves it. Having said that, it contains one of the greatest songs ever written: 'God Only Knows', which is melancholic yet uplifting, pure yet fucked-up. But the rest of the record is a total let down – I felt that way from the very first listen. *Pet Sounds* is a million miles away from *Sgt Pepper* or *Dark Side of the Moon*. I do appreciate the lyrics, and I know it's an album about getting older, but as a concept album, it doesn't quite add up. Good tunes, yes – 'Wouldn't It Be Nice' is a great pop song – but most of the other tracks just don't resonate for me. I apologise unreservedly to everyone who loves every word and note, every last crackle, on this album, but that's how it is. Oh, and it's got the worst sleeve of any major album, ever. Feeding time at the zoo? I don't think so.

The Stone Roses, *The Stone Roses*
Nominated by Eddie Argos of Art Brut
They're totally overrated. Plus they covered 'Scarborough Fair'. I don't understand why people still play their music in nightclubs – it makes me really angry. When I'm drunk in a club I usually end up arguing with the DJ who's playing them. The Stone Roses were

an awful, awful band. They were uncharismatic, their lyrics are nonsensical and their music is dreary. Also, we have them to thank for Oasis, although at least Noel Gallagher is funny and Liam is a bit of a pop star. The Roses make me think of kids older than me swaggering around with bowl haircuts and affecting Manchester accents. It makes my skin crawl. And all their fans are so smug: 'Oh, you don't understand it.' I do understand it! It's ridiculous that it regularly gets voted in at the top of those 'greatest British album ever' polls. They spawned a new thug-boy pop culture.

The Strokes, *Is This It*
Nominated by Ian Williams of Battles
The Strokes were just rich kids from uptown New York; the children of the heads of supermodel agencies who formed a rock band and thought they deserved respect because of that. Suddenly the downtown, older form of punk rock got co-opted by the system. If ever there was a point where Gucci and rebellion were married together, it was right there. The Strokes have, basically, been responsible for five or six years of a new form of hair metal, in the guise of something more tasteful. Their music is post-9/11 party music because it came out that week and everybody wanted to dance. They're seen as the rebirth of rock in the UK – but it's a very conservative, old-fashioned idea of rock for the 21st century. As for their punk credentials, I'm not going to say anyone's more authentic than anyone else . . . But the Strokes are the new Duran Duran; the new decadence for the new millennium.

Television, *Marquee Moon*
Nominated by Alex Kapranos of Franz Ferdinand
People expect us to love Television the way they think we love Gang of Four and were influenced by them – but we don't and we weren't! *Marquee Moon* is one of those records that I thought I loved, but it was only after a few years I realised I didn't love the album, just the first ten bars of the title track, which are pretty astonishing. Those guitars that play off each other and the way the instruments go into wonderful places and the guitars are

totally insane and that big cascade of drums – it's incredible. Then your attention wanders. You know when a boring guy is explaining to you the technical spec of a car, the fuel injection system and the leather seats, and his voice becomes so much background noise? Once I took the needle off this record, I realised I hadn't heard it at all.

But what annoys me is the way people pontificate over the album; it's one of those staples of student halls of residence. People wax lyrical about it, but the reason it's so popular is because it's a prog rock album it's okay to like. Because the words 'punk' and 'New York' and '1977' are associated with it, it's deemed cool. Really, though, they're a band who give guys who like 20-minute guitar solos an excuse. They were the Grateful Dead of punk, and I always hated all that jam-band stuff. They have the ethos of a jam-band but the aesthetic of a New York outfit. If anything, the Strokes took the look of Television, the aesthetic – and the Converse sneakers – and ignored the jam-band aspect. They took those first 10 bars of 'Marquee Moon' and did something great with it! Tom Verlaine's lyrics didn't have much impact on me. I'm always uneasy when singers in bands profess to be poets – they can veer into pomposity and pretentiousness. But I've got to be careful: I once said something about Jim Morrison and the Doors, about their pseudo-poetry, and immediately all these articles on the Internet appeared saying, 'Kapranos slams Morrison!' I'm not slamming Television – I respect them. But *Marquee Moon* is an album I admire more than enjoy.

The Beatles, *Sgt Pepper's Lonely Hearts Club Band*
Nominated by Billy Childish, prime mover of British garage rock
I was a big Beatles fan – I had a Beatles wig and Beatles guitar when I was four – so I know what I'm talking about, but Sgt Pepper signalled the death of rock 'n' roll. Rock 'n' roll is meant to be full of vitality and energy, and this album isn't. It sounds like it took six months to shit out. The Beatles were the victims of their success. This is middle-of-the-road rock music for plumbers. Or people who drive round in Citroens – the sort of corporate hippies who ruined rock music. I bought it the day it came out: it was

ideal for a seven-year-old. These days, well, it's my contention that it represents the death of the Beatles as a rock 'n' roll band and the birth of them as music hall, which is hardly a victory.

The main problem with Sgt Pepper is Sir Paul's maudlin obsession with his own self-importance and Dickensian misery. (Paul McCartney is the dark one in the Beatles, not John Lennon, because he writes such depressing, scary music.) It's like a Sunday before school that goes on forever. It's too dark and twisted for anyone with any light in their life. Then again, when he tries to be upbeat, it rings false – like having a clown in the room. The best thing about the album was the cardboard insert with some medals, a badge and a moustache. But the military jackets they wore on the front made them look like a bunch of grammar-school boys dressed by their mummy. When I was in Thee Mighty Caesars we did a rip-off of the sleeve for an album called *John Lennon's Corpse Revisited*, featuring the Beatles' heads on stakes. This isn't the greatest album ever made; in fact, it's the worst Beatles album up to that point. *Live at the Star Club* trounces it with ease.

Abba, *Arrival*

Nominated by Siobhan Donaghy, former Sugababe turned solo artist

I love the Beatles, the Beach Boys, Burt Bacharach, all those great pop melody-writers, but there's something about Abba that I hate. Maybe it's going to parties with shit DJs for most of my childhood that has made me hate them. Abba were forced on people from my generation, so there's a natural resentment towards them. Through my mum I discovered Pink Floyd and Jimi Hendrix, and if I'd done that with Abba maybe I'd have appreciated their brilliant pop songs. On *Arrival*, the particularly annoying songs are 'Dancing Queen', 'Knowing, Me Knowing You' and 'Money, Money, Money'. And if we're talking about the reissue, you can add 'Fernando'. Nick Hornby may well say they're part of the canon now, but I still don't have to listen to them. Yes, they wrote some of the catchiest melodies of all time. But then, 'The Birdie Song' is catchy, too.

Arcade Fire, *The Neon Bible*
Nominated by Green Gartside of Scritti Politti
People who enjoy this album may think I'm cloth-eared and unperceptive, and I accept it's the result of my personal shortcomings, but what I hear in Arcade Fire is an agglomeration of mannerisms, clichés and devices. I find it solidly unattractive, texturally nasty, a bit harmonically and melodically dull, bombastic and melodramatic, and the rhythms are pedestrian. It's monotonous in its textures and in the old-fashioned, nasty, clunky Eighties rhythms and eighth-note basslines. It isn't, as people are suggesting, richly rewarding and inventive. The melodies stick too closely to the chord changes. Win Butler's voice uses certain stylistic devices: it goes wobbly and shouty, then whispery – and I guess people like wobbly and shouty going to whispery; they think it signifies real feeling. It's some people's idea of unmediated emotion. I can imagine Jeremy Clarkson liking it; it's for people in cars. It's rather flat and unlovely. The album and the response to it represent a bunch of beliefs about expression and truth that I don't share. The battle against unreconstructed rock music continues.

Pink Floyd, *Dark Side of the Moon*
Nominated by Tjinder Singh of Cornershop
This album is a sort of lab experiment, put together by scarf-wearing university types. There's a certain irony in a song like 'Money' that takes pot-shots at greedy corporations, when this album made so much money. There's also irony in these super-wealthy elite prog musicians positing themselves against The Man, having a go at the machine. The light shows, all the technology and white-coated technicians at their disposal, make them very much part of the machine. I appreciated the early stuff Pink Floyd did with Joe Boyd, but this is a bloated concept album that made punk necessary. It says, 'What a crazy world it is!' and 'Everyone's demented!' It's meant to be imbued with the spirit of Syd Barrett, God rest his soul. I'm amazed that it's up there in the pantheon, because I can't see any virtue in it whatsoever. Lyrically, it's banal and doesn't say anything beyond 'greed is

bad'. Radiohead are the 21st-century Floyd, which says it all really.

The Doors, *LA Woman*

Nominated by Craig Finn of the Hold Steady

In America when you're growing up, you're subjected to the Doors as soon as you start going to parties and smoking weed. People think of Jim Morrison as a brilliant rock 'n' roll poet, but to me it's unlistenable. The music meanders, and Morrison was more like a drunk asshole than an intelligent poet. The worst of the worst is the last song, 'Riders on the Storm': 'There's a killer on the road/ His brain is squirming like a toad' – that's surely the worst line in rock 'n' roll history. He gave the green light to generations of pseuds. A lot of people told him he was a genius, so he started to believe it. The Velvets did nihilism and darkness so much better – they were so much more understated; what they did had subtlety, whereas the Doors had little or none: they were a caricature of 'the dark side'. I actually like Los Angeles, but the Doors represent the city at its most fat, bloated and excessive. Morrison's death does give rock some mythic kudos, but that doesn't make me want to listen to the music. In fact, if it comes on the radio, I change the station.

The Smiths, *Meat Is Murder*

Nominated by Jackie McKeown of 1990s

I'm a Smiths fan and I like most of their records, but this is the weakest link in the canon. With the debut and *The Queen Is Dead*, you could cut up Morrissey's lyrics and they could be pages from the same book. For *Meat Is Murder*, he seemed to make a list of topics to write about. It was a protest album, which defeats the idea of Morrissey as romantic. The cool-guy cover with *Meat Is Murder* written on his helmet rams it down your throat. The title track is offensive, not least because of the loud, gated drums and Eighties production that you get on Huey Lewis and the News records. Morrissey was obviously suffering from a loss of nerve or lack of faith when he wrote these songs. It took him years to write the first album in his bedroom. By the second album, he started panicking and pointing fingers at teachers at school and thinking up things like, 'Oh, meat is murder and, oh, we're going to get attacked by thugs in Rusholme.' 'Barbarism Begins at Home' is where the Smiths betray their jazz-funk session-guy roots; it's absolutely treacherous to listen to, even if it was brilliant fun to record. You can just see the rolled-up jacket sleeves. It's everything Morrissey hated. *Meat Is Murder* is Red Wedge music for sexless students. It's like being stuck in a lift with a Manchester University Socialist Workers' Party convention.

Captain Beefheart and the Magic Band, *Trout Mask Replica*
Nominated by Peter Hook, ex-New Order and Joy Division
Steve Morris, New Order's drummer, was a great fan of his, but Beefheart was one of those things I found unlistenably boring. I desperately wanted to like it because Steve loved it so much, but I had to admit defeat. Ian Curtis found it easier to convert us to the Doors, put it that way. *Trout Mask* wasn't a work of untutored genius, it was untutored crap. When you're beginning as a musician, people try to educate you with music like this, but I never understood the allure of Captain Beefheart. I certainly didn't last all four sides. There are very few records I gave up on, apart from Lou Reed's *Metal Machine Music* and *Trout Mask Replica*. It sounded like somebody taking the piss. But then, I've never been a great fan of jazz, and this erred on the selfish side of jazz. It sounds like you feel when you've taken the wrong drugs, like going to your mate's dope party on speed. I'd listen to it with my head in my hands. *Trout Mask* was highly regarded by post-punk bands because of its idiosyncratic approach to rhythm and song construction – but those bands were full of shit, weren't they? I wouldn't have put it at the front of my record pile to impress people; it would have been at the back with my Alvin Stardust and Bay City Rollers records that they sent me from the record club I belonged to at the time. These days, I would rather listen to the Bay City Rollers than Beefheart.

The Velvet Underground, *The Velvet Underground & Nico*
Nominated by novelist and music lover Ian Rankin
This is a sacred cow but that doesn't mean it can't be turned into hamburger. You can start before you even listen to the music. The front of the album bears the name Andy Warhol and a yellow banana – there's no mention of the band whatsoever. The back of the album says it was produced by Andy Warhol alongside the Velvets, so straight away I'm annoyed. It's one of the worst-produced albums of all time – put it on a modern hi-fi and you'll think: this sounds like shit. It's muddy, the volume comes and goes, the guitars are all out of tune, as is the viola. John Cale is one of the great Welshmen, but the viola on 'Venus in Furs' sounds like a Tom and Jerry sound effect. And Nico's voice is flat throughout – she sings English the way I sing German. Talk about looks being everything: she was a supermodel trying to sing in a rock band, but she couldn't sing – she gave good dirge.

It all flags up that the Velvet Underground were just part of Warhol's circus, his Factory; just another product. Once you start thinking about the Velvets being part of that, the notion of them waiting around for the man is ludicrous. As far as introducing the idea of nihilism to rock, the first Doors album, which came out the same year, was far better produced, far darker, and more nihilistic. Ditto the first Mothers of Invention album. Those two were from the west coast; the Velvets were from New York. And this was New York trying too hard. There's a line in 'Venus in Furs' about 'ermine furs adorn imperious'. Those are four words that should never appear in a rock song and here they are put together. And the last two tracks are completely unlistenable: 'The Black Angel's Death Song' and 'European Son', which constitute 11 minutes and one fifth of the album.

Nevertheless, as Brian Eno said, almost no one bought this album but the ones who did put a band together, so it was important – as the beginning of the black raincoat brigade.

11 May 2007

I WAS NO LONGER A LOSER

Craig Finn

People often ask me if there's a message in the band I front, the Hold Steady. I guess there is, and I guess it's the same one I learned more than 20 years ago when I heard a band who came from my hometown of Minneapolis, Minnesota.

October 1984 found me 13 years old and drudging away in the eighth grade at Valley View junior high school in Edina, Minnesota, a suburb just outside Minneapolis. Valley View was a terrible place, designed to let seventh, eighth and ninth graders sit and spin while they waited out puberty. The teachers were often the trophy-winning athletics coaches from the adjoining Edina senior high school, a sports powerhouse. Most classes began with the lights shutting off, followed by the hum of a film projector, and a movie that may or may not have anything to do with the ostensible subject of the class. In the hallway, the small and bespectacled of us moved hurriedly between classes, avoiding the eyes of the bullies and the jocks who seemed only to love two things in life: sadistic acts of terror and spitting.

I had shown up at Valley View for seventh grade thinking I was a normal kid, friends with everyone equally, as I had been in my grade school. Not the first to be picked for a baseball game, but also not the last, and certainly not an outcast. But over the summer, as if it had been decided in a forum I hadn't attended, I was deemed a 'loser'. That was a self-fulfilling prophecy. I retreated deeper into books. I became more timid. I spoke less. But I also started spending more time playing the guitar I had received as a gift for my 12th birthday, and started seeking out music. However, in the time before the internet, this was a different game. Rock 'n' roll, outside of classic rock radio, was but a whisper on the wind. Information came in the form of unreliable rumours, most often centred on what animal Ozzy Osbourne had defiled that week. Heavy metal all seemed quite silly to me, but I found a humour and excitement in the Ramones.

I dug their self-deprecation, their refusal to pander, and mostly their fast and samey music, which echoed the monotony of the suburbs. Like Woody Allen movies, there was something inherently New York about the Ramones, which caused a slight divide between them and a midwestern 13-year-old. However, there was something brewing closer to home.

Early in the summer before the eighth grade, a friend had hipped me to a band called the Replacements. Apparently his older sister knew the bass player, Tommy Stinson, who was just a few years older than us. He told me the band lived in nearby south Minneapolis, and was 'sort of like the Ramones'. I picked up their *Hootenanny* album. It was sloppy and fun rock 'n' roll, with wild lead guitars and a great sense of humour. The second song on the record, 'Run It', advised recklessness in the form of running red lights, naming south Minneapolis streets: 'Lyndale, Garfield, Run It!' It was a revelation that such excitement lived so close to me, just a few miles east, an easy bicycle or bus ride. I picked up their remaining records as quickly as I could. It took a 45-minute bus ride to south Minneapolis, to a shambling record store called Oar FolkJokeOpus (diagonally opposite from the CC Club, where the Replacements supposedly drank). But the journeys into the city were part of the excitement, and part of the folklore that existed around the band, both for real and in my head.

Back at school in September, I met a few other kids who were into the Replacements, if not at the same obsessional level as I was. They introduced me to other bands that you didn't hear on the radio stations: Hüsker Dü and Soul Asylum were the other big bands in the Minneapolis scene, but there were others – Otto's Chemical Lounge, Outcry, Rifle Sport.

From California, I discovered the punk bands of the SST label: Minutemen, Black Flag, the Descendents, and there were more from other parts of the country. The local bands were always the most exciting, though, because of the hometown connection (as with the Replacements, you'd often find a friend's older sister who knew them). I had never before considered that rock music could be made any place near the green idylls of Edina, and never would have expected there was an endless number of great bands playing every night within a few miles of home. Because of liquor laws and age restrictions, live rock 'n' roll was still mostly untouchable to us, but soon I started attending shows – the 'all-ages hardcore matinee shows' we sing about in the Hold Steady – at First Avenue, the legendary nightclub featured prominently in the movie *Purple Rain*, a building that still is the heart and home to my idea of rock 'n' roll.

Going to these shows, and going to uptown Minneapolis to buy records, was the highlight of the week. It made the abuse and dire boredom of my daily school life bearable, almost. I had become a poor student – nothing captured my attention like my records. After school I would retreat to my room, put them on the turntable and try to play along with my candy apple red Stratocaster copy that never sounded like it contained a millionth of the power of a Hüsker Dü record.

But if I wasn't succeeding at school, I had at least created an identity I could live with. I was no longer just a 'loser', I was a music fan. I spoke a language that set me apart from the other kids at school. I could talk about labels, EPs, the Athens music scene. There were even some girls our age that liked rock, although they mostly would tell you they only liked the Smiths. They would stand in line smoking cigarettes and sometimes smile at you. It was heartening, if still vaguely threatening. But it made me feel human in a way school rarely did.

October 1984 brought a change to my life, and also to Minneapolis. It was around this time that I started noticing the graffiti of the local street gangs the Gangster Disciples and the Vice Lords, our local chapters of the national Crips and Blood gangs. Within a year, they had murdered a high school girl in Martin Luther King park, and many years and many murders later, the *New York Times* dubbed my hometown 'Murderapolis'. Our city's biggest celeb, Prince, had finally become a megastar with *Purple Rain*. And the Replacements released *Let It Be*, which still stands as my favourite ever record.

Like most records, it arrived on a Tuesday, but I wasn't able to get to the store until Saturday. The anticipation was killing me. I didn't even know what the cover looked like. I convinced my father to drive me to the store, and he did me one better by buying the record for me. Even he could tell this one was 'important'. The cover art was a thing of beauty, the coolest known band in the universe just sitting on a roof, looking dishevelled and uninterested. I scanned the song titles: 'I Will Dare', 'Favorite Thing', 'We're Coming Out'. My father raised his eyebrows at the title 'Gary's Got a Boner' but still shelled out. The record store clerk was kind enough to turn down the volume and point to each of us: 'Cool dad. Cool kid,' he said. I am sure my father doesn't remember that, but I always will.

Of course, things eventually got better for me. They do for everyone, when greater confidence helps you overcome the awkwardness of early teendom. I eventually switched to a private school that was more kind to creative types. I got my first girlfriend. I started a band. Not in that order.

But still to this day when I hear *Let It Be*, and especially the songs 'Unsatisfied' and 'Sixteen Blue', it gives me a bit of the creeps. While lots of rock 'n' roll makes you think that your teens should be all about riding in a convertible with the top down, Paul Westerberg, the leader of the Replacements, is somehow magically able to capture the part of being teenage that is scary and embarrassing.

And when I hear it, I know what we're trying to do, too: let people know that everything is going to be OK. And when it isn't, rock 'n' roll can help.

13 June 2008

FOR THOSE ABOUT TO ROCK

Chris Salmon

From bringing on the marching band and the robots to curling up backstage in fear, top pop acts explain how to handle the biggest gig of your life: headlining a festival.

Treat it like a big deal

Alex Kapranos, Franz Ferdinand

Headlined Reading/Leeds (2006)

When we headlined Reading and Leeds, we definitely wanted it to be a bit of an event. We spent quite a while discussing the props and the stage decoration. We had this big sign and these abstract, Hannah Höch-inspired robots with lights for heads. I think you've got to put that extra bit of effort in for a headline slot. But the most important thing is that you give a fantastic performance. Some bands come out with that nonsense about, 'If we enjoy it, that's all that matters, if anybody else enjoys it, that's a bonus.' It's really not like that. You have to realise it's a big deal, because then the adrenaline courses through you in a way that stimulates you to give the right kind of performance. There's nothing worse than seeing a band going through the motions. Before shows like that, it feels like you're standing on the edge of the highest board in the swimming pool. You're crapping yourself. I suppose it's just difficult to comprehend playing to that many people. But when the first chords ring out, the rush is phenomenal.

Hire a marching band

Clint Boon, Inspiral Carpets

Headlined Reading (1990)

If anyone asks what the highlight of the Inspirals' career was, I'll usually say headlining Reading on the Saturday night in 1990. It was a phenomenal experience. We pushed the boat out a bit with that show. Before we came on, we sent a pantomime cow out, which, legend has it, had our roadie Noel Gallagher in it. We also blew a load of our fee, which was about £40,000, on fireworks that the band couldn't even see because the stage was covered. But the thing most people remember is the drum majorettes, the Hornchurch Haverettes. They'd been in the video for 'She Comes in the Fall', and we got the full troupe to march on stage at Reading during that song. They went down incredibly well. Too well, actually. They were used to marching up and down high streets in shitty little towns, so being on stage with 50,000 people screaming at them was a bit much for them. Several of them fainted backstage afterwards.

Write a new song especially
Chris Martin, Coldplay
Headlined Glastonbury (2002)
It was definitely a risk on the part of the Eavis family to ask us [to headline]. We'd only released one album and we were still getting the whole 'bedwetters' thing thrown at us. But although we thought they were crazy, we said yes. We took a lot of heat for not being the right act to do it, but it was kill or be killed and we spent a long time preparing for it. In fact, we wrote the song 'Politik' specifically for Glastonbury. We knew we were going to be so nervous that we'd want to bash things really hard, so we wrote a bashy song and opened the set with it. Actually, I think we played seven new songs and seven old ones, which, in retrospect, was just plain stupid. But it went down really well, and there's no doubt that gig changed our career. It was our equivalent of being in the *Pop Idol* final. And luckily we were Girls Aloud rather than One True Voice.

Bide your time
Tim Burgess, the Charlatans
Headlined Phoenix (1997), V (1998), Reading (1999)
When our first album came out, we were asked to headline lots of festivals, but it was too early. We felt that one day we would be worthy of headlining a festival and that we should wait until then. It was probably a bit risky, but I think it paid off. The first big headline slot we did was Phoenix, then we did V and Reading.

The Reading one was probably our biggest triumph. We were on to our sixth album by then, and it was an incredibly euphoric show. I felt like how the Stone Roses must've felt at Spike Island. You definitely feel the pressure when you headline, but, in a weird way, you also know that a lot of people won't be paying as much attention as they would if you were on earlier; people are so pissed by the end of the night that you actually have to try harder to be memorable. But it's definitely a brilliant feeling to be the last band on.

Beef up your light show
Ed Simons, Chemical Brothers
Headlined Glastonbury (2000)
I think when you headline, you have to do something to mark it as an occasion, production-wise. Our shows are always about the music and the visual aspect, so when we headlined Glastonbury, we really stepped it up, because we were playing to such a big space. We had a couple of meetings, hired tons of gear and then set it off at opportune moments. I've always liked those big sky-cannon searchlights from going to raves in 1989, so we got two of those to light up the sky behind the stage while we were playing. They were so big, they needed their own lorries. Michael Eavis always says that 200,000 people were there for that show, because it was the last year without the fence and a really sunny weekend. It was an incredible sight, with the flags and the fires at the top of the hill. And it was a pretty crazed reaction to our set. I remember being on stage thinking: 'I must remember how this feels, I should store this somehow.' I haven't really been able to do that, but I know it was an amazing night.

Remember you've been asked to headline for a reason
Fran Healy, Travis
Headlined Reading (2001)
Just before we headlined Reading, we suddenly got the fear. We were like, 'Why are we headlining this? It's a rock festival. People are gonna throw bottles of piss and socks of shit at us.' We were genuinely terrified. Then I made the mistake of going up to the

stage to see the band before us, which was Green Day. They were setting fire to their drum kit, and the place was going mental. I was thinking, 'Fuck, man, how can we follow this?' I was at the Big Day festival in Glasgow in 1990 when Sheena Easton came on stage with this weird transatlantic accent, and the entire crowd turned on her. She had to leave the stage and she hasn't played in Scotland since. That was flashing through my mind backstage at Reading. But something amazing happened. We went on and everyone got really into it. I guess there's something universal about melody. Anyway, we didn't get bottled off – on the contrary it was one of the best festivals we ever played. I suppose it proves that if you're headlining something, you're headlining it for a reason.

Don't rant at the organisers
Jim-Bob, Carter the Unstoppable Sex Machine
Headlined Glastonbury (1992)
I look back at our Glastonbury headline slot with a certain amount of embarrassment. We had a big encore planned, with cannons firing foam balls into the audience. But when we finished our main set, they said: 'That's it, there's no time for more.' Various bands had overrun and it had cut into our time. I think they eventually let us do one song, but the crowd wanted more, so it was agreed that our guitarist, Fruitbat, could go on, apologise and say we'd run out of time. Instead, he went on and launched into a big anti-Glastonbury rant. The way I remember it, we were asked to leave, although we had to leave anyway, cos we had another festival the next day in Germany. We definitely did get thrown out of that one. We were obviously going through a phase. I'm not sure whether we were actually banned from Glastonbury, although we certainly told everybody that. But I do know that about a year later at an *NME* awards thing, I got really drunk and was quite abusive to Michael Eavis. With hindsight, headlining the Pyramid is a massive thing, but I don't think it felt like it at the time. I sort of regret that I didn't think more of it, but when you're there you're a bit big-headed from the mere fact that you're in a position to be headlining. We enjoyed it, but I don't think I

thought it was an honour and privilege, whereas now I'd probably feel a lot different. Basically, what I'm saying is that I was a bit of a wanker back then, but I'm not any more.

Ignore Primal Scream
Felix Buxton, Basement Jaxx
Headlined Glastonbury (2005)
We were originally second on the bill, but we moved up a slot when Kylie had to pull out. Bands don't make money from doing Glastonbury – it's just something that you really want to do, because it's such a special festival, so it was a real honour to headline. Primal Scream were on before us and I think they were a bit pissed off that they weren't doing the lead slot. Beforehand, they were saying embarrassing things on TV about our singers being fat and that sort of thing. It was quite disappointing that they were being so small-minded. Then, during their set, they were shouting, 'Who do you want? Us or Basement Jaxx?' and people were going, 'Basement Jaxx!' Bobby Gillespie threw the mic down and stormed off the stage, because they were trying to go on longer. But I think that all made it more exciting for us. When we walked on stage, I was just bowled over by the crowd's amazing reaction. It's the only time I can remember when my breath was literally taken away. It turned out to be one of the best gigs we've ever done.

Treasure the memory – it might be your biggest gig
Skin, Skunk Anansie
Headlined Glastonbury (1999)
Headlining the Pyramid Stage was definitely the pinnacle of our career. I'm pleased to say I have really vivid memories of the whole set – it didn't flash by at all. That could be because we never drank before we went on stage. But I also kind of had a premonition that it was gonna be our biggest gig. I actually remember walking on stage thinking: 'I wonder if we'll ever do this again?' We played really, really well and the audience reaction was phenomenal. It's unbelievable to see that many people, especially when you could see them jumping up and down all the way to the back. We came

back on to do an encore and I asked if we should do one more. The entire crowd just went 'YES!' It was such an ego trip. That was undoubtedly one of the best gigs we ever played, but it was almost a little bit deflating afterwards, like, 'How are we ever gonna top that?' I still remember what an amazing feeling it was, though. It's nice to know that we got there.

Save the fear for afterwards
Mark Chadwick, the Levellers
Headlined Glastonbury (1994)
Before we headlined the Pyramid I was totally relaxed. We were so busy, it just seemed like the most natural thing in the world for us to be doing, even though we were playing to the biggest crowd they'd ever had – 140,000 people or something. The fear kicked in straight after we finished. My stomach totally cramped up. I've never had it before in my life, or since. I remember I went straight to my tent behind the stage and curled up in a ball, screaming in agony. It was absolutely terrible. My girlfriend didn't understand it at all. She was going: 'You've just headlined Glastonbury, you can go out there and party like a motherfucker and you're lying in your tent wailing.' I just told her to go away. I stayed there all night until the Sunday morning. I think I'd obviously put the whole thing out of my mind, and once I'd done it, my body went, 'Right! Now you're getting all that stress that you've been putting off in one hit! Bang!' Well, it was either that or a dodgy beanburger.